MY (HALF) LATINX KITCHEN

MY (HALF) LATINX KITCHEN

Half Recipes, Half Stories, All Latin American

KIERA WRIGHT-RUIZ

HARVEST

An Imprint of WILLIAM MORROW

HarperCollins books may be purchased for educational, business, or sales promotional use. For information, please email the Special Markets Department at SPsales@harpercollins.com.

FIRST EDITION

Design: Tai Blanche
Photography: Lauren Vied Allen
Culinary Photoshoot Director: KC Hysmith
Production Assistant: Savannah Shoemake
Prop Styling: Lauren Vied Allen
Illustrations: Zyan Méndez

Speech bubbles on page ix © sveta/stock.adobe.com
Dotted texture on pages ii, vi, vii, 85, 147, 185 © dule964/stock.adobe.com
Heart with sparkle emoji on page 113 © vadymstock/stock.adobe.com
Sparkle emoji on pages 205 and 254, and envelope emoji on page 254 © Adono/stock.adobe.com

ISBN 978-0-06-329253-6

25 26 27 28 29 IMG 10 9 8 7 6 5 4 3 2 1

For my mom, who won't be in the book
much but to whom I owe everything.

For the rest of my family. This story
is as much theirs as mine.

And for anyone who has ever had to check
off the "other" box: this one's for us.

CONTENTS

INTRODUCTION

This is the question that has followed me my entire life. My skin's a shade of brown that easily deepens in warm summers. My dark brown eyes curve at the corners like a gentle smile. My ethnicity has always been a topic of curiosity to many people I've interacted with. No one has ever accurately guessed my cultural identity, though many have tried—from friends to coworkers to complete strangers—starting in childhood and continuing to this very day. For a long time I couldn't understand why. At times, the question weighed so heavily that it even made me question myself.

There are also two other questions almost as bad as the first:

If you're reading this now, you may be wondering the same thing—*what are you?*

I am half Ecuadorian and half Korean—half Latinx and half Asian. It feels ironic to write so openly about my ethnicity, let alone create an entire book on the subject, when the question makes me so uncomfortable. But here I am!

My origin story is as follows: My dad, along with his six siblings and parents, uprooted their lives from the humid port city of Guayaquil, Ecuador, immigrating to New York City in 1969. They were in search of more, like so many others before and after them. In the same year, my mother was adopted from Seoul, South Korea, and was moved to the sprawling fields of rural Pennsylvania. In the 1980s, my parents met and fell in love in New York City. Shortly after, I was born, and eventually, my little brother followed.

Though I am a first-generation American, I didn't have the usual experience often tied with that identity. I didn't grow up in a home where food and traditions from our cultures were passed down from one generation to the next, from either of my parents. I can't even speak Spanish! (Although my grandma claims it was my first language.) And for a large portion of my life, outside of my family, the only other person I knew of who was Ecuadorian was Christina Aguilera. (Yes, the singer. She's also half.) But you can say Christina and I are not really close.

I so deeply wish this book was about how I stood in the kitchen watching my Ecuadorian dad whip up bubbling stews from his homeland, dishes that transform the toughest cuts of meat into luscious textures as long as you put enough time and heart into them. But it's not. I didn't grow up much with my dad, who would have been the traditional person to pass on his Ecuadorian culture to me.

My family is riddled with more problems than average, and the chain of "my mother taught me a recipe, which was taught to her by her mother, and her mother before that" has been broken for a very long time. The role of "parent" has been played by many people in my life: my actual parents, then just my mom, then just my dad, then my mom again, then my dad again, foster parents (four to be exact), grandparents, and finally my mom again. Most of the people who raised me were from various parts of Latin America. Each of them taught me more about what it means to be Latinx through their cooking. Both my Asian and Latinx identities shape how I view the world, but the Latinx side was always present in my life in a way my Asian side wasn't. This cookbook is a celebration of Latin American dishes and about how the journey to embrace a culture isn't always linear.

Most of my childhood was spent growing up in the heavy air of West Palm Beach, where crunchy ham croquettes and pastelillos de guayaba y queso were always staples. But I developed a much more intimate relationship with Cuban dishes in Miami while in foster care. My main foster parents were an elderly Cuban couple who seemed to have once lived an adventurous life (at least that's what the framed photo of them on desert camels suggested), before settling down for a sleepy life in their old age. Arroz con pollo was dinner after school. Lunch meant picadillo. Leftover picadillo became fried papas rellenas to eat as snacks. I often accompanied my foster mom to her nonstop doctors' appointments, where tall stacks of bocaditos and glossy pastelitos de carne would keep me company in the waiting rooms. But the food in that house didn't feel like it was made out of love. More like obligation. Despite the isolation and loneliness I felt, I still connected with the food and culture, and I learned that even through sadness, food can touch your heart.

My grandparents' house was an entirely different story. They became my guardians after I left foster care. They gave me and my brother, Thor, a real place to call home. The house was always filled with joy and plantains in every color and stage of ripeness. Green, when they were the starchiest and could endure enough pressure from a tostonera to be smashed and fried into tostones; their sides cracked and became as golden as the Florida sunshine outside. Yellow plantains spotted with tiny brown freckles let me know that if I just held out a little longer—and waited until they were black—I would be rewarded with glistening maduros that caramelized from the natural sugars and formed clusters of sweet edges, shattering from the smallest bite. While my grandfather didn't cook, he would always request Ecuadorian dishes: encebollado de pescado, ceviche with a little bit of ketchup (because that's how Ecuadorians like it), and plátanos asados con queso.

My grandma did all the cooking, which included the Ecuadorian dishes my grandpa craved, but making Mexican food is what made her the happiest. It reminded her of growing up in Mexico City, her home before she immigrated to the US. (Technically, she's my step-grandma, but she and my grandpa were married before I was born. By all accounts, she's my "full" grandma.) Her version of weeknight dinners meant achiote-stained meats and pickled escabeche that cut the richness, alongside cups of chilled sour agua de tamarindo to wash it all down. Special occasions would bring handmade tamales steamed with fatty bites of pork and chiles, or pozole that would take the better part of a day to make but was always, always worth it. A lot of my happy childhood memories were made when I lived with my grandparents, Thor, and my half-uncle George (who was also like a brother to me). The reason why I even understand some Spanish is because of them—and partly due to the constant hum of Telemundo that would play for what seemed like twenty-four hours a day. What can I say? My grandparents love their telenovelas.

My (Half) Latinx Kitchen is a bit different from a traditional recipe book. It's a mix of personal essays (some about food, some not) with recipes from all over Latin America. Some memories I've had to sort through are over twenty years old, so I've written everything to the best of my recollection, letting the food lead the way. The story will loosely follow the chronology of my life (so far), with a heavy focus on the people who taught me about the culture through the dishes they cooked. The first chapter is more focused on my initial understanding of being Ecuadorian and the issues I faced having multiple ethnicities. The last one is a reflection on the outlook I have today and a lot about Tokyo, where I've been living and writing the last couple of years. But the chapters in between are odes to the people who taught me more about Latinx culture through their immigration stories, our relationship, and, most of all, food. In a way, it's sort of like a culinary genealogy project.

Culture isn't just defined by who raised you. It's also the environment, music, movies, books, community, ex-partners, and so much more that shape an identity. While these are some of the biggest influences in my life, they aren't the only things that made me embrace my Latinx side: there were also the parties filled with laughter and a little too much alcohol at the home of my aunt TT, who is arguably the best cook in the family. Or my first move across the country to LA, where late nights were fueled by carne asada fries topped with mountain-high guacamole. Or my brief chonga phase, where I repped my Ecuadorian side at the expense of concealing my other half. Each moment brought me closer to where I am today. This is a taste of my journey through a culture I love and am proud to be a part of, even though I've had a backward way of getting there.

I am not an expert on all things Latinx. When it comes to cookbooks covering diverse cultures within the US, there is huge pressure on authors to make their books encompass all aspects of whatever culture they're writing about. This book doesn't do that, nor does it try to. For example, there isn't a single Brazilian recipe, although that country makes up half of South America's entire population. This book is not a catchall for Latin American recipes. That would require many, many encyclopedia-length cookbooks. Even within the cuisines of the handful of countries I do explore, I offer a very small view into their vast and regional cuisines. I am writing only through the lens of my personal experience and the dishes I ate along the way. My journey will inherently be different from yours. But I hope that through the struggle, joy, and love in these recipes and stories, you see yourself, too.

This book contains details that I've kept private, even from some of my friends. It's not that I think they can't handle it, but it makes me uncomfortable to think someone's opinion of me might change because of my past. If someone has a negative opinion, well, there's nothing I can do about that. But even positive "you are so strong" comments have always irked me—going through life, and at points enduring it, doesn't make me stronger than anyone else. It only means I kept going, not in an inspirational way but in an I-had-no-choice way. To some, maybe that is moving in itself, but to others who have been in a similar position, they probably understand that going forward doesn't always mean something profound; it simply means you did.

I wanted to write this book to show people how I became proud to be Latinx. And although I'm half, it doesn't mean I'm any less Latinx than others. I also wanted to share Ecuadorian history through its delicious dishes; Ecuador is overlooked in so many ways, but it deserves the same recognition as any other country. And I wanted to make it clear that it's OK to learn about your cultural identity in an untraditional way. And that untraditional ways exist in the first place!

Right now, we are living through a mini food-writing renaissance. For the first time, people from all backgrounds are able to tell their own stories through food. Though it is very far from perfect, and we still have such a long, long way to go, it's a huge victory that more diverse voices are finally sharing their food stories.

That said, I still haven't seen many stories that reflect who I am: someone who is mixed. And diversity also extends far beyond ethnicity. It includes geographical and economical diversity, too, both of which I often see lacking in cookbooks and food writing in general. There's an inherent assumption within the food-writing world that the reader has money to buy the flaky sea salt and nice extra-virgin olive oil, but what if they don't? I hope my story can help show some of the depth of diversity, because it's not just about being Latinx or half Latinx; it encompasses all other aspects of who I am, where I grew up, the money I had at times and the other times I didn't.

I am putting so much of myself out there in the hope that people relate to my story and know they're not alone, whether from a class, geographical, racial, multiracial, cultural, or ideological perspective. Thank you for taking the time to read this book. I'm so glad you're here.

Although I'm half, it doesn't mean I'm any less Latinx.

A note about the title:

The term Latinx is contentious within the Latin American community, but it is how I personally identify culturally. The Spanish language was adopted in Latin America after it was colonized by Spain. It uses gender as a foundational structure. Girl is niña; boy is niño. Kitchen is cocina; money is dinero. Over time, many people have come to view the gendered parts of Spanish as commonplace and take no issue with them, but others have. Using Latinx or Latine is a way to make the labeling of a group of people more gender neutral by replacing the *a* (feminine) or *o* (masculine) suffix with an *x* or *e* (neutral).

Its usage attracts criticism because, well, sometimes people don't like change. But even among people who welcome the idea of inclusivity, it doesn't change the fact that Latinx doesn't easily translate into the phonetics of Spanish. There is a common misconception, even within the Latin American community, that the term Latinx was created by non-Spanish-speaking white people. But it couldn't be further from the truth. Latinx first emerged from the Spanish-speaking queer community online in the early 2000s. To believe otherwise erases its creators.

Currently, the largest group of people who use the term Latinx are younger, college-educated, and live in the US. The majority of people of Latin American descent still use Hispanic when referring to themselves (fun fact: Hispanic is a term that first widely appeared on the 1970 US Census and stuck from there), but Latina/o, Latine, and referencing the specific country or Indigenous community a person is a part of are also used. To sum it up, everyone has different preferences, so just ask how someone would like to be referred to.

Like sexual orientation and gender itself, I view cultural identity as an extremely personal, intimate journey. And because it is a journey, I may use another term in the future, but for today, I identify as Latinx. The *x* replaces more than just gender to me; it also means removing the stigmas around what it means to be Latina or Latino (or never being enough of either), and allows me the chance to define that experience for myself.

INGREDIENTS

Whenever I look into a pantry, I feel like I'm peeking into someone's soul. Raiding my family's kitchen cabinets allowed me to understand them on a more personal level. The bags of Mexican dried chiles and bundles of canela hastily packed into my grandparents' pantry gently perfume the shelves with sweet and floral scents. Inside the laundry room extending from their kitchen sits a big glass jar of dried chamomile flowers my grandma reaches into every evening to make cinnamon chamomile tea, the same kind she's been making since I was a kid, at least. However, Aunt TT's pantry is organized like a Michelin-starred restaurant. Packets of Goya sazón are lined up like soldiers ready for duty. Each jar of achiote, adobo seasoning, and ají has a place on her lazy Susan carousel tucked away on a shelf. It's a pantry that's equipped to feed two just as easily as one hundred.

Though there are many shared ingredients and techniques throughout Latin America, the Latinx pantry is not homogeneous. Every country—and every country's region—is vast and diverse. The ingredients below do not remotely encompass every ingredient out there (very far from it, in fact!). But they reflect what's to come in the book and can be used as a shopping guide.

Ingredient sections in cookbooks are always strange to me because they often seem to assume that the reader has zero knowledge about anything. So I'm going to do something different and load this section with as many interesting facts about each ingredient as possible. Even if you already cook with these ingredients every day, I'm hoping there's something new you can pick up and impress people with:

Achiote: Known as annatto in English, achiote are the red seeds of the Bixa orellana tree, more commonly called a lipstick tree. They grow inside fuzzy, teardrop-shaped pods that look like they're straight out of a Dr. Seuss book. When crushed, the seeds transform into a burning sunset color that naturally gives food a vibrant orange-red glow. One of the key ingredients in this book—please take note—this seed is popular throughout Latin America, the Caribbean, and some parts of Asia. In ancient times, Mayans used it in many ways (anything from drinks to body paint!), but today it can be commonly found in cheddar cheese (giving it an extra-orange hue). You can buy it whole or crushed into a powder, infused in oil, or mixed into seasoning blends (hello, sazón). Tastewise, it is mild with a subtle, earthy flavor; some even describe it as sweet and peppery.

Adobo Seasoning: This prized seasoning makes a frequent appearance in Latinx dishes. The term adobo itself comes from the Spanish verb adobar, which means "to marinate." Due to Spanish colonization, adobo can mean many things in different cultures around the world. But in this book, it always refers to the dry seasoning that's usually a combination of garlic powder, onion powder, cumin, oregano, salt, pepper, and turmeric, the last giving it that signature golden color. This kind of adobo blend is inspired by a Puerto Rican variation that became further popularized by Goya in 1966 when it started selling a similar version.

Ají Amarillo: If Peru were a pepper, it would probably be a golden ají amarillo. This long, slender pepper is thought to have originated in central Bolivia, and it's believed that the Incas used these peppers to flavor dishes thousands of years ago. Today in Peru, it is considered one of the most culturally significant ingredients in the country's cuisine. The name translates to "yellow chile pepper," but as the pepper ripens, the skin becomes a glowing orange color that resembles a sunrise. When it is green and unripe, it is also referred to as ají verde in Peru. It can be difficult to find fresh ají amarillos in the US, but many Latin American stores and online shops sell them frozen whole or blended into a puree. Ají amarillo has a similar spice level to tabasco and cayenne peppers (according to the Scoville scale a.k.a. official pepper spiciness ranking) but more fruitiness, which helps balance out its heat.

Canela: In the US, the most commonly used cinnamon is known as cassia, familiar as the hard, curled sticks poking out of hot ciders and the kind that's ground and stuffed inside cinnamon rolls. But in Mexico, it's a canela world. Also known as Ceylon cinnamon, canela is a lot gentler, sweeter, and more floral—unlike the harsh notes of cassia. If cassia were a towering cinnamon tsunami, canela would be a calm stream nestled between butterfly floral beds in a sunlit forest. Beautiful but without trying too hard. The texture of canela also varies drastically from its cassia counterpart. Ceylon cinnamon sticks are very brittle, making them easy to break apart and simmer away in tasty liquids.

Hominy: Hominy is the soaked kernels from white or yellow maize, or field corn, the main ingredient in grits and corn tortillas. To create hominy first requires soaking dried kernels in an alkali solution traditionally made from wood ash, lye, or slaked lime until the outer shells are soft enough to remove easily. This process is called nixtamalization, a method and term from Nahuatl (the language of the Aztec and Toltec people) invented by the Indigenous people of Mesoamerica, who have used this technique since 1000 BC. Once the hominy is soaked and cooked, the kernels grow to be about three times as big as those of sweet corn. Besides softening the kernels, nixtamalization also awakens the corn's inner nutty flavor and unlocks nutritional benefits, making it one of the most important food discoveries. You can find hominy available frozen or canned in most grocery stores.

Masa Harina: Like hominy, masa harina is created using the ingenious three-thousand-year-old Mesoamerican technique of nixtamalization, except with a few more steps. After nixtamalization, the corn is then ground into masa. In Nahuatl, nixtli means "ashes," and tamalli means "corn dough." The flour made from dried, ground, nixtamalized corn is masa harina. It is the base for many essential recipes like tamales (page 128), champurrado (page 137), and corn tortillas. There are many types of masa harina available today. Maseca, a popular brand, was my grandma's go-to as a kid because of its availability, but it does have preservatives. Personally, I adore Masienda's masa harina because it uses single-origin ingredients sourced from Mexico.

Naranjilla: Originally grown in the Andean region of South America, naranjilla (pronounced "na-rahn-HEE-ah") is a tiny, orange-colored fruit that resembles a cross between a tomato and persimmon upon first glance. But once cut open, the green-tinted flesh is entirely different. It tastes like a tarter mixture of an orange, pineapple, and passion fruit all in one. In Ecuador, it's a key ingredient in anything from drinks to seco (one of the country's more cherished stews). In Colombia, where it's also commonly used, it's called lulo. The name is derived from lulum, a term used by the Incas, who are believed to have enjoyed it, too. The fresh fruit is rare to find in most of the US, but many Latin American stores and sections will carry the pulp blended and frozen. The name itself means "little orange" in Spanish, but its flavor is anything but small.

Piloncillo, or Panela: Piloncillo is raw, unrefined pure cane sugar. It's created by boiling sugarcane until it thickens, and it's then poured into molds, where it is left to cool and harden. It can usually be found formed into cones or discs wherever Latin American ingredients are sold. Throughout the book, I will alternate between calling it piloncillo and panela because the name varies depending on the region: in Mexico, people refer to it almost exclusively

as piloncillo, but in Colombia, it is often called panela. Brown sugar and piloncillo are both dark in color, but they are very different. Raw, pure cane sugar possesses a rich caramel depth with a little natural smokiness. Brown sugar gets its flavor and color from being mixed with molasses. In a pinch, brown sugar can be substituted, but if you can, get the real stuff. It's much better.

Plantains: While technically plantains are part of the same plant family as bananas, they are not bananas. Repeat: plantains are not bananas! But they do share many similarities. Plátanos, as they're called in Spanish, are a fruit that is believed to have originated in Southeast Asia before spreading around the globe. In the green, unripe stage, they're at their starchiest and have a thick peel. But as they ripen, more sugars develop, turning the peel softer and darker, reflecting the sweetness inside. You can eat plantains countless ways in any stage of ripeness, making them one of the most versatile and magical ingredients. Their many uses illustrate that whatever stage you are at in life is not only good enough but also delicious. They continue to be a staple food in Latinx, African, Caribbean, and Southeast Asian communities.

Salt: For all of the recipes, I used Diamond Crystal Kosher Salt. But, of course, any salt you have will work with some adjustment. If you're using a salt other than Diamond Crystal, start with half of the amount listed in any recipe. You can easily adjust to your taste. Remember, it's easier to fix a dish that needs a little more salt but much harder to save one that's been oversalted. Salt liberally but with caution!

Sazón: If you want to cook from this book, you *need* sazón. Sazón simply means "seasoning," but it really is one of the most beloved elements of Latinx cuisine. It's usually a combination of salt, cumin, garlic (granulated or powdered), coriander, pepper, oregano, and—the key ingredient—achiote, which gives it that orange hue it's so famous for. There are many kinds of sazón out there (some without annatto), but for this book, you need the version with achiote in it. I grew up with the Goya culantro y achiote variety that's spiked with MSG and artificial color. For many Latinx home cooks in the US (including my grandparents), it was the most accessible way to get achiote. But nowadays, there is a wider range of sazón on the market. For a more natural and organic option, I really love Loisa. And, of course, you can also make your own blend at home and adjust it to your liking.

Tajín: Tajín (pronounced "ta-HEEN") is a Mexican seasoning made of dehydrated lime, salt, and a combo of dried chiles de árbol, pasilla, and guajillo. The taste is a little salty, a little citrusy, and a little smoky, with just a tinge of heat that makes it the perfect complement to sprinkle onto juicy fruits or to coat the rims of iced micheladas. It is a spice that embodies the flavors of Mexico.

Yuca: Also known as cassava, yuca is an indigenous root vegetable commonly used throughout Latin America, Africa, the Caribbean, and Southeast Asia. Its starchy white flesh is coated in dark brown skin that almost looks like a zoomed-in view of tree bark. Once peeled and cooked, it softens similarly to a potato and has a subtle floral sweetness. You can easily find yuca precooked and frozen in the US. And it's readily available fresh at many grocery stores. When yucas are in their whole state, just be sure to generously peel them (the skin is often coated in a thin layer of wax) and thoroughly check for discoloration. Important note: If you find a fresh yuca with dark veins running through it, discard it because it can be poisonous. And, do NOT eat yuca raw, because it's also poisonous in that state. (But I promise yuca is not scary! Just some small things to look out for.) It was most likely first cultivated by the Maya in Yucatán, Mexico, but is now found worldwide and used as a vegetable (duh), tapioca, flour, and even laundry starch.

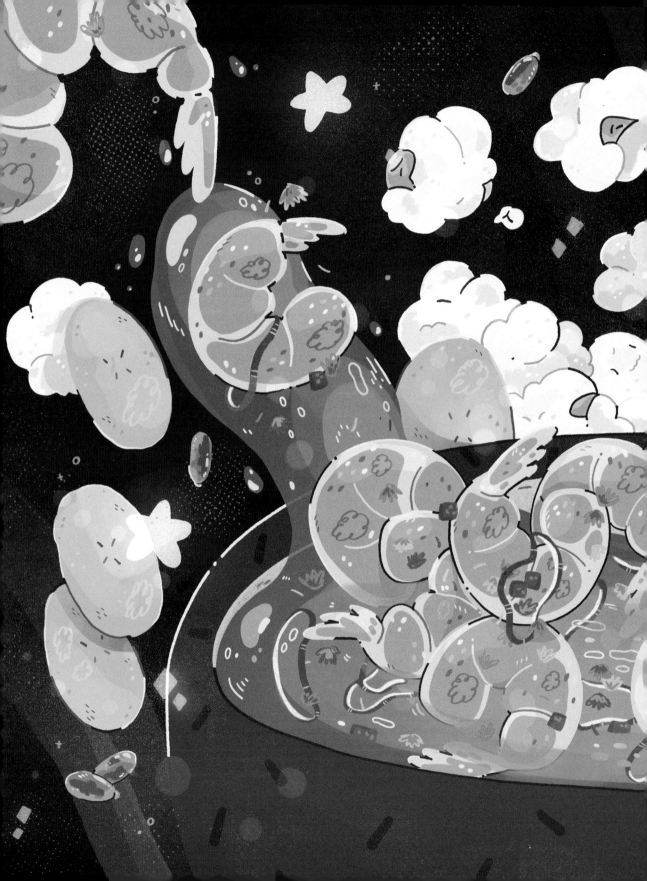

CHAPTER 1

GROWING UP (MOSTLY) ECUADORIAN

The only two bedtime stories I remember my dad telling me as a kid were (1) the entire plot of *Star Wars* and (2) the story of the majesty of the Andean condor, Ecuador's national bird. It appears on the country's flag, standing proudly on top of a coat of arms with its massive wings spread open to symbolize strength, centered among yellow, blue, and red horizontal stripes in the background. He told me what each color in the flag represents: yellow for fertile land, blue for the ocean, and red for the lives lost while fighting for independence. Andean condors are the largest flying birds on earth, with a wingspan as big as 10.5 feet. Because of their hefty size, they prefer to live in windy areas and catch the breeze to fly along the Andes Mountains, which span Ecuador and six other countries.

It is believed that the Incas considered the condor to be part of a sacred trinity that divided the world: snake for the underworld, puma for the earthly world, and condor for the higher world. Because of the height at which condors soar, it was thought that they were messengers of the heavens. Today the condor remains an important bird in Latin America and is sometimes referred to as the king of the Andes.

My dad told me this story filled with so much excitement. I still remember his eyes glittering as he spread his arms open as much as he could to show my then four-year-old self just how mighty the condor is. It was one of the only things I learned from him about Ecuador.

I was five years old when my parents separated. It didn't take long for their relationship to unravel due to the drug problem my dad secretly nursed in private. There's no easy way to talk about addiction. If someone close to you has a problem, you already know how insidious a disease it is. It festers like an oozing wound and grows so fast and violently until it rips apart friendships and families, leaving only ruins.

All this is to say that I didn't grow up much with my dad. The last time I had regular contact with him, I was twelve years old. But I didn't lose just a father then; I lost my only direct link to Ecuador and all things Latinx.

For most of my childhood (and sometimes still in adulthood), when I would reluctantly answer someone's question about my ethnicity with "I'm Ecuadorian," they would almost always respond with "What's that?" It was awful, but maybe slightly better than other people refusing to acknowledge that I'm also Korean by saying, "So, you're Chinese, right?"

The only two things I had that connected me to Ecuador were that condor story and the food. I've often felt that people imagine that my childhood was full of every kind of Ecuadorian and Korean food—half a table covered in luscious stews and the other half scattered with colorful banchan. In reality, it was neither. I rarely saw most of my greater Ecuadorian family because they lived in different states and we didn't have the money to make frequent flights. The people I saw most often were my dad's parents: my Ecuadorian grandfather, who was too old to cook regularly, and my Mexican step-grandmother, who made dishes that blended both of their cultures with ingredients and techniques picked up in the US. But despite that, some Ecuadorian staples would appear: seco de pollo, guatita, ceviche de camarón, tortillas de yuca, and lots of plantains. While they offered me a look into the expansive world of Ecuadorian cuisine, it was only a fleeting glimpse. Recipes for all these dishes and more will follow in this chapter.

Being a specific ethnicity doesn't guarantee knowledge of a culture. I may have inherited some common Ecuadorian features like my dark hair, tan skin, and shorter height (the national average height for women is often cited to be about five feet), but these features are limited only to physical traits. Language, customs, and traditions didn't transfer. I've found, though, that being born a certain ethnicity does often spark curiosity about your background—at least it has for me. And as an adult, I wanted to answer the question of "What are you?" for myself.

In 2017, I went to Ecuador for the first time. I visited Quito, the capital, and Guayaquil, the city my family is from. I wanted to learn more about the country and see firsthand where my roots started (and I also wanted to eat). Stepping off the plane right into Quito's 9,350-feet-above-sea-level elevation immediately made me nauseous with altitude sickness. But as I climbed up a steep hill and looked behind me, I saw the city lights flickering wildly. In the night sky, I could make out the outline of mountain ranges with the thousands of building lights that resembled star constellations acting as guides to where the peaks and valleys were. When I stood on the terrace of the apartment I stayed in, I felt like I was on a grand stage with a sea of lighters shining back from adoring fans. "I finally made it," I thought. Going to Ecuador to learn and experience some of the culture firsthand had been a lifelong dream. And here I was in my family's home country after so many years of wondering if I was even Latinx enough to visit.

Ecuador is nestled snugly in the northwest of the continent between Colombia to the north and Peru to the east and south. It gets its name from the equator, which cuts through the capital city. Although Ecuador is one of the smallest countries in South America, its landscape is vast and diverse. The country's geography has four distinct regions: the Amazon rainforest, the Andean mountains, the Pacific coast, and the famous Galápagos Islands (which will hopefully ring a bell as a source of inspiration for Charles Darwin's theory of evolution). Within these regions is a wealth of ecosystems and biodiversity. Ecuador is classified as one of only seventeen megadiverse countries, according to a list by Conservation International of nations that cover 10 percent of the world's surface yet host 70 percent of Earth's recognized species. Ecuador is a country that fully embodies the saying "Size isn't everything."

The people of Ecuador are just as complex as its land. A few years back, my brother took a DNA test and shared his full ethnicity results with me (I didn't want to pay for my own and figured it was basically the same). On our Ecuadorian side, the results were 25 percent Indigenous and 25 percent general European (a.k.a. Spanish), a common result for many people of Latinx background. In a 2010 survey, more than 70 percent of the seventeen million people in Ecuador identified as mestizo, a term used for people with mixed Indigenous and European roots. It's been over five hundred years since Spain colonized Latin America, but the lingering results are forever present in my blood.

Beyond mestizo, there are many communities of Indigenous and Afro-Latinx people, who still face extreme hardships and injustices due to systemic racism within Ecuador and broadly in Latin America. But without Indigenous and Afro-Latinx people, Latin American cuisine would simply not exist.

There is a common misconception that Latin America is a monolith. Just looking at Ecuador's facts alone, it is far, far from it.

There is a common misconception that Latin America is a monolith. Just looking at Ecuador's facts alone, it is far, far from it.

In Quito, Spain's colonial presence is felt everywhere, but especially so in the architecture. The city is often split up into "Old Town" and "New Town." Old Town is filled with European-style buildings constructed in the fifteenth through eighteenth centuries. New Town has more modern restaurants, bars, and shopping areas with little to no look of Spanish colonialism. But located in the heart of Old Town is Plaza de la Independencia, a large outdoor square that's been reclaimed to honor those who fought for Ecuador's independence. In the center is a tall monument adorned with decorative pillars leading to a statue of a woman holding a blazing torch to commemorate El Primer Grito de la Independencia, or the first cry for freedom. In 1809, Ecuador became the first Hispanic American nation to declare its independence from Spain. It wouldn't be until 1822 that Ecuador gained its full independence, but it is often said that its initial uprising against Spain helped inspire other countries to follow. To this day, El Primer Grito de la Independencia is celebrated as an Ecuadorian national holiday.

One of my favorite memories on the trip was eating at Quitu Identidad Culinaria. Quitu is a fine-dining restaurant that specializes in contemporary Ecuadorian gastronomy created by chef Juan Sebastián Pérez. I dined like a king on what remains one of the most memorable meals of my life. Every dish highlighted locally sourced ingredients that mirrored the diverse landscape. Fruits from the Amazon rainforest, potatoes from the Andean mountains, and herbs from the nearby markets. Course after course dazzled, but it all led up to dessert: corn, twelve ways. Corn foam, corn dehydrated chips, corn silk spun like sugar, corn ice cream, and more. Each bite was a beautiful ode to such a cherished Latinx ingredient. It was the first time I had ever eaten Ecuadorian food in a fine-dining environment, and it made me emotional. For so long, I had to explain to people what Ecuador even was, and now I was eating foods I grew up with that could compete with dishes at any of the best restaurants in the world. While the fine-dining scene in Ecuador is still fairly new, it has begun to gain international attention. In 2020, Nuema was the first-ever Ecuadorian restaurant to be on the World's 50 Best Restaurants list. It still holds a spot as I write this in 2023.

In Guayaquil, I explored the city by foot, sticking to the paths that hugged the water. The air was wet with humidity and embraced me the same way it does in Florida. I feasted on a mountain of locally caught red crabs smothered in a garlic-achiote sauce. I fed pieces of torn iceberg lettuce from a twenty-five-cent bag to the famous iguanas in the town square, where hundreds gather to bask in the sun. And I climbed the 444 steps of Santa Ana Hill to take a look at Las Peñas, a neighborhood with hundreds of colorful homes built into the hill. From a distance, the scenery looks like a jar of rainbow jelly beans, each building bursting with color and competing for attention. I thought about my family. What their life here was like, what could have been if they hadn't left, and what opportunities they got because they did. As a kid of immigrants, I was reminded of my family's sacrifice and my heart filled with gratitude. That feeling on the hill has never fully left.

There are almost no cookbooks about Ecuadorian cuisine written in English. While this book explores many other dishes from different countries, I wanted to do my best to share a little about what I've learned about Ecuador with you as the proud Ecuadorian I am. Its beauty, food, and culture are things I am still getting to know myself, but I hope this has inspired you (and made you hungry) to learn more. Even if I spend the rest of my life fully dedicated to learning about Ecuador, I doubt it would be enough. Ecuadorian culture, like all cultures, is constantly evolving, always offering something new. But the fact of that perpetual change is what keeps me coming back for seconds.

CEVICHE DE CAMARÓN

Ceviche de camarón is one of two Ecuadorian dishes I ate the most when I was growing up (the other is seco, page 9). Ceviche is a Latin American dish made by combining seafood and citrus in a variety of ways. While its origins are still debated, there is evidence that the first kinds of ceviche were made over three thousand years ago by fishermen. The dish is an integral part of Ecuadorian cuisine and is present in one form or another in all twenty-four provinces of the country, changing to fit what's in season and continuing to adapt to local tastes. Usually, the fish (the most common seafood of choice for ceviche) is raw and bathed in fresh lime juice (also the most common citrus). The acid from the limes cures the fish while it soaks, slightly firming up the raw surface, and leaves the fish with a kinda-cooked-yet-still-tender texture in the process. But Ecuador's famous ceviche de camarón is special because it doesn't fully include or do either.

It is made with just-cooked shrimp, fresh orange and lime juice, red onion, cilantro, and (the thing that truly makes it Ecuadorian) a little ketchup. For those who have only had Peruvian ceviche before, I understand why the ketchup might sound surprising. But you just have to trust me and all the Ecuadorian people who have been doing this for a long time—it's really good. The ketchup adds a touch of sweetness and color, giving the ceviche a recognizable blush look. Like any country-specific recipe, it varies slightly from region to region and cook to cook. No orange, lots of orange, more limes, fewer limes, little mustard, extra ketchup. This recipe is the combination I personally like the best, but you can tweak it to fit it to your own taste. One thing that is not essential but strongly recommended is eating it with chifles (plantain chips), popcorn (yes, popcorn!), or maíz tostado (little toasted corn nuts). These are common to eat with ceviche in Ecuador. For the true Ecuadorian experience, though, it's better to have a combo of all three, alternating between salty, crunchy, and citrusy tastes with every bite.

This is a dish that is best eaten the day it's made, so avoid making too much if you can; it scales down as easily as it scales up. On many occasions, I've made this as one serving by quartering or halving the recipe (depending on my appetite), and it's never let me down.

Time: 15 minutes ● **Serves:** 3 to 4

Ingredients

1 pound medium or large shell-on shrimp

4 limes, juiced (about ⅔ cup)

½ orange, juiced

3 tablespoons ketchup

½ teaspoon Dijon mustard (optional)

1½ teaspoons kosher salt, plus more to taste

¼ large red onion, halved and thinly sliced

1 medium tomato, diced

½ cup packed finely chopped cilantro leaves

1 ripe avocado, sliced (optional)

Recipe continues

Directions

1 Prepare the shrimp. Remove the shells and reserve them for later. Using a paring knife, carefully devein the shrimp.

2 Place the shrimp shells in a small saucepan with enough water to fill about three-quarters of the pan. Bring to a boil over medium-high heat, reduce the heat to medium, and cook for 5 minutes. Using a fine-mesh strainer, strain the shrimp stock and reserve the liquid.

3 Return the shrimp stock to the same saucepan and bring it to a boil over medium-high heat. Once boiling, add the shrimp and cook until just pink all around, about 10 seconds. Using tongs, place the cooked shrimp into a large bowl or on a plate to cool at room temperature. Reserve ¼ cup

of the shrimp stock in a measuring cup and set aside to cool. Store the remaining stock for another use, if desired.

4 While the shrimp is cooling, mix together the lime juice, orange juice, ketchup, mustard (if using), and salt in a large bowl. Add the onion and let the mixture soak for at least 10 minutes.

5 Add the tomato, cilantro, shrimp, and reserved ¼ cup shrimp stock to the lime mixture. Taste and adjust for salt, if needed. Stir until fully incorporated. Serve at room temperature or chilled. Garnish with the avocado, if using, neatly arranged on the side of the bowl.

Make It Vegan

Ceviche de chochos is a very common variation in Ecuador. Instead of seafood, the protein is chocho (lupini beans), making it fully vegan. This recipe works just as well with cooked chochos; just ditch the shrimp and stock.

SECO DE POLLO

In every culture, there's that one dish with the superpower to fix your worst day, heal your body when you're weak, and bestow the ultimate feeling of coziness. For me, this is the Ecuadorian recipe that does it all, and the first Ecuadorian dish I ever learned to make.

Seco is a thick stew made with beer, naranjilla, achiote, tomato, and sofrito (onion, green bell pepper, and garlic). It's typically served with a side of yellow rice, maduros, and avocado slices. There are many seco variations out there made with different kinds of meat, like gallina (older hen), carne (beef), chivo (goat), and borrego (lamb). Each one is delicious and requires slight tweaks to the base recipe, but it's always thick and always rich. I grew up with the chicken version the most, hence the variation here.

In Spanish, seco literally means "dry," the exact opposite feeling of this dish: every piece of chicken is lush and juicy. But it's popularly believed to refer to the thick-but-not-too-liquidy consistency of the stew itself. You want to see the blended sofrito texture blanketed over the chicken after a good amount of the liquid has evaporated; the plate should not be swimming in a flood of broth.

A great seco is about the balance of flavors. The classic preparation calls for chicha, an ancient fermented corn drink, instead of beer. But beer is more common today. It adds bitterness, while naranjilla—a citrusy fruit native to the region whose taste is often described as a cross between pineapple and lemon—balances it out with subtle sweetness. You can usually find frozen naranjilla pulp in Latin American grocery stores, but fresh orange juice is a solid substitute in a pinch. The stewed chicken adds a heaviness, and the shower of cilantro gives it a brightness. Each ingredient has a counterweight, making this dish harmonious in every way.

Time: 1 hour ● **Serves:** 4

Ingredients

1 large yellow onion, roughly chopped

1 large green bell pepper, roughly chopped

4 garlic cloves, roughly chopped

One 4-pound whole chicken, cut into 8 pieces (or 3 to 4 pounds bone-in, skin-on chicken pieces of your choice), patted dry

1 tablespoon plus 2 teaspoons kosher salt, plus more to taste

2 tablespoons extra-virgin olive oil

One 12-ounce can lager beer

4 ounces frozen naranjilla pulp (also called lulo), or ½ cup fresh orange juice (from 1 to 2 oranges)

1 tablespoon sazón with achiote

1½ pounds tomatoes, roughly chopped

1 tablespoon plus 1½ teaspoons white vinegar

1 cup packed finely chopped cilantro leaves and stems (about 1 bunch)

Recipe continues

●

9

Directions

1 Prepare the sofrito mixture. In a blender or food processor, combine the onion, bell pepper, and garlic until fully blended into a thick puree. Leave in the blender or food processor and set aside.

2 Season the chicken all over with 1 tablespoon of the salt.

3 Heat the oil in a large Dutch oven or large pot over medium-high heat. Once the oil is shimmering, add the chicken, skin side down, in batches as necessary to avoid overcrowding the pot. Cook until it's a deep brown color, about 5 minutes. Flip the pieces and cook on the other side until browned, another 4 to 5 minutes. Place the chicken on a plate and set aside.

4 Reduce the heat to medium and add the sofrito mixture (reserve the blender or food processor for the tomatoes), being careful not to splatter. Using a wooden spoon, scrape up any browned bits from the bottom of the pot. Cook until fragrant, about 5 minutes, stirring frequently to avoid browning.

5 Increase the heat to high and add the beer, naranjilla pulp, sazón, and remaining 2 teaspoons salt. Stir until fully incorporated. Bring to a boil.

6 While you wait for the mixture to boil, prepare the tomatoes. Add the tomatoes to the blender or food processor and blend until they're a thick puree. Pour the blended tomatoes directly into the pot and stir until fully incorporated. Return the mixture to a boil.

7 Add the chicken and any accumulated juices back to the pot, being sure to fully submerge the meat in the broth. Cover with a lid and reduce the heat to medium-low, stirring occasionally to evenly cook the meat and avoid scorching. Cook until the chicken starts to become tender and just begins to loosen from the bone, about 20 minutes. Remove the lid and increase the heat to medium-high. Cook uncovered until the liquid reduces and thickens, about 25 minutes (or until the desired texture is reached). Taste and adjust the salt. Remove from the heat.

8 Just before serving, add the vinegar and cilantro, letting the residual heat wilt the herb. Mix until the cilantro is evenly distributed. Serve while hot.

Plantains 101

Tostones and maduros are made from opposite sides of the same plantain coin. When green (I'm talking about 100 percent green, no yellow at all), plantains are unripe and are the starchiest. But over time they transform like the phases of the moon. Like bananas, plantains develop more sugars as they ripen—but please do not confuse plantains for bananas. These sugars will turn a green plantain yellow, then yellow with brown spots, and eventually, fully black. Maduros are best made with fully black plantains, when they're the sweetest and can caramelize easily from all the natural sugar; tostones are best made with fully green plantains, when they're the starchiest and can withstand being squished and fried twice. Essential to Latin American, Caribbean, Indian, and African cuisines, plantains are edible and beautiful at every color and stage of ripeness.

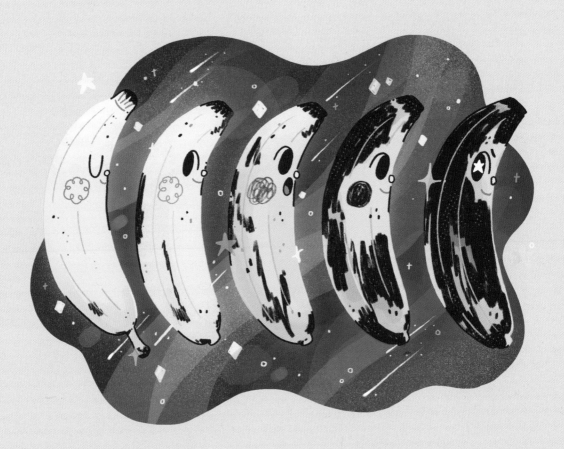

TOSTONES

Tostones go by many names. Known as patacones in Ecuador, frito verde in the Dominican Republic, and bannann peze in Haiti (just to name a couple), the dish always follows the same basic steps: green plantains, fried, flattened, and fried again. There are variations of this recipe out there that call for a bath of garlic and salt water between frying steps, but I have always grown up eating them made without it, so here we are. For the crunchiest and most golden tostones, use only the greenest unripe plantains. If your plantains have already begun to ripen and turn yellow, save them for maduros or another recipe. Eat tostones with guacamole, topped with ceviche, or just on their own, fresh from frying.

Time: 10 minutes ● **Serves:** 2 to 4

Ingredients

2 fully green (unripe) plantains

Vegetable oil, for frying

Salt

Directions

1 Peel the plantains. Cut off and discard the ends. Using a paring knife, cut a slit along the length of the plantains, carefully avoiding cutting into the flesh, and then remove the peels. If the peel is too firm, use a spoon to lift the edges. Slice the plantains crosswise into 1-inch thick rounds (6 to 8 pieces per plantain, depending on how long they are).

2 Heat about ⅓ inch of oil in a large skillet over medium heat. Once the oil is shimmering, add the plantains flat side down. Fry until they just start to turn golden but not brown, about 1 minute per side.

3 Turn off the heat, but keep the skillet on the burner. Using a slotted spoon or tongs, transfer the plantains to a cutting board. Working with one piece at a time, use a tostonera (a tool specifically made for this purpose!) or a large flat-bottomed cup to gently flatten each plantain to about ½ inch thick, being careful because they will still be hot. Do not wait until they cool off or they will be more difficult to flatten and may break. If using a cup, keep it as centered as possible to evenly flatten them. If any plantain gets a little stuck to the bottom of the cup, you can remove it gently with a knife.

Growing Up (Mostly) Ecuadorian

Recipe continues

4 Reheat the skillet over medium heat, adding a little more oil if necessary to keep it about ¼ inch full. Working in batches, fry the flattened plantains again until evenly golden and the edges are crisp, about 1 minute per side.

5 Using a slotted spoon, transfer the tostones to a paper towel–lined plate. Immediately sprinkle with salt to taste. Serve while hot.

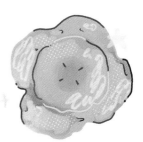

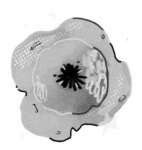

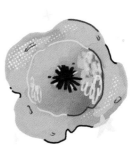

MADUROS

I know it can be hard to be patient when waiting for plantains to ripen, but you *really* should wait until they are fully black to make the best maduros. The riper they are, the more caramelized, burnt edges you'll get, and the sweeter each piece will be. This recipe is based on the most common way to cut maduros, but there are many ways to slice them: small rounds, halved lengthwise, quartered, or butterflied. Usually, I like eating these with heavier meats or dishes with tomato-based sauces to balance out the savoriness. But fried whole and drizzled with a little condensed milk is equally tasty.

Time: 10 minutes ● **Serves:** 4

Ingredients

2 very ripe, blackened plantains

Vegetable oil, for frying

Salt (optional)

Directions

1 Peel the plantains. Cut off and discard the ends. Using a paring knife, cut a slit along the length of the plantains, carefully avoiding cutting into the flesh, and then remove the peels. Slice the plantains at an angle crosswise into ½-inch-thick pieces (about 10 pieces per plantain).

2 Heat about ¼ inch of oil in a large skillet over medium-high heat. Once the oil starts to shimmer, add half the sliced plantains.

Fry until the middles are golden brown and the edges are dark brown, turning once, about 2 minutes per side. Each plantain should be fully caramelized on both sides with crisp edges but still-tender centers.

3 Using a slotted spoon, transfer the maduros to a paper towel-lined plate. Repeat with the remaining sliced plantains. Immediately sprinkle with salt to taste, if using. Serve while warm.

Dear plantains,

Do you remember the first time we met? You had just arrived from the store, still unripe, green, and full of starch. From the moment I saw you, I loved you. I love that as you've aged, you've done it with so much grace . . . turning yellow as you sweeten, then, eventually, a deeper shade with brown specks like sun-kissed freckles. Finally, you fully ripen and become all black with so much sugar that the sweet scent seeps from your skin. At every stage, you have always been beautiful and perfect.

No food is more versatile than you. Green and unripe means chips or tostones. Your starchiness gives you the ability to hold your shape and thicken whatever you're placed in. But even after being cooked and mashed, you can become Dominican mangú, Puerto Rican mofongo, bola-shaped Ecuadorian plantain dumplings, or empanada wrappers (fully replacing flour!). And when grated you can become a banana-leaf-steamed pastel or a bubbling cazuela. Your yellow in-between stage is best for a little-but-not-too-sweet sweetness and a tender-but-not-too-tender bite. And at your ripest, the possibilities are as endless as your youthful green phase. When you're sliced and fried as maduros, tiny clusters of caramelization form along your edges, sparking delight. But there's also pastelón, a lasagna-style dish in which the layers of pasta are replaced with thin slices of sweet plantain. Then you can be simply baked whole and stuffed with cheese or slowly cooked in sugar for cakes or sweet rolls. You can do anything.

I'm writing this to just say thank you. My life wouldn't be the same if we had never met. Every day I feel thankful we did. Although I don't see you as much (you don't really come here to Japan that often), I always think about you and wonder when we'll be reunited. Because when we are, I know it will have been worth the wait.

Until then,

Kiera

ENCOCADO DE CAMARÓN

This is a coastal Ecuadorian recipe that is so damn good that I wish I had eaten more of it growing up. Also commonly found along the Pacific coast of Colombia, encocado is a seafood dish made with achiote-spiced coconut milk (its name means "coconutted") that really makes it taste like a coconut hit you on the head (in a good way). I prefer shrimp for this—hence camarón—but fish like corvina and halibut are equally delicious. Just swap some skinless fillets for the shrimp to make pescado encocado. Most encocado variations use chopped tomatoes, but I use cherry ones here for the extra bursts of brightness. And the bonus is that this recipe takes only 15 minutes to make. Serve with white rice, sliced avocado, and tostones.

Time: 15 minutes   ●   **Serves:** 3 to 4

Ingredients

1 tablespoon extra-virgin olive oil

1 tablespoon unsalted butter

½ cup finely diced red onion

¼ cup finely diced red bell pepper

¼ cup finely diced green bell pepper

Handful of fresh cilantro, leaves and stems divided and finely chopped (about ½ cup)

2 scallions, thinly sliced, white and green parts divided

3 garlic cloves, finely chopped

One 13.5-ounce can coconut milk

1½ teaspoons kosher salt, plus more to taste

1½ teaspoons sazón with achiote

1 teaspoon ground cumin

½ teaspoon cayenne pepper (optional)

1 pound medium to large shrimp, peeled and deveined

½ cup halved cherry tomatoes

1 lime, quartered

Directions

1 Heat the oil and butter in a medium pot over medium-high heat. Once the butter is melted, add the onion, both bell peppers, the cilantro stems, scallion whites, and garlic. Cook, stirring frequently to avoid browning, until the onion is tender and translucent, about 3 minutes.

2 Add the coconut milk, salt, sazón, cumin, and cayenne (if using). Stir until the mixture is an even orange color. Bring to a boil and reduce the heat to medium-low. Simmer uncovered until the coconut milk reduces slightly and thickens enough to coat the back of a wooden spoon, 5 to 8 minutes.

Recipe continues

3 Increase the heat to medium-high. Add the shrimp and cherry tomatoes. Cook, stirring occasionally, until the shrimp is just cooked through with no visible pink color, about 2 minutes. Remove from the heat and immediately add the cilantro leaves and scallion greens. Taste and adjust for salt if desired. Mix to evenly distribute. Serve immediately with the lime wedges on the side.

AREPAS DE CHOCLO

Arepas are one of the quintessential Latin American foods, but this is the only recipe I have for them in this book. Mostly because I didn't grow up eating them very often—except for the ones at the South Florida Fair. For a middle schooler in West Palm Beach then, there were only three places in life that mattered: the movie theater, the mall, and this fair, which comes every January and proclaims itself to be "17 outrageously fun days," according to the official website. It was the social event of the season. Everyone who mattered was there, and they wore their best outfits in case their crush spotted them. For me, that meant my prized Ecuadorian beaded necklace with a metal medallion of a cartoon boy decked out in a backward hat in the yellow, blue, and red of the flag. When you arrived at the fair, a sea of other cartoon boy necklaces in various colors, representing different Latin American countries, would act as a welcoming committee. If you were Latinx, this was what you wore.

As at any good fair, the food was always deep-fried and decadent. But I usually walked past all the fried candy bars and Italian sausages to the carts selling sweet-smelling arepas de choclo: Colombian corn arepas stuffed with cheese. There are tons of variations out there, but these lean toward the sweeter and more buttery side, just like the fair's version. For some ingredient specifics: Most arepas are made with masarepa, a precooked and ultrafine corn flour that can be found in Latin American grocery stores. Fresh sweet corn is ideal if you can get it, but frozen works fine. And I personally like to use cheddar, even though it's not traditional, because of the sharpness and how it looks like grilled cheese. I guess my middle school tastes have not changed much.

Time: 40 minutes   ●   **Makes:** 7 arepas

Ingredients

2 cups corn kernels (from 2 to 3 ears of sweet corn)

1 cup whole milk, plus more as needed

2 tablespoons unsalted butter, melted, plus more for cooking

¼ cup sugar

Pinch of kosher salt

2 cups masarepa (preferably white P.A.N.), plus more as needed

1 cup shredded or crumbled cheese (such as queso fresco, mozzarella, or cheddar)

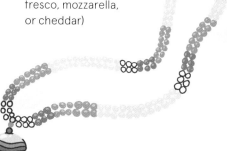

Recipe continues

Directions

1 In a blender, combine the corn, milk, melted butter, sugar, and salt. Blend until smooth.

2 Transfer the corn mixture to a large bowl. Add the masarepa and mix with a wooden spoon until fully combined. Cover and let rest for 10 minutes. After resting, the dough should have the same consistency as fresh Play-Doh and should not be sticky. If it's a little too wet, add another tablespoon of masarepa at a time until that consistency is reached. If it's too dry, add another tablespoon of milk.

3 Form the arepas. Divide the dough into seven equal portions, about ¼ cup each. Take a portion and roll it into a ball, then flatten into a disc, about ⅓ inch thick. Add about 2 tablespoons of cheese to the center and enclose the cheese in the arepa. Reform the ball and flatten it into a ½-inch-thick disc that's about 3 inches wide. Smooth out any cracks with your fingertips; you can also dip your fingers in a little bit of water to help with the smoothing if necessary. Repeat with the remaining dough.

4 Cook the arepas. Melt 1 tablespoon of butter in a large nonstick skillet over medium-low heat. Once melted, add half the arepas. Cook until both sides are browned, 4 to 5 minutes per side, adding more butter if necessary to avoid sticking. When a side is browned correctly, it will be easy to flip. If it's not ready yet, it will stick a little. Repeat with the remaining arepas. Serve while warm.

VEGAN GUATITA

So, the thing is . . . guatita isn't vegan, at least not traditionally. The name means "little belly" in Spanish because it's typically made with tender beef tripe. It's paired with potatoes and simmered in a peanut butter sauce that blankets everything with a nutty flavor. Because of its heartiness, it's a popular Ecuadorian hangover food.

That said, this version *is* vegan. I love the original and eat a lot of it whenever I'm visiting my family, but when I'm cooking at home, I sometimes like to eat less meat. Since I moved to Japan, my love for the umami meatiness of maitake mushrooms has grown tenfold, especially when they're seared just right. This vegan guatita is still guatita in all regards; it just swaps maitakes for the tripe, the mushrooms in some ways mirroring the tripe's soft texture. The sear on the mushrooms is key to bringing the same beef-like depth to the sauce, so be patient. I promise it's worth it.

Plate with white rice. And if you're looking for even more, add Cebollas Encurtidas (page 44), sliced avocado, and Maduros (page 15).

Time: 30 minutes ● **Serves:** 4 to 6

Ingredients

3 tablespoons extra-virgin olive oil

8 ounces maitake mushrooms, rinsed and torn into bite-size pieces

½ large yellow onion, chopped

½ large red onion, chopped

1 large green bell pepper, chopped

6 garlic cloves, chopped

1½ teaspoons sazón with achiote or ground achiote

1½ teaspoons ground cumin

2 teaspoons dried oregano

½ cup unsweetened creamy peanut butter

4½ cups unsalted vegetable stock or water

2 large (or 3 to 4 medium) Yukon Gold potatoes, peeled and cut into 1-inch pieces

Kosher salt and freshly cracked black pepper

1 cup packed finely chopped cilantro leaves and stems

Directions

1 Heat 2 tablespoons of the oil in a large Dutch oven or large pot over medium-high heat. Once the oil is shimmering, add the mushrooms and cook, stirring occasionally, until the moisture evaporates and the mushrooms become a deep brown color, about 6 minutes. Transfer the mushrooms to a bowl or plate and set aside.

Recipe continues

2 In the same pot, add the remaining 1 tablespoon oil, both onions, the bell pepper, garlic, sazón, cumin, and oregano. Stir frequently to evenly distribute the seasonings and avoid browning. Cook until the onions are translucent and tender, about 3 minutes. Remove from the heat.

3 In a blender, combine the cooked sofrito, peanut butter, and about half the vegetable stock. Blend until smooth. Add the blended mixture and remaining stock back into the same pot and bring to a boil.

4 Add the potatoes and reduce the heat to medium. Cook until the potatoes are tender and the broth is thick enough to lightly coat the back of a wooden spoon, 10 to 12 minutes.

5 Reserve about ¼ cup of the cilantro for garnish. Add the reserved mushrooms and remaining ¾ cup cilantro directly into the guatita. Then season with salt and black pepper to taste. Mix until well combined. Serve hot and garnish with the reserved cilantro.

TORTILLAS DE YUCA

If you've never eaten yuca before, you need to make this dish. And if you've eaten yuca a million times already, you *still* need to make this dish. Hands down, this is one of my favorite recipes in this book, and whenever I've made it for anyone, they instantly fall in love, too.

Tortillas de yuca are fried Ecuadorian yuca and cheese patties dyed orange from achiote. Traditionally, these are made with mashed cooked yuca as the base, but this recipe uses grated yuca, a method my grandparents developed together. They were inspired by muchines, another kind of Ecuadorian yuca patty that is shaped like a football and deep-fried. I'm sticking with the name tortillas de yuca, but truly, they are about half of each.

Queso fresco is Ecuador's go-to cheese choice for these. But in my house we sometimes swap it for cheddar, which complements the subtle floral sweetness of yuca beautifully. Eat them by themselves as a snack, appetizer, dinner side, or even for breakfast paired with eggs. Really any excuse to eat them is a good enough reason.

A word of advice: Grating 2 pounds of yuca by hand will be an arm workout, so this is a good time to recruit a friend for extra help. In return for their assistance, they will be rewarded with what will probably become everyone's favorite yuca dish.

Time: 45 minutes ● **Makes:** 8 to 10 tortillas

Ingredients

2 pounds yuca, peeled, halved, and deveined (see note)

2 cups crumbled queso fresco or shredded extra-sharp cheddar

1 tablespoon sazón with achiote

1½ teaspoons kosher salt

Cooking spray

¼ cup vegetable oil, plus more if needed

Directions

1 Using a box grater, grate the yuca on the side with the second smallest holes. The texture should be thinner than hash browns, with each grated piece being about the width of a spaghetti noodle (not fettuccine). Once grated, place in a fine-mesh strainer and squeeze out any excess liquid.

2 Transfer the strained yuca to a bowl. Add the cheese, sazón, and salt. Mix with a wooden spoon until fully combined and an even orange color.

3 Form the tortillas de yuca. Divide the mixture into 8 to 10 equal portions, about ½ cup each. Using your hands, roll each portion into a ball. Then with your palm, gently flatten each ball to form a patty about ½ inch thick.

Recipe continues

4 Preheat the oven to 350°F. Lightly coat a baking sheet with cooking spray.

5 Heat the oil in a large nonstick skillet over medium-high heat. Once the oil is shimmering, add half the tortillas de yuca. Cook until browned, 2 to 3 minutes per side. When a side is browned correctly, the patty will be easy to flip. If it's not ready yet, it will stick a little. Place the browned tortillas de yuca directly onto the prepared baking sheet. Repeat with the remaining patties, adding another tablespoon or two of oil as needed.

6 To finish cooking, bake for 10 to 15 minutes. Once cut, the color should be an even shade all the way through.

If it's not, continue to bake until it's one color throughout. Serve while warm.

Note: I prefer the texture of fresh yuca for this, but you can use whole thawed frozen yuca. Just be sure to thoroughly strain the frozen yuca by squeezing out the liquid after it's thawed and grated because it holds extra water.

For both the fresh and frozen yuca, be sure to remove the vein from the center. To do so, cut it in half and cut at an angle to remove the center fiber, doing your best to avoid cutting too much of the yuca flesh itself. Remember, this vein can be poisonous, so do not skip this step!

There's No One Way to Empanada

If you google "empanada recipe," about 38,100,000 results will appear in half a second—and those are just the ones the search engine can locate in English. Empanadas, one of Latin America's favorite dishes, have no limit. The filling, the flour dough, the not-flour dough, how to cook them . . . The list and its combinations go on forever.

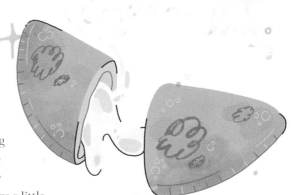

Here are four empanada variations (and a dough!) to start with that will encourage you to keep exploring the vast, beautiful empanada cinematic universe. The kimchi, chorizo, and cheddar empanadas are the only vaguely Korean recipe (which is my other half). They're a little spicy, and the fermented cabbage cuts the richness of the chorizo. The second recipe has spinach and cheese, a common vegetarian option you can find at a lot of Latin American restaurants. Then a classic beef, inspired by Argentina, the birthplace of empanadas. Finally, an Ecuadorian version called empanadas de viento, or cheese-stuffed empanadas topped with sugar. Viento translates to "wind," referring to the delicate and airy quality of the dough as it puffs up in hot oil. A little savory, a little sweet, and a whole lot of perfect.

KIMCHI, CHORIZO, AND CHEDDAR EMPANADAS

Time: 35 minutes, plus 30 minutes cooling   ●   **Makes:** 10 empanadas

Ingredients

8 ounces Spanish or Mexican fresh pork chorizo

⅓ cup strained and chopped napa cabbage kimchi

1 cup shredded cheddar

Ten 5-inch empanada wrappers (fresh or thawed), store-bought or homemade (see page 34)

Vegetable oil, for frying

Recipe continues

Directions

1 Squeeze the chorizo from its casing directly into a large skillet and then discard the casing. Cook the chorizo over medium-high heat, using a wooden spoon to break it into small pieces, until some parts begin to lightly crisp, 12 to 15 minutes. Remove from the heat and transfer to a large bowl.

2 Let the chorizo cool at room temperature or uncovered in the refrigerator for 30 minutes (you don't want the residual heat to melt the cheese). Once the chorizo is about room temperature, add the kimchi and cheddar. Mix until fully combined.

3 Working with one empanada wrapper at a time, place 2 tablespoons of the filling into the center of the wrapper. Using your finger, wet the edges of the dough with water and fold the wrapper over the filling, forming a little half-moon shape and gently pressing out as much air as possible. Then use the back of a fork to crimp the edges

of the empanada closed. Repeat with the remaining empanadas.

4 Heat ½ inch of vegetable oil in a large skillet over medium heat. Once the oil reaches 365°F and is shimmering, add the empanadas in batches, making sure they don't touch and adjusting the heat as necessary. Cook until golden brown, about 2 minutes per side. Transfer to a paper towel-lined plate and repeat with the remaining empanadas. Serve while hot. You can also store the cooked empanadas in the freezer for up to 3 months and reheat in the oven from frozen at 425°F for about 15 minutes, until warmed all the way through.

SPINACH AND CHEESE EMPANADAS

Time: 25 minutes, plus 15 minutes cooling ● **Makes:** 10 empanadas

Ingredients

1 tablespoon extra-virgin olive oil

5 garlic cloves, minced

13.5 ounces fresh spinach (one and a half 9-ounce bags)

Kosher salt

1⅓ cups shredded low-moisture mozzarella

Ten 5-inch empanada wrappers (fresh or thawed), store-bought or homemade (see page 34)

Vegetable oil, for frying

Directions

1 Heat the oil in a large skillet over medium heat. Once the oil is shimmering, add the garlic. Cook, stirring frequently, until the garlic is tender and fragrant, about 1 minute.

2 Add the spinach one handful at a time. Cook until it's just wilted, 1 to 2 minutes. Season with salt to taste. Remove from the heat and let cool for 15 minutes, then transfer to a fine-mesh strainer lined with a paper towel or cheesecloth and drain the excess liquid.

3 Transfer the spinach to a cutting board and chop it into smaller pieces. Place in a large bowl and mix in the mozzarella.

4 Working with one empanada wrapper at a time, place about 2 tablespoons of the filling into the center of the wrapper. Using your finger, wet the edges of the dough with water and fold the wrapper over the filling, forming a little half-moon shape and gently pressing out as much air as possible. Then use the back of a fork to crimp the edges of the empanada closed. Repeat with the remaining empanadas.

5 Heat ½ inch of vegetable oil in a large skillet over medium heat. Once the oil reaches 365°F and is shimmering, add the empanadas in batches, making sure they don't touch and adjusting the heat as necessary. Cook until golden brown, about 2 minutes per side. Transfer to a paper towel–lined plate and repeat with the remaining empanadas. Serve while hot. You can also store the cooked empanadas in the freezer for up to 3 months and reheat in the oven from frozen at 425°F for about 15 minutes, until warmed all the way through.

ARGENTINIAN-INSPIRED BEEF EMPANADAS

Time: 40 minutes • **Makes:** 10 empanadas

Ingredients

2 large eggs

1 tablespoon extra-virgin olive oil

3 tablespoons finely diced yellow onion

3 tablespoons finely diced red bell pepper

3 garlic cloves, minced

12 ounces lean ground beef

2 tablespoons raisins

¾ teaspoon ground cumin

¾ teaspoon paprika

½ teaspoon kosher salt, plus more to taste

½ teaspoon dried oregano

Pinch of cayenne pepper, plus more to taste (optional)

Ten 5-inch empanada wrappers (fresh or thawed), store-bought or homemade (see page 34)

Vegetable oil, for frying

Directions

1 Hard-boil the eggs. Place the eggs in a small pot and cover with water. Bring to a boil over high heat and cook for 10 to 12 minutes. Drain and rinse the eggs in cool water. Peel, chop into ¼-inch pieces, and set aside.

2 Heat the oil in a large skillet over medium-high heat. Add the onion, bell pepper, and garlic. Cook, stirring frequently to avoid browning, until the onion is tender and translucent, about 3 minutes.

3 Add the ground beef, raisins, cumin, paprika, salt, oregano, and cayenne (if using). Cook, stirring occasionally, until the beef is cooked through and begins to crisp in some areas, about 10 minutes. Remove from the heat and transfer to a large

bowl. Add the chopped eggs and mix until combined. Taste and adjust for salt.

4 Working with one empanada wrapper at a time, place about 2 tablespoons of the filling into the center of the wrapper. Using your finger, wet the edges of the dough with water and fold the wrapper over the filling, forming a little half-moon shape and gently pressing out as much air as possible. Then use the back of a fork to crimp the edges of the empanada closed. Repeat with the remaining empanadas.

5 Heat ½ inch of vegetable oil in a large skillet over medium heat. Once the oil reaches 365°F and is shimmering, add the empanadas in batches, making sure they don't touch and adjusting the heat as necessary. Cook until golden brown, about 2 minutes per side. Transfer to a paper towel–lined plate and repeat with the remaining empanadas. Serve while hot. You can also store the cooked empanadas in the freezer for up to 3 months and reheat in the oven from frozen at 425°F for about 15 minutes, until warmed all the way through.

EMPANADAS DE VIENTO (CHEESE EMPANADAS TOPPED WITH SUGAR!)

Time: 20 minutes ● **Makes:** 10 empanadas

Ingredients

1½ cups crumbled queso fresco

½ cup shredded low-moisture mozzarella

Ten 5-inch empanada wrappers (fresh or thawed), store-bought or homemade (recipe follows)

Vegetable oil, for frying

2 teaspoons sugar

Directions

1 Combine the queso fresco and mozzarella in a medium bowl.

2 Working with one empanada wrapper at a time, place about 2 tablespoons of the filling into the center of the wrapper. Using your finger, wet the edges of the dough with water and fold the wrapper over the filling, forming a little half-moon shape and gently pressing out as much air as possible. Then use the back of a fork to crimp the edges of the empanada closed. Repeat with the remaining empanadas.

3 Heat ½ inch of vegetable oil in a large skillet over medium heat. Once the oil reaches 365°F and is shimmering, add the empanadas in batches, making sure they don't touch and adjusting the heat as necessary. Cook until golden brown, about 2 minutes per side. Transfer to a paper towel–lined plate and immediately sprinkle some sugar on top. Repeat with the remaining empanadas. Serve while hot. You can also store the unsugared cooked empanadas in the freezer for up to 3 months

Recipe continues

and reheat in the oven from frozen at 425°F for about 15 minutes, until warmed all the way through. Sprinkle with sugar before eating.

EMPANADA DOUGH

This dough recipe is adapted from the empanadas found on Layla Pujol's food website, Laylita's Recipes. She was the first Ecuadorian food writer I found online who shared the recipes I grew up eating, and is someone I return to often when I'm looking for new dishes to cook. Don't get me wrong: I am a firm believer in the store-bought-is-fine mentality, so if you can get frozen empanada dough, do what you gotta do. But if you want a small DIY dough project, this one is easy. The sparkling water creates tiny air pockets that give the fried product a lighter texture. And the cold cubes of butter make these way more buttery than store-bought varieties.

Time: 15 minutes, plus 30 minutes resting ● **Makes:** 10 empanada wrappers

Ingredients

2 cups all-purpose flour, plus more as needed

¾ teaspoon baking powder

½ teaspoon kosher salt

5 tablespoons cold unsalted butter, cut into ½-inch cubes

6 tablespoons cold sparkling water, plus more as needed

1 tablespoon any neutral oil

Directions

1 In a food processor, add the flour, baking powder, and salt. Pulse a couple of times to fully combine. Add the butter and pulse until combined. Then add the sparkling water and pulse again until a dough starts to form. The consistency should resemble Play-Doh. If the dough is not coming together and looks too dry, add more sparkling water as needed, 1 tablespoon at a time, being careful to not make the dough too wet.

2 Lightly coat the bottom of a large bowl with the oil. Transfer the dough to a lightly floured or nonstick surface and knead until it is smooth and does not stick to your fingers, about 3 minutes. Roll the dough into a ball and place into the bowl. Cover and let rest at room temperature for 30 minutes.

3 Form the empanada rounds. Divide the dough into 10 equal pieces (about 40 g per portion) and roll each portion into a little ball. Working with one piece at a time, transfer a ball to a lightly floured or nonstick surface. Use a rolling pin to roll out the dough to be about 5 to 5½ inches wide, alternating rolling directions to keep it as circular as possible (but it's OK if it's not perfect!). Place the round on wax or parchment paper so it doesn't stick and tear. Repeat with the remaining dough, layering wax

or parchment paper between each one so they don't touch. Use immediately (see note) or wrap in plastic wrap and chill in the refrigerator for same-day use. You may also store them in an airtight container in the freezer for up to 3 months. Just thaw in the refrigerator before using.

Note: You can use the dough right away without any issues, but the crimped edge will lose some of its definition. For high-def crimps, chill your dough for 30 minutes to 1 hour before filling and frying. The cold dough will retain its shape the best.

THE CHONGA YEARS

Chonga
noun—chonga / CHON • ga /
A girl who identifies as Hispanic and lives in South Florida. The Spanish-derived term was popularized around 2004. As stated by Wikipedia, it was often used to describe young women who adopted a specific look that involved tight pants, bold jewelry, and gelled hair. As it grew in popularity, it became a small subculture in the region.

In middle school, I was a chonga. Though being a chonga requires multiple elements, my twelve-year-old interpretation was: skin-tight pants called Brazilian jeans with tiny pockets to accentuate the back, baggy T-shirts, Reeboks with shoelaces that color coordinated with my T-shirt, lots of gold bangles for both of my wrists, a fake-gold nameplate necklace that said "Kiera," purchased from the flea market, and gold hoop earrings so big I could fit my whole hand through them.

The makeup and hair were elaborate but essential to complete the transformation. The goal was straightforward—to look like a cute Bratz doll with exaggerated features like heavily lined eyes and perky lips. But the makeup execution took lots of practice that was well beyond my adolescent skill set, so I dumbed it down with heavy black eyeliner to tightline my upper lash line and waterline my bottom. To really bring out the eyeliner's inky quality, I would pop into the school bathroom and use a lighter to heat up the eyeliner tip so it melted (a trick I picked up from my fellow chongas), causing the occasional leakage into my eyes and momentary blindness. It felt like a small price to pay to look cool. When I dared to be extra brave, I would also take a dark brown liner, trace the outline of my lips, and use the shiniest dollar-store lip gloss I could find to fill in the middle.

The hairstyle was supposed to accentuate a naturally curly texture, but as someone who has almost pin-straight hair, it made zero sense for me to try. Nonetheless, I did it anyway. Every day before school, I would blast Ivy Queen (the reggaeton icon) and start the long process. I put handfuls upon handfuls of curly hair products into my straight-ass hair, doing my best to scrunch and press it into curls. Occasionally small swiggles would form and harden from the copious amounts of gel, but usually my hair looked like millions of wet spikes.

It was a look. And from twelve to fourteen years old, this was what I (and many other Latinx girls in my middle school and South Florida at large) wore every day. Dressed as a chonga, I could fully represent being Ecuadorian, feel like I was part of a larger Latinx community for the first time, and hide that I was also half Asian. I had been called racial slurs since I was a kid, and the tight pants and scrunchy hair felt like a full-body suit of metal armor against the world.

I spent some of my childhood living in the rural part of West Palm Beach, far from the shores and even farther from the rich neighborhoods of the city. The farther west you drove, the denser the woods became and the dustier the streets were. The only home my parents ever bought together was on a dirt road in this neighborhood. But they soon sold it after they split only a couple of years later. And when I eventually returned to Florida to live with my grandparents in middle school, I was back in the same rural part of town on another dirt road not far from the first one. It was still an underdeveloped area, so you could buy a lot of land and build a house for a fair price. But it meant not being around much of what I enjoyed.

Parts of the land were beautiful, though. The pine trees grew so tall that they towered over even the largest house. The ponds scattered everywhere always had tiny ripples along the surface from the fish catching bugs. And at night, the soft stirrings of various woodland creatures hummed out soothing ambient sounds to help me drift off to sleep. But it wasn't until I was older that I noticed, hidden among the trees, the many Confederate flags on people's houses, on trucks, and on clothing. Honestly, I didn't even know that this was unusual until I left Florida altogether.

There were almost no Asian people where I grew up, so I always stood out, no matter where I was. The slurs started as far back as elementary school. There's no need to repeat them because they're so hateful (but whatever you're imagining they are, you are probably correct). Some kids in my class would pull their eyes back and laugh as they made fun of my physical features, something that continued even after college. As a child with no one else around who looked like me, the racism that engulfed me made me hyperaware that I was different from everyone else. And the message I was being sent was that I should feel bad about it.

Those conflicted feelings about my looks and ethnicity weighed heavily on me and grew stronger with each passing year. By the time I became a preteen, my already wavering confidence collapsed into itself like a black hole.

In middle school, with the move to my grandparents' house, I became the new kid again. Unlike in my elementary school, kids in this middle school were loud about their cultural identities. Although there was still no Asian community, it was the first time I saw Latinx students be proud of their ethnic backgrounds—and I wanted to be a part of it.

Whatever people assume I am, others have guessed the opposite. To some there was no mistaking that I was Asian, but another person could guess I was fully Latinx. Back then, the concept of being somewhere in the middle was not discussed. Ethnicity felt only black-and-white, even if there's an infinity of colors in between. In this new school, I decided to abandon my Asian identity in an attempt to get rid of the racist trauma. From then on, I was only Ecuadorian. The idea of choosing to be only one identity when you're more is, of course, ridiculous and impossible. But adopting the chonga look gave me the ability to lead with one half of myself and finally get a chance to blend in. When people asked then, "What are you?" I would reply with "Ecuadorian" and omit the Korean half completely.

The exact origin of chongas is not well documented, but the subculture is believed to have been created by the Cuban American community in Miami and may have begun as early as the 1990s, even though it didn't build widespread momentum until the early 2000s. The looks and interests associated with chonga culture seem to draw inspiration from the established Mexican Chicana and Black communities in the US. In 2007, a video called "Chongalicious" went viral and pushed the topic of chongas into the national spotlight for the first time. It was a parody of Fergie's hit song "Fergalicious" with a stereotypical portrayal of chongas, but it was made by two women who did not identify with the subculture. Instead of celebrating it, they made fun of it, damaging the image of not just chongas but all Latinx women by enforcing harmful beliefs. Now, almost two decades later, the video has over 8 million views on YouTube.

Little to no academic research has focused on chonga subculture, except for the extensive work by Dr. Jillian Hernandez, who studies Blackness and Latinidad as relational formations. In her book *Aesthetics of Excess: The Art and Politics of Black and Latina Embodiment,* she begins with a first-person story about her own experience with chonga culture and why it's also an example of an aesthetic of excess, then she explores the meaning and significance behind some over-the-top appearances within these larger minority groups and what they reflect about our society. "To exceed is to trespass," she writes. With so many different kinds of societal pressures, deifying things like gender expectations and fashion norms can be a way for some people to find liberation. A short excerpt from the book:

> **Aesthetics of excess embrace abundance where the political order would impose austerity upon the racialized poor**

and working class, viewed as excessive as in unnecessary, unproductive ... This is why artist Kehinde Wiley poses young working-class Black men against floral baroque patterns and ornate gilded frames, why performer Celia Cruz wore spectacular gowns and wigs, why the late Chicana singer Selena bedazzled her bras with sequins and rhinestones.

Dr. Hernandez's concept of being hypervisible through excess in spite of the white supremacist state of surveillance on Black and Latinx consumption really resonated with me. Being a chonga meant putting what people asked you to hide on the loudest volume for the world to see. As part of the Latinx community, I felt empowered to own my identity in an area that didn't welcome people with diverse backgrounds. But there was this internal irony because, while I was proud on one hand, I also felt scared to own my Asian identity the same way because of the past.

I don't really remember how or why I stopped scrunching my hair with buckets of gel, stopped sliding into the tightest pants I owned, or stopped using dark brown liner to outline my lips, but I did. All the places where I used to shop slowly faded away with time. The flea market where I bought my fake gold became an empty building. The mall with my favorite Brazilian pants closed, like so many other malls. Now it's a Whole Foods.

Looking back, I have complicated feelings about my chonga phase. I feel uncomfortable about how I claimed my Ecuadorian culture when I didn't know it then, and not just because I was twelve. Even now, as an adult writing a book on the subject, I still have so much to learn. While I feel happy that I was able to find confidence at such a tender stage in my life, I mostly feel sad because I felt then that I had to conceal my Asian identity to find any kind of acceptance. To be honest, the other chongas in my school probably wouldn't have cared that I was also Asian, but I was too scared to find out and lose the one community I was a part of. My chonga phase acts as a reminder to never hide again, either side.

Some people may believe that our "phases" fade away and leave us forever, but I don't. Like a tattoo, they're a reminder of who we were and how we got here, even if we're a different version of ourselves now.

It's been twenty years since my chonga days. All of those clothes and fake jewelry are long gone. But I recently bought a pair of big hoop earrings again for the first time in a long time, and the weight gently tugging on the bottom of my earlobes just felt right.

LLAPINGACHOS IS THE BEST WORD TO SAY

There's no breakfast dish with a better name than Ecuadorian llapingachos. Pronounced "yah-peen-GAH-chos," these fried potato and cheese patties are traditionally mixed with achiote, which is how they get their orange hue. In this version, sazón gives them the same vibrance while adding even more flavor.

No plate would be complete without salsa de maní spooned over the top of each patty. The peanut butter–based sauce is a little sweet and rich, helping balance the savory elements of the llapingachos themselves. For the full hearty breakfast experience, eat with eggs, chorizo, and avocado slices.

Time: 35 minutes ● **Makes:** 6 llapingachos

Ingredients

SALSA DE MANÍ

1 tablespoon extra-virgin olive oil

1 scallion, thinly sliced

2 garlic cloves, minced

¼ cup chunky unsweetened peanut butter

½ cup plus 2 tablespoons whole milk

½ teaspoon ground cumin

¼ teaspoon kosher salt

Pinch of light or dark brown sugar

Freshly cracked black pepper

Cayenne pepper (optional)

2 tablespoons finely chopped cilantro leaves

LLAPINGACHOS

1 pound Yukon Gold potatoes, peeled and cut into 1-inch pieces (about 2 medium potatoes)

1½ tablespoons kosher salt

1 tablespoon unsalted butter

¼ cup all-purpose flour

1½ teaspoons sazón with achiote

½ teaspoon onion powder (optional)

¼ teaspoon ground cumin

Scant ½ cup shredded low-moisture mozzarella

2 teaspoons extra-virgin olive oil

2 tablespoons finely chopped cilantro (optional)

Directions

1 Make the salsa de maní. Heat the oil in a small saucepan over medium heat. Once the oil is shimmering, add the scallion and garlic. Cook, stirring frequently to avoid browning, until the garlic is tender and fragrant, about 1 minute.

Recipe continues

2 Reduce the heat to medium-low and add the peanut butter. Cook, stirring frequently to keep the garlic from burning, until the peanut butter is mostly melted, about 1 minute. Add the milk, cumin, salt, brown sugar, black pepper to taste, and cayenne to taste (if using). Stir until fully combined. Increase the heat to medium, bring the mixture to a boil, and cook for 2 minutes, or until slightly thickened. The consistency should be spoonable but not runny. Remove from the heat and stir in the cilantro. Serve at room temperature. Store in the refrigerator for up to 3 days.

3 Make the llapingachos. Add the potatoes and salt to a small pot. Fill the pot with water and place over high heat. Bring to a boil and cook until the potatoes are fork-tender, about 9 minutes. Drain and place the potatoes back into the same pot for mashing.

4 With a potato masher or the back of a fork, mash the potatoes until smooth, adding the butter halfway through so it melts into the potatoes. Add the flour, sazón, onion powder (if using), and cumin.

Using your hand or a wooden spoon, mix just until the flour and sazón are evenly distributed. Avoid overmixing the potatoes or the texture could become gummy.

5 Form the llapingachos. Divide the potato mixture into 6 equal portions, about ⅓ cup each. Roll each portion into a ball, then flatten it into a disc about ½ inch thick. Place 1 tablespoon of cheese in the center and enclose it in the llapingacho. Reform the ball and flatten it into a ½-inch-thick disc that's about 3 inches wide. Smooth out any cracks or uneven parts with your fingertips.

6 Heat 1 teaspoon of the oil in a large nonstick skillet over medium heat. Once the oil is shimmering, add half the llapingachos. Cook until both sides are browned, about 4 minutes per side. Try not to flip them too early because the surfaces are fragile and may tear if turned before they're fully browned. Repeat with the remaining half. Serve while warm with salsa de maní generously spooned over the top and garnish with the cilantro, if using, 2 to 3 llapingachos per serving.

ARROZ AMARILLO

Yellow rice is white rice's golden, more flavorful cousin. It's my go-to rice for many Ecuadorian dishes, and it's particularly good for soaking up seco. It gets its yellow/orange color from the achiote in sazón. Personally, I like mine on the extra-vibrant side—hence the big tablespoon of sazón—but feel free to halve it for a truer gold shade.

I'm not going to lie, I have been using a rice cooker exclusively to make my rice for years now. (It's one of those singing Zojirushi ones, so how can I not use it?) This recipe, though, is written to make fluffy rice on the stove. But if you have a rice cooker you love, use it because it's easier.

Time: 35 minutes ● **Serves:** 4 to 6

Ingredients

2 cups long-grain white rice

1½ teaspoons extra-virgin olive oil

1 tablespoon sazón with achiote

1 teaspoon kosher salt, plus more to taste

Directions

1 Wash the rice. Using a fine-mesh strainer, rinse the rice with tap water, using your hand to swirl the grains around. Repeat at least three times, until the water runs clear.

2 Add the drained, rinsed rice to a medium pot. Add 3 cups water, the oil, sazón, and salt. Mix to evenly distribute the sazón. Bring to a boil. Cover, reduce the heat to low, and simmer until all the water has been absorbed, about 15 minutes.

3 Remove from the heat. Let the rice sit covered to steam for another 15 minutes. Uncover and fluff with a fork before serving. Taste and adjust for salt, if needed.

CEBOLLAS ENCURTIDAS (LIME-PICKLED ONIONS)

This is one of those recipes that almost feels too easy to even be called a recipe. Like, literally all you have to do is mix lime juice, salt, and red onion together. But the outcome is beautiful: once the onions start to soak in the acid, the red color spreads and dyes the slices neon fuchsia until they resemble tiny party streamers. This "recipe" is for the fastest method possible, but there are a few ways to switch it up. The thinner the onion, the more quickly it will begin to change color. The longer the onions soak, the brighter the color will become. Overnight yields good results, but two-day encurtidas look like they're ready to dance in a rave.

There are so many ways to enjoy these: in a leafy salad, over toast, on top of Pernil (page 193), with Vegan Guatita (page 21), tossed with tomatoes, spooned over Tamale Soup (page 139), and more. I use extra lime juice in this because a couple of spoonfuls only helps brighten the flavors of whatever you're eating, so don't let it go to waste.

Time: 5 minutes, plus soaking ● **Makes:** About 2 cups

Ingredients

4 limes, juiced (about ⅔ cup)

1½ teaspoons kosher salt

1 large red onion, halved and thinly sliced (⅛-inch slices cut with a knife or as thin as you like with a mandoline)

Directions

1 Combine the lime juice and salt in a large bowl. Add the onion and mix until coated. Try to submerge most of the onion in the lime juice, but it's OK if they're not all completely soaked.

2 Cover and let marinate in the fridge until the onions soften and become fluorescent pink, about 30 minutes. The longer you let them sit, the more vibrant they will become. Eat right away or store in the fridge for up to 3 days.

CHAPTER 2

GRANDPA'S FAVORITES

D o you know what your grandpa's everyday routine is? Like, *truly* know it? I didn't until I went back to Florida to learn my grandparents' recipes for this cookbook. Because I didn't have access to my own car, I stayed in their house during the day for two weeks, the longest time in over a decade. I closely observed my grandpa in his natural habitat, like a nature documentary, and it felt like a privilege to see his daily activities so up close and personal. Here is the result of my research, what a normal Tuesday looks like for him:

7:30 a.m.	Wake up and start watching the news, preferably Telemundo.
8:00 a.m.	Drive my grandma to work.
9:00 a.m.	Eat the breakfast of leftovers she portioned out for him the night before.
9:30 a.m.	Snack on a fruit cup, and drink hot chocolate.
10:00 a.m.	Shuffle around the kitchen putting dishes away. He says it's his exercise and that this is his main job. Sometimes the dishes are not put in the right spot.
11:00 a.m.	End up on the "Explore" page of Instagram and fall down a rabbit hole of weird funny videos of people falling.
12:00 p.m.	Go to sleep in the chair in front of the TV.
1:00 p.m.	Move to bed and nap some more.
4:00 p.m.	Pick up my grandma from work.
5:00 p.m.	Eat an early dinner that's usually leaner than what my grandma eats. This could be a small serving of rice and precut steak so it's easier to chew.
6:00 p.m.	Catch up on various family dramas, juggling different phone calls from his various daughters.
6:30 p.m.	Read a book about wellness.
7:00 p.m.	Watch the nightly Telemundo programs with Grandma.
8:00 p.m.	Get ready for bed.
9:00 p.m.	Zzzz.

My grandpa, Jorge Ruiz, is well into his nineties now, so life is calmer and slower. But his younger years in Ecuador were anything but.

Jorge was born in the 1930s in Guayaquil, Ecuador's second largest city, main port, and most important economic center. It currently has a population of over three million, but while Jorge was growing up, it was under five hundred thousand from what he can recall. The city today is a hub for many businesses, with modern skyscrapers dotted throughout its historic downtown area. In the 1930s, it looked very different: sparser, with modest homes inland and colonial buildings along the Río Guayas, a huge river that crawls its way through the city. Jorge hasn't gone back to Ecuador since 1970, a year after he immigrated to the US, but if he did, he probably wouldn't recognize his first home.

At fifteen years old, Jorge was recruited to start boxing at a neighborhood gym. He was a little over five feet tall, a seeming disadvantage against taller fighters, but with Ecuador's average height being five feet, four inches, he fit right in. He was in the category gallo (Spanish for "rooster") and was already a local champion by the age of sixteen. Instead of a cash prize, he received only fabric and shoes, but to this day, he talks about his time in the ring with so much pride.

Boxing eventually led him to become a lucha libre wrestler and compete in matches all over Guayaquil. Just as WWE (World Wrestling Entertainment) and Olympic wrestling differ, lucha libre skews toward the more dramatic WWE style. Lucha libre is a popular style of wrestling created in Mexico, where fighters battle it out in the ring in a performance that's as physical as it is campy. Wrestlers, often in colorful masks that fully enclose their heads with only their eyes, nose, and mouth poking out from behind metallic fabric, soar from great heights across the ring to body-slam opponents. Although lucha libre originated in Mexico, many places throughout the world carry on its legacy. And in Jorge's Ecuador, it was what everyone wanted to see. He went by the name of El Indomable (The Indomitable) because he never lost. Through his wins, he gained some local notoriety, drawing as many as ten thousand people to local stadiums, where they'd cheer him on every other week. Today his lucha libre days live on through the weathered newspaper stories and black-and-white photos he keeps safely tucked away in one of his many photo albums.

During his decade-plus of wrestling, Jorge also became a cop. Without a high school degree, he wasn't supposed to join the force, but one of the officers recognized him as a luchador, which I guess was enough to bend some rules back then. While on the job one night in 1955, he was accompanying a politician by motorcycle when a car slammed into him. This accident would shape the rest of his life. Immediately afterward he was rushed to the hospital, where they performed surgery. All he says about it is that his leg is now metal inside. He had to stay in the hospital for a year to recover; he learned to walk again.

My grandpa has had a severe limp as far back as I can remember. When he got older, he started to use a cane, and eventually that cane was replaced by an electric scooter that he zips around in. For the first time ever, he's faster than me.

Looking through his stacks of photo albums, I've felt a disconnect between the grandpa I know today and the version of him from his youth. Was this suave young man the same person I know now? But I am quickly reminded that he is whenever it's time to go out.

Every moving-to-America story is unique, but they usually have one common throughline: the pursuit of a better life. And my grandpa was able to find that in the US.

His closet is stuffed with tailored pants, dress jackets, button-ups, vests, suspenders, hats, and neckties in every pattern. No matter how small or big the occasion, Jorge cleans up. He always slicks back his still mostly black hair and color coordinates his outfits. When I got married during the pandemic, he attended my ceremony via Zoom (where it really didn't matter what people wore to the video call) and still showed up in a freshly pressed three-piece suit.

In 1969, Jorge and his then-wife, Patricia (my "blood grandma"), immigrated to New York City. He followed his cousin and younger brother who settled there first, among the thousands of Ecuadorians in the initial mass migration to the city. His seven kids came in batches after him because he didn't have enough money to fly everyone over all at once. But with Patricia and Jorge both working, they were able to save enough that by the end of their first year in New York, the family was back together again. And by the second year, they could buy bikes for the kids and a large TV, which would not have been possible in Ecuador.

When I asked my grandpa why he wanted to move to the US, his answer was simple—money. At that time in Guayaquil, he would earn monthly about 3,000 sucre (Ecuador's currency from 1884 to 2000 before the economy collapsed and it was switched to the US dollar). According to Wikipedia, 3,000 sucre was equivalent to about $150 USD then, less than $2,000 for an entire year. But in the US, even a very low-paying job could earn him much more.

Because he had almost no English-speaking abilities, finding work proved to be difficult. He first worked for security in New York's JFK airport alongside other people who spoke only Spanish. But later he landed a gig as a handyman through another Ecuadorian immigrant he met in the city. "Just tell them you have experience with electricity," he encouraged Jorge to say. So Jorge did. Although he didn't have any real qualifications at the time, he grew into the role by learning on the job, and it became his lifelong career. He retired only when he was physically unable to work any longer.

I'm sharing all of this because I really admire everything my grandpa did to move our family to the US. As someone who has also relocated to another country (although my situation is much different and more privileged in every way), I now know firsthand how difficult it can be—let alone with seven kids. Every moving-to-America story is unique, but they usually have one common throughline: the pursuit of a better life. And my grandpa was able to find that in the US.

Although I grew up mostly with my grandpa's second wife, Veronica (a lot more about her in the next chapter!), doing almost all the cooking, Jorge knows his way around the kitchen, too.

Shortly after he settled in New York, he and Patricia got divorced. He started to cook on a regular basis to feed his large family. At a young age back in Ecuador, he had learned to cook out of necessity. He stopped going to school altogether because his family was unable to afford shoes. With no classes or homework to fill his days, he worked at an extended family member's restaurant in exchange for free meals. The first dish he learned to make was rice. He began by washing the rice, rinsing it under water until the water ran clear, getting rid of the excess starch. Then he cooked it in a pot until it was light and fluffy. He's made rice the same way ever since. Working there, he watched how different stews and marinated meats were prepared, and how many of the dishes were paired with slices of ripe avocado.

My food memories of him when I was growing up are of eating big piles of crabs for celebrations and watching him cut into long strips of still-sizzling churrasco by the poolside. Seeing him bake whole ripe plantains until they're fully caramelized before stuffing them with cheese for breakfast. Or my grandma Veronica and him tag-teaming to make ceviche. She's allergic to lime skins, so my grandpa would cut and juice all the limes while she did the rest. I can still clearly envision the large silver juicer whirring its sharp blades on their kitchen table and squirts of lime juice flying in the air. This chapter is dedicated to all the foods he loves and taught me to love, too.

As I've grown older, our time together has become less frequent. The farther I move away from South Florida, the less close contact I have with him. I will mention this a couple of times throughout the book because I think it's important: you don't need to write a book to find the time to learn and collect your grandparents' stories. But I am very grateful that this project finally pushed me to spend more time with my grandpa.

ENCEBOLLADO

Ecuador is one of the largest tuna-producing nations in the world. It's no surprise that encebollado is among the country's most famous dishes. It's a fish soup made with chunks of fresh albacore, yuca, tomatoes, and herbs that's popular along the country's coastal region. The giant bites of tuna that infuse the soup with the flavor of the sea are the main star. The full name of the dish is encebollado de pescado, which roughly translates to "onioned fish soup," but it is often just called encebollado. If it seems odd to you that onion can be a verb, that's only because you haven't tried this dish yet. Each bowl is topped with a big pile of red onion and cilantro, which is then doused in lime juice. As you spoon the oniony mixture over, the lime juice adds to the richness and brightens each ingredient. Encebollado can be enjoyed for breakfast, lunch, or dinner: anytime is a good time. While the chifles, or plantain chips, are optional, you don't want to miss the crunch.

Time: 40 minutes • **Serves:** 8

Ingredients

3 tablespoons extra-virgin olive oil

½ large green bell pepper, roughly chopped (about 1 cup)

¼ large red onion, roughly chopped (about ½ cup) plus 1 medium red onion, thinly sliced (about 2 cups) for garnish

4 garlic cloves, chopped

1 tablespoon dried oregano

1 tablespoon ground cumin

8 ounces Roma tomatoes, roughly chopped (about 2 large tomatoes)

One 1-inch piece ginger, peeled and chopped

1 tablespoon sazón with achiote

1 tablespoon kosher salt, plus more to taste

¼ teaspoon cayenne pepper (optional)

2 pounds fresh albacore tuna

¼ bunch parsley, tied in a bundle (see note)

¼ bunch cilantro, tied in a bundle (see note) plus ½ cup packed finely chopped cilantro leaves for garnish

1 pound yuca, peeled and halved (fresh or frozen)

2 limes, cut into wedges

Chifles (optional)

Directions

1 Heat the oil in a large pot over medium-high heat. Add the bell pepper, chopped onion, garlic, oregano, and cumin. Cook, stirring frequently to avoid browning, until the onion is soft and translucent, about 3 minutes.

2 Add 8 cups water, the tomatoes, ginger, sazón, salt, and cayenne. Bring to a boil. Once boiling, add the tuna and herb bundle and reduce the heat to medium. Cook until the tuna is no longer pink in color and is easy to separate, 10 to 15 minutes. Turn off the heat. Using tongs or a slotted spoon, transfer the tuna to a large plate to cool for at least 10 minutes. Remove and discard the herb bundle.

3 While the tuna is cooking and cooling, make the yuca. Fill a separate large pot with water and bring to a boil over high heat. Once boiling, add the yuca. Boil until fork-tender, about 20 minutes for fresh yuca or according to the package instructions for frozen. Drain and transfer the yuca to a cutting board to cool. Once cool enough to handle, remove the middle fibers and cut into 2-inch pieces. Set aside until serving.

4 Use an immersion blender to blend the soup mixture until smooth, about 3 minutes. Season with salt to taste. (You can use a regular blender, but be very careful with the hot liquid and be sure to remove the middle center piece from the top to allow the steam to escape. If you don't, you may have a hot, dangerous mess. Use a kitchen towel to loosely cover the top while you blend to avoid splatters.)

5 Once the tuna is cool enough to handle, break it into bite-size pieces. It's easiest to use your hands and break it along the natural grooves of the flesh, but you can also use a knife if you prefer.

6 Rewarm the soup if necessary. To serve, place some yuca and tuna in a bowl and ladle the hot broth over them. Top with the sliced red onion and cilantro leaves and serve with the lime wedges and chifles (if using) on the side.

Note: To create the herb bundle, stack the parsley and cilantro and wrap them tightly with butcher twine. Alternatively, you can put the herbs in a cheesecloth and tie it with butcher twine or a piece of ripped cheesecloth. But personally, if some herbs fall into the soup, I'm not mad.

GUAYAQUIL GARLIC CRABS

My grandpa is happiest when he's cracking open a mountain of crabs. For his birthday, he usually goes to the Chinese buffet and throws down the most crabs I have ever seen anyone eat in one sitting. I grew up hearing about the legendary seafood in Guayaquil, his hometown in Ecuador, but I didn't know how special it was until I saw it myself.

Red crabs are the crab of choice (and arguably, of all seafood) in Guayaquil. They are bigger than the small blue crabs easily found in the US and have much more rounded heads that almost look like tiny blown-up balloons. Nestled along the shore, they live in holes hidden among mangrove roots, where skilled catchers gather them into huge bundles for local markets. Unlike the US blue crabs that are blue all around, uncooked red crabs look like a burning sunset: eight eggplant-purple legs, two lavender claws, and a bright orange-red head that fades into a dusky blue in the center. But they transform to that familiar neon tangerine color once cooked. If Maryland blue crabs were a cursive font, Guayaquil red crabs would be big bubble letters.

I knew I had to try some when I visited Guayaquil, so I ventured to the Red Crab, a local seafood institution that's been around for over twenty-five years. From the moment I arrived, the scale of everything disoriented me. On top of the entrance rests a monstrous ten-foot-wide crab that made me feel as if I were its meal. Circling the top of the building are sky-blue waves outlined in neon lights. And right under the crab's massive claws, the words "red crab" are scribbled in neon with the same flourish as someone signing off with "all my love" at the end of a letter. Inside the restaurant, the scale is normal—at least until the food arrives. I have never been served a plate of crabs as big before. Stacks of bubbly red crabs were layered on top of each other and blanketed with a thick orange sauce studded with minced garlic. As I stared at the pile of crabs, I again felt small.

When I think back to that meal, all I remember is being in a crab/sauce/garlic vortex. Time stopped as I cracked, pried open, and slurped each crab. I could have been there for two hours or two days; it's hard to tell. This recipe is an ode to those crabs.

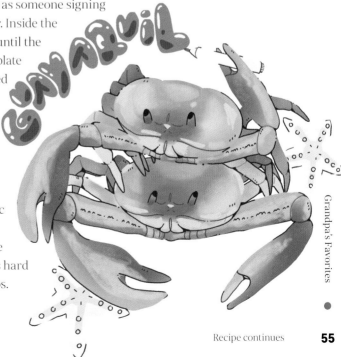

Grandpa's Favorites

Recipe continues

Because those specific red crabs are so difficult to find in the US, I use blue crabs here. I am not entirely sure what Red Crab uses in their sauce, so this is my take on it, complete with twenty cloves of garlic.

Time: 25 minutes ● **Serves:** 2 to 3

Ingredients

2 pounds fresh crabs, rinsed (about 8 blue crabs)

4 tablespoons unsalted butter

20 garlic cloves, finely chopped (about 2 heads garlic)

½ cup dry white wine

½ cup unsalted chicken stock

1 cup heavy cream

1½ tablespoons sazón with achiote

Kosher salt

Directions

1 Bring a large pot of water to a boil over high heat. Once boiling, add the crabs. Cook until fully red, 5 to 6 minutes. Drain and set aside.

2 Melt the butter in a large, deep skillet over medium heat. Once melted, add the garlic. Cook, stirring frequently, until tender and fragrant but not yet browned, 2 to 3 minutes.

3 Add the wine. Boil until the raw alcohol smell has cooked off, about 2 minutes. Then add the chicken stock, cream, and sazón. Cook until the sauce is thick enough to evenly coat the back of a wooden spoon, 5 to 7 minutes. Season with salt to taste.

4 Remove from the heat. Immediately, add the crabs to the pan and spoon sauce over them to coat. (You may need to do this in batches.) Transfer to a serving plate and pour extra sauce directly over the crab tops. Serve immediately.

LOCRO DE PAPA

Over four thousand potato varieties grow in the Andean highlands that span Ecuador, Peru, and Bolivia, according to the International Potato Center. (I love that there is an International Potato Center.) Locro de papa is an Ecuadorian soup that celebrates potatoes and cheese. Popular across Ecuador's mountainous region (including Quito, the capital), this creamy vegetarian dish is the perfect thing to eat as the weather cools. If you're looking for extra texture or a little sweetness, try adding a cup of corn, a popular variation of the soup.

A quick word of caution: You can use a regular blender instead of an immersion blender for this recipe. But please let the soup come to room temperature before blending. The heat causes the container to expand and could result in the top popping off and hot soup flying everywhere. If you're using an immersion blender, proceed as written!

Time: 25 minutes ● **Serves:** 4 to 6

Ingredients

3 tablespoons unsalted butter

1 large yellow onion, diced

4 garlic cloves, finely chopped

2 teaspoons ground cumin

1 teaspoon dried oregano

1 tablespoon sazón with achiote

2 pounds russet potatoes, peeled and diced

4 cups unsalted vegetable stock or water

2 teaspoons kosher salt, plus more as needed

1 cup shredded or finely crumbled white cheese (such as queso fresco or mozzarella), plus more for garnish

1 cup whole milk

½ cup heavy cream

½ cup packed finely chopped cilantro leaves and stems

1 ripe avocado, sliced

Directions

1 Melt the butter in a large pot over medium heat. Once melted, add the onion, garlic, cumin, oregano, and sazón. Cook until the onion is tender and translucent, about 3 minutes.

2 Add the potatoes and mix to coat evenly. Then add the vegetable stock and salt.

Increase the heat to medium-high and bring to a boil. Cook until the potatoes are fork-tender, about 10 minutes. Remove from the heat.

3 Using a slotted spoon, reserve about one-quarter of the cooked potatoes (it's OK to eyeball it here!). Add the cheese

Recipe continues

to the pot. Using an immersion blender, blend the soup with the cheese until the potatoes are smooth. If some of the cheese hasn't totally blended, it's OK; it will continue to melt. Place the pot back over medium heat.

4 Add the milk, cream, and reserved potatoes. Cook until the soup is thick enough to coat the back of a wooden spoon, about 5 minutes.

5 Add ¼ cup of the cilantro to the soup and stir until fully combined. Taste and adjust for salt. To serve, ladle the soup into bowls and top with the avocado slices (the soup should be thick enough to support the avocado's weight), crumbled queso fresco, and the remaining ¼ cup cilantro.

PLÁTANO MADURO ASADO CON QUESO

There are a million different ways to cook plantains. This happens to be my grandpa's favorite way to eat them for breakfast. And mine, too.

He gently tosses super-ripe plantains in a light coating of oil and bakes them whole in a toaster oven. Once they become soft and turn a deep brown color, he cuts a slit into them and stuffs them with mozzarella, making cheese-stuffed plátanos maduros. Every bite is a balance of sweet and savory and leaves trails of cheese.

My method generally follows the same steps but with two changes: a regular oven for ease and salted butter for extra richness. For the sweetest results, use completely blackened, almost too-soft plantains, which have more sugar and create more caramelized clusters along the surface.

Time: 30 minutes ● **Serves:** 2

Ingredients

3 tablespoons salted butter

2 very ripe, blackened plantains

¼ cup shredded low-moisture mozzarella

Directions

1 Preheat the oven to 425°F and line a baking sheet with aluminum foil. While the oven is preheating, melt the butter in a microwave-safe bowl in 10-second increments until melted.

2 Prepare the plantains. Using a paring knife, cut off the ends. Carefully cut a slit along the length of the plantains, avoiding cutting into the flesh. Remove and discard the peels. Place the whole plantains on the prepared baking sheet and evenly coat them with the melted butter by pouring it or spooning it over the tops.

3 Transfer to the oven and roast until the plantains are tender and browned, 20 to 25 minutes, flipping over once about halfway through.

4 Once the plantains are caramelized on both sides, remove them from the oven but leave the oven on. Make sure the plantains are curved side up, then, using the tip of a paring knife, cut a shallow horizontal slit along the length of the plantain without puncturing the bottom. Using a spoon, gently spread each plantain open and stuff with the cheese. Bake for an additional 2 minutes, or until the cheese is melted. Serve immediately.

BOLÓN DE VERDE

Breakfast in Ecuador means a cup of coffee and a big bolón de verde. These plantain balls are made with mashed green plantains, when they're in their starchiest state. The mashed plantains are then mixed with a little peanut butter for creaminess, cheese for richness, and chicharrón because, well, fried pork belly makes everything tastier. After you form baseball-size balls (but I've eaten ones as big as softballs!) from the mixture, you fry it to melt the cheese and add more crunchy texture to the outside. You know it's made correctly if you get a cheese pull that trails and trails on the first bite.

The origins of this Ecuadorian dish are not well documented in English, but mashed plantains similar to bolón can be found throughout the Caribbean and Latin America. In Cuba, fufú de plátano is a popular dish. Made with many of the same ingredients and with a similar technique, it can be traced back directly to its African roots.

Because of my grandpa's age, this is his special-treat breakfast now. Although queso fresco is the most common cheese to use in the Ecuadorian version, my grandpa prefers his with shredded cheddar. He often skips the chicharrón and final frying step, but he washes his bolón down with hot coffee, like he always has.

Time: 25 minutes ● **Serves:** 2

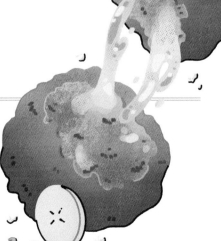

Ingredients

2 green (unripe) plantains

2 garlic cloves, minced

¼ cup crunchy unsweetened peanut butter

½ cup crumbled or shredded cheese (such as queso fresco or cheddar)

½ cup chopped chicharrón or crushed pork rinds (optional)

Kosher salt

Vegetable oil, for frying

Directions

1 Peel the plantains. Cut off and discard the ends. Using a paring knife, cut a slit along the length of the plantains, carefully avoiding cutting into the flesh, and then remove the peels. If the peel is too firm, use a spoon to lift the edges, then discard the peel. Slice each plantain into quarters. (It doesn't have to be pretty; just make the pieces roughly the same size.)

2 Bring a medium pot of water to a boil. Once boiling, add the plantains and cook until fork-tender, 10 to 12 minutes. Drain and immediately transfer them to a large bowl. Using a potato masher or majador, mash the plantains while still hot until they reach a smooth texture, like mashed potatoes. (If you let the plantains cool before mashing, they will harden and not become the right texture.)

3 Add the garlic and peanut butter. Mix or mash until well combined. Then add the cheese and chicharrón (if using). Combine with your hands or a wooden spoon. Season with salt to taste.

4 Form the bolónes. (One plantain should make one large bolón, but if your plantains are on the larger side or you just want a smaller portion, you can make two from each.) Divide the plantain mixture in half. Then scoop up a half with your hands and form it into a ball, patting the outside to tightly pack it together. Repeat with the other half. Each bolón should be about the size of a baseball.

5 Heat about ½ inch vegetable oil in a large skillet over medium heat. Once the oil is shimmering, add the bolónes. Fry, rolling occasionally to cook evenly on all sides, until a thin but firm crust forms on the outside, about 5 minutes. Using a slotted spoon, transfer the bolónes to a paper towel-lined plate and let cool for 3 minutes. Serve immediately with coffee.

Note: If you're using chicharrón and want even more texture, you can add another ¼ cup chicharrón to roll the bolónes in before frying. Make sure the pieces are stuck well into the exterior before frying so they don't fall out.

GOING HOME

Whenever I look at the palm trees in my hometown, I feel funny. They haven't changed since I was a kid. The trees' slender trunks are the color of a sun-bleached, worn T-shirt, a familiar tan-gray shade. The long palm leaves billow from the top and look like the bounciest head of hair. Each frond flickers between its natural green and a shimmering gold as it catches the light. Never as tall as the LA palm trees, but tall enough to catch my eye and remind me I'm home. Since I left Florida, I have changed. Every time I go back, I am a new version of myself. And when I look at the palms swaying in the breeze, I'm reminded of how different I am from the last time I took in the same sight.

I knew I had to cook alongside my family in real life to learn the recipes and stories for a lot of this cookbook. Zoom wasn't going to cut it! So I flew from Tokyo (where I'm currently based) to the US to cook with my grandparents for two weeks, the longest time I've spent with them in over ten years, as I've mentioned.

I spent most of my childhood in Florida, and for almost all of that time, I couldn't wait to leave. Maybe it was the constant feeling of being othered, or maybe it was because I have so many not-so-happy memories tied to the Sunshine State, but I knew from a young age I wanted to be somewhere else. When I finally got my chance to move away for good after college—a full-time gig at Taco Bell's corporate offices in California—I snatched it as fast as I could.

During the first few years, I would make it a point to go back multiple times a year. Eventually I went back less and less often. Even my annual Christmas trip began to shorten. What used to be at least a weeklong break became a three-day stopover. Though I wanted to see my family, my desire to continue to live the new life I had built for myself was a little stronger. Also, I got a dog, which always makes travel harder.

Going back home to cook with my grandparents felt so familiar yet new in many ways. Their house looked the same. The usual photos of family members were still plastered along the walls, smiling at me, and the kitchen cart was bursting with fresh oranges. But as I greeted my grandparents, I saw that their faces had deeper wrinkles or more sunken cheeks than the last time I had seen them. Probably one of the things that sucks the most about being over thirty is that I finally notice their faces aging more with each visit. And sometimes I think about how many times I will still be able to look upon these people I love so much.

This time, my visit was the most different to date, though. I was working on a cookbook, which took years and years of hard work. I had come from Tokyo, my new home, after exerting so much effort to get there. And we were all still navigating the uncharted pandemic.

On my first day, I made a cooking schedule with my grandma and clustered the recipes that made sense to cook together, balancing out weekdays versus weekends and the logistics of going to various Latin American grocery stores. On one of the bigger shopping days, we piled into the car to go to Supermercados El Bodegón, a superstore that carries a huge array of products from seemingly every Latinx country. It feels like a food amusement park. When we arrived, I helped my grandma assemble the electric scooter for my grandpa. She and I took turns pushing the shopping cart and lifting commercial-size cans of hominy, while my grandpa put his cart on the fastest setting as he whipped around the store like a pinball. Before heading back home, they both insisted on getting something to drink from the agua fresca stand.

I didn't go back home only to cook; it was also to replenish my heart.

I sipped on a sweet horchata while my grandparents shared a fresh coconut, my grandpa giddily lifting it up to show that it was the same size as his head. It had been years since I had done such a normal errand with them.

I have been in the kitchen as they cooked a million meals before, but this trip felt like the first time I had ever paid any attention. When my grandma sliced up ingredients, the thumping of the blade against her worn cutting board didn't fade into the background for me like it used to. And as my grandpa shuffled in and out of the kitchen looking at different stews bubbling away like potions, my eyes didn't glaze over; instead, I soaked in his every movement. As a kid, I would watch TV while they cooked, but now they were the main event.

Of the two of them, my grandma has always been the primary cook. But when my grandpa was younger, he would make certain dishes. All the recipes he learned how to cook, he taught my grandma, so his dishes live on through her. Most of the day when I was cooking alone in their kitchen, I would bring my grandpa little bites to taste as he rested on his soft recliner. Although he is in his nineties, his eyes and taste buds are as sharp as ever. With a single spoonful, he would tell me how the balance of flavors needed to be adjusted. *Too sweet. Too salty. More fruit. Less peanut butter.* And from a quick glance at a pot of soup, he would know how much more time it needed to thicken to the right texture. *A few more minutes, but don't forget to take the cabbage out or it will thicken too much.*

After I returned to my home in Japan, I found that sourcing ingredients for my cookbook there was difficult, and finding Latin American ones felt almost impossible. My feelings of loneliness from moving across the world became amplified as I struggled to cook the foods of my childhood. I remember the first time I cut a fresh lime in my new kitchen, my eyes watered as the bright scent of the citrus oil unlocked old memories. I didn't go back home only to cook; it was also to replenish my heart.

In between prepping ingredients and sautéing, my grandparents told me stories, many of which I had never heard before. Where they first learned a recipe, who they used to cook it for, what their preferred way to eat it is, or when their favorite time we shared it was. I should not have waited for a book to learn these stories, but I am so happy it led us to this moment.

Looking at the palm trees on this last trip, I felt different in the usual way, but new thoughts crept in. "Were they always this beautiful?" I wondered as I admired their gentle sway. For the first time, I was happy to be back home.

COLADA DE AVENA CON NARANJILLA

Until the day I saw my aunt Sandy order it from an Ecuadorian restaurant, I had never tried colada de avena con naranjilla. "Un Quaker, por favor," she said, referring to the drink by its nickname. The waiter brought out a tall glass filled with a thick liquid the same color as a tan autumn coat. "It's my favorite," she said. I tried a sip—it tasted like a mixture of orange, pineapple, and passion fruit layered with a subtle flavor of oatmeal that mellowed out the tart, bright notes. The tang comes from naranjilla, also known as lulo, a small fruit native to the Ecuadorian and Colombian region. Drunk both hot and cold, the beverage is a staple in Ecuador.

Like his daughter Sandy, my grandpa loves this drink. When I was testing this recipe, he was relaxing in his favorite chair. I would ask him to taste the drink in between his catnaps. *Needs more oatmeal. Needs more naranjilla. More sugar.* I continued to tweak the amounts until I gave him one final cup. "This is it," he said, as a huge smile spread across his face.

Time: 20 minutes, plus cooling ● **Makes:** About 7 cups

Ingredients

1 cup rolled oats

14 ounces frozen naranjilla pulp (also called lulo)

One 4-inch cinnamon stick (preferably Ceylon)

1 teaspoon vanilla extract

4 whole allspice berries, or ¼ teaspoon ground allspice

4 whole cloves

8 ounces piloncillo, or 1 cup packed dark brown sugar

Ground cinnamon, for serving (optional)

Directions

1 In a medium pot, combine 6 cups water, the oats, naranjilla, cinnamon stick, vanilla, allspice, cloves, and piloncillo. Bring to a boil, reduce the heat to low, and let simmer for 15 minutes. Remove from the heat and let cool for 15 minutes, or until about room temperature.

2 Transfer the liquid to a blender, working in batches if necessary to avoid overfilling. Blend until the solids are finely ground and the colada is smooth, about 3 minutes. Using a fine-mesh strainer, carefully strain the drink into a pitcher for serving. Store in the refrigerator for up to 3 days. To serve, top each glass with a sprinkle of ground cinnamon, if desired. Enjoy hot or chilled with ice, depending on your preference.

CALDO DE BOLAS

Imagine plantain dumplings the size of tennis balls filled with tender beef and sofrito and bobbing alongside corn and cabbage in a peanut butter–spiked broth. You've just envisioned caldo de bolas de verde, an Ecuadorian stew that's beloved in Guayaquil and, of course, by my grandpa. The name, which means "ball stew," refers to the enormous dumplings, the star of the dish. Making it is a labor of love that requires an equal amount of both cooked and grated raw green plantains to give the bolas just the right texture to hold their shape and remain tender. But what I adore the most about this caldo is how it shows off the true versatility of plantains. People sometimes assume that green plantains can only be used for tostones, but they can be used for so many things, even plump dumplings.

After I cooked this with my grandma, we gave my grandpa a bowl. "Oh wow," he said. "Please mail me food from Japan."

Time: 2 hours   ●   **Serves:** 8 to 10

Ingredients

1½ pounds bone-in beef shanks

1 pound bone-in beef short ribs or flanken ribs

4 tablespoons kosher salt, plus more to taste

4 tablespoons extra-virgin olive oil, plus more as needed

1 tablespoon plus 2 teaspoons sazón with achiote (3 packets of Goya)

½ large red onion, diced into ¼-inch pieces (about 1 cup)

¼ large green bell pepper, diced into ¼-inch pieces (about ½ cup)

¼ large red bell pepper, diced into ¼-inch pieces (about ½ cup)

8 garlic cloves, finely chopped

1½ teaspoons ground cumin

1½ teaspoons dried oregano

½ teaspoon freshly cracked black pepper, plus more to taste

1½ cups unsweetened creamy peanut butter

¼ bunch fresh basil

¼ bunch parsley

¼ bunch cilantro, plus ½ cup packed finely chopped for garnish

¼ bunch mint

8 green (unripe) plantains

½ head green cabbage, cut into bite-size pieces

2 ears corn, cut into 2-inch-thick rounds

Directions

1 Sear the beef. Pat the beef dry with a paper towel and season with 1 tablespoon of the salt. Heat 2 tablespoons of the oil and ½ teaspoon of the sazón in a large

Recipe continues

stockpot over medium-high heat. Once the oil is shimmering, add half of the shanks and half of the short ribs. Cook, flipping occasionally, until the meat is seared, with some dark brown crust, about 7 minutes. Transfer to a plate. Add the remaining 2 tablespoons oil, another ½ teaspoon of the sazón, and the remaining meat. Sear and transfer to the plate.

2 Reduce the heat to medium. If the pot is looking a little dry, add a little more oil. Then add the onion, both bell peppers, the garlic, ½ teaspoon of the cumin, and ½ teaspoon of the oregano. Cook, stirring frequently to avoid browning, until the onion is tender and translucent, about 5 minutes. Remove half of the sofrito and set it aside in a medium bowl for the filling later.

3 Add 12 cups water, 2 tablespoons of the salt, 2 teaspoons of the sazón, the remaining 1 teaspoon cumin, remaining 1 teaspoon oregano, and the black pepper. Mix to evenly distribute the seasonings. Increase the heat to high and bring to a boil.

4 While waiting for the caldo to boil, prepare the peanut butter and herb bundle. In a blender, combine 3 cups water and 1 cup of the peanut butter. Blend until smooth, then pour directly into the pot. Next, make the herb bundle. Stack together the bunches of basil, parsley, cilantro, and mint and wrap them tightly together with butcher twine (you can also use cheesecloth!). Add the herb bundle to the pot.

5 Once the caldo is boiling, add the reserved meat. Then cover and reduce the heat to low. Cook, stirring occasionally, until the meat is tender, 45 minutes to 1 hour.

6 While the caldo is cooking, prepare the plantains. Cut off and discard the ends. Using a paring knife, cut a slit along the length of the plantains, carefully avoiding cutting into the flesh, and then remove the peels. If the peel is too firm, use a spoon to lift the edges. For the half that will be cooked, cut four plantains in half crosswise and add them to the soup while the meat is cooking. Cook until the plantains are tender and you can easily pierce them with a fork, about 30 minutes.

7 Remove the cooked plantains with tongs or a slotted spoon (too much liquid will mess with the bola consistency, so really shake it off) and place them into a large bowl. Immediately mash the plantains with a potato masher or the back of a wooden spoon until smooth. Cover with a clean kitchen towel. Grate the remaining four raw plantains using the second-to-smallest option on a box grater. Immediately mix in 1½ teaspoons of the sazón to prevent the plantains from oxidizing. In the large bowl with the mashed plantains, add the grated plantains with 1 tablespoon salt and the remaining ½ cup peanut butter. Mix until fully incorporated. It should have a consistency similar to Play-Doh (the texture will look different, though). Cover with a damp paper towel or kitchen towel until you're ready to form the bolas.

8 Make the filling. After the meat is tender, remove it from the pot and cut it into small pieces, discarding the bones. In a bowl, mix the meat with the remaining ½ teaspoon sazón and the reserved sofrito. Season to taste with salt and black pepper.

9 Remove and discard the herb bundle. Next, skim off any foam or fat that has risen to the top of the caldo. Then, add the cabbage and corn to the pot. Cover and continue to simmer as you proceed with the rest of the steps.

10 Assemble the bolas. Place the meat filling and a small bowl of water near your bolas station. Using your hands, take about ½ cup of the plantain mixture, roll it into a ball, and flatten it into a ½-inch-thick disc. Next, take a very generous tablespoon of the meat filling and place it into the flattened center. Then enclose the filling by folding the edges of the plantain mixture toward the center so no filling is showing. You can dip your fingertips in a little bit of water to smooth out any rough or cracked areas along the surface. Each bola should be roughly the size of a tennis ball. Repeat with the remaining plantain mixture until you have about 12 bolas. Reserve any remaining filling.

11 Skim off any foam that has formed at the top of the caldo. Then add the bolas and any remaining filling to the broth. Each bola should be mostly submerged. If not, you can add hot water, ½ cup at a time, until the liquid almost covers the tops of the bolas. Increase the heat to medium. The liquid should be at a gentle boil. Cook uncovered until the bolas are cooked through, about 15 minutes, until the internal temperature reaches 140°F. Do not stir, because the bolas are fragile, but you can occasionally use a ladle to pour some of the hot liquid over the tops. Taste the broth and adjust for salt.

12 Serve in bowls with 1 or 2 bolas per serving. Garnish with the chopped cilantro.

CHURRASCO

Each time I go home, my grandparents make churrasco, grilled marinated steak. Because the meat can be on the pricier side, it's a special-occasion meal reserved only for honored guests. Although churrasco originated in Argentina and Brazil, many countries throughout Latin America have their own take on the popular dish.

The flavorful overnight marinade is my grandma's recipe and combines ingredients like orange juice, garlic, sazón, and cumin. It also helps tenderize the meat. Skirt steak is the most popular cut to use, but flank is a great substitute; just be sure to get it on the thinner side so you can have those nice charred edges. Eat with a big mound of rice, sliced avocado, and maduros.

Time: 25 minutes, plus overnight marinating ● **Serves:** 4

Ingredients

1 large orange, juiced (about ½ cup)

4 garlic cloves, smashed to a paste

1½ teaspoons sazón with achiote

½ teaspoon ground cumin

½ teaspoon dried oregano

1½ teaspoons kosher salt

½ teaspoon freshly cracked black pepper

1½ pounds skirt steak or flank steak, cut into 4 equal pieces

½ large white onion, thinly sliced

Extra-virgin olive oil

Flaky salt (optional)

Directions

1 Combine the orange juice, garlic, sazón, cumin, oregano, kosher salt, and pepper in a medium bowl or a gallon zip-top bag. Add the steak and onion, and toss to evenly coat the meat. Next, seal the bowl or bag completely, and refrigerate overnight. Take the steak out 1 hour before grilling to come to room temperature.

2 If using a charcoal grill, start by building a fire with kindling, then adding charcoal once the fire is going. Allow the coals to get hot. If using a gas grill, set the temperature to high.

3 Once the grill is ready, remove the steaks from the marinade and onion mixture. Lightly drizzle them with oil and place on the hottest part of the grill. Reduce the heat to medium and sear each side for 3 to 4 minutes, until it has a dark char and nearly burnt edges and the inside is medium-rare (135°F internal temperature).

4 Remove the steaks from the grill and let rest for 5 minutes. (While the steaks are resting, you can cook the onion from the marinade on the stove until tender if you'd like.) Serve the steak immediately whole or sliced with a sprinkle of flaky salt, if using.

CALDO DE PATA

Caldo de pata is another Ecuadorian stew that shows how time and low heat can deliciously transform an often overlooked cut of meat: cow feet, or patas in Spanish. And of course, this is another soup my grandpa can't get enough of. The patas are cut into chunks and mixed into a simmering jacuzzi of adobo and other seasonings. Over time, the tough chunks of meat break down to a texture so soft it's almost slurpable. Chickpeas and hominy are added to the golden broth for contrast and body. When it's time to serve, every bowl is topped off with a very generous garnish of white onion, cilantro, and lime that cuts the richness of the dish. Once you've eaten a bowl, you'll wonder why you haven't been eating patas this whole time.

If you're having a hard time finding the right cut of meat, try a local Latin American, Caribbean, or Asian market. Or befriend a local butcher (it's a good relationship to cultivate).

Time: 4 hours   ●   **Serves:** 6 to 8

Ingredients

FOR THE BROTH

¼ bunch parsley

¼ bunch cilantro

2 pounds cow feet, well rinsed and cut into 2-inch chunks (see note)

½ large red onion, roughly chopped

4 garlic cloves, crushed but whole

1 teaspoon dried oregano

1 teaspoon ground cumin

1 teaspoon adobo seasoning

1 teaspoon kosher salt

FOR THE SOUP

2 tablespoons extra-virgin olive oil

½ large white onion, diced

4 garlic cloves, minced

1½ teaspoons sazón with achiote

½ teaspoon dried oregano

½ teaspoon ground cumin

3 cups cooked and drained hominy, rinsed

1¾ cups cooked and drained chickpeas, rinsed

1 cup whole milk (optional)

Kosher salt

FOR THE TOPPING

¼ large white onion, finely diced

½ cup packed finely chopped cilantro leaves and stems

3 limes, juiced (a little more than ¼ cup)

Directions

1 Make the broth. Tie the parsley and cilantro together with butcher twine. Fill a large pot with 10 cups water. Add the herb bundle, cow feet, red onion, garlic, oregano, cumin, adobo, and salt. Mix and then bring to a boil over high heat. Once boiling, cover and reduce the heat to low. Cook, stirring once an hour, until the cow feet are super tender and the meat starts to fall off the bone, about 3 hours. If your cow feet are on the slightly thicker side, it may take an additional 30 minutes. Transfer the cooked cow feet to a cutting board to cool.

2 Place a colander in a large bowl. Strain and reserve the broth. Discard the aromatics.

3 Make the soup. In the same pot, heat the oil over medium-high heat. Once the oil is shimmering, add the white onion. Cook, stirring frequently to avoid browning, until the onion is tender and translucent, about 4 minutes. Then add the garlic and spices. Continue to cook, stirring frequently, until the garlic is tender and the spices are fragrant, about 1 minute.

4 Add the reserved broth, ½ cup water, the hominy, and chickpeas. Bring to a boil and then reduce the heat to medium-low. Cook for 20 minutes.

5 While the hominy and chickpeas are cooking, cut the cow feet into ½-inch pieces, making sure to remove and discard the bones. Add the meat and milk (if using) to the soup. Cook for another 5 minutes. Season with salt to taste.

6 Make the topping. In a small bowl, combine the white onion, cilantro, lime juice, and 3 tablespoons water. Mix until fully combined. Serve the caldo in bowls and spoon over the topping and its juices.

Note: The easiest way to get the cow feet into the right size is to ask your butcher to cut them for you. You can cut the softer top part on your own at home, but most grocery store butchers will have no issue cutting them for you. Another good reason to get to know your local butcher!

MOJARRA FRITA
WITH PINEAPPLE SALSA

If my grandpa isn't eating crabs, he's eating fish—preferably whole and lightly fried until it's golden. This Mexican mojarra frita is from my grandma, who learned it while working at her family's restaurant in Cancún. It has a crisp exterior that resembles copper flakes and a tender interior that releases little curls of steam as you cut it open. It gets the name mojarra from being made with a freshwater fish like tilapia, which is my grandma's go-to. But what gives this dish its flavor is the aromatic marinade made of onion, garlic, and spices. If tilapia isn't your thing, you can swap another light fish like snapper or porgy.

I know many, many places in the world pair fruit with fish, but it's always felt like a Florida thing to me. The pineapple salsa is my addition and pays tribute to the countless plates I've eaten at home that combine fish and fruit. Although this recipe makes quite a bit, I think the perfect balance is an almost 1:1 ratio of fruit to fish. But if you have any pineapple salsa leftovers, save them to eat with chips. The salsa alone is something you may want to double just to have for later.

Time: 30 minutes, plus marinating ● **Serves:** 1 to 2

Ingredients

FOR THE FISH

¼ large onion of your choice, roughly chopped

2 garlic cloves

½ teaspoon ground cumin

½ teaspoon adobo seasoning

¼ teaspoon dried oregano

One ¾-pound whole tilapia, cleaned, scaled, and gilled

Vegetable oil, for frying

FOR THE PINEAPPLE SALSA

¾ cup diced fresh pineapple

½ jalapeño, finely diced (seeds to taste)

½ Roma tomato, diced

3 tablespoons finely diced red onion

2 tablespoons packed finely chopped cilantro

½ lime, juiced

1 tablespoon fresh orange juice

Kosher salt

Directions

1 Make the marinade. In a molcajete or food processor, combine the onion, garlic, cumin, adobo, and oregano until a paste forms.

2 Prepare the fish. Make four shallow crosswise cuts on both sides of the fish, then transfer to a large plate or resealable

76   Recipe continues

bag. Rub the marinade all over the fish, into the skin and cavity. Add any extra marinade on top of the fish. Let marinate for 30 minutes at room temperature.

3 While the fish is marinating, make the pineapple salsa. Place the pineapple in a large bowl and add the jalapeño, tomato, onion, cilantro, lime juice, and orange juice. Mix until fully incorporated. Season with salt to taste. Store in the refrigerator until it's time to serve.

4 Heat 1 inch of oil in a large pan over medium-high heat. Once the oil is around 350°F and shimmering, pick up the fish, shake off the excess marinade, and carefully lower it headfirst into the oil. Be careful: the oil will splatter at first, so use a splatter guard. Fry until golden brown, 5 to 10 minutes, carefully spooning some oil onto the exposed parts of the fish to evenly cook it if needed (there's no need to flip!). Using a spatula, very carefully transfer the fish to a paper towel–lined plate or baking sheet to drain. Let rest for 2 minutes.

5 Transfer the fish to a serving dish. Garnish the center of the fish with the pineapple salsa. If you have leftovers, remove the remaining fish from the bones, then store in the refrigerator for up to 3 days. It makes a mean taco.

CALDO DE SALCHICHA

Let's get it out of the way: you need two pounds of pig offal to make this stew. I know offal is not everyone's thing—but it should be. So many dishes throughout Latin America (and around the world!) showcase the beauty of transforming parts of the animal that are often thrown away into something new and delicious.

Caldo de salchicha is a hearty stew made of vegetables, peanut butter, offal, and morcilla, or blood sausage (a food beloved by my grandpa). Within two hours, magic happens, and one of the most flavorful soups I have ever eaten is created. This recipe serves ten but can easily be scaled down if you want to make a smaller amount.

Morcilla is the salchicha in this stew, and there's no true replacement. You can find it at Latin American or Spanish grocery stores.

Offal-based dishes are often born when resources are tight, but they speak to the ingenuity and resilience of a culture's cuisine. This caldo is no exception.

Time: 1 hour 45 minutes ● **Serves:** 10

Ingredients

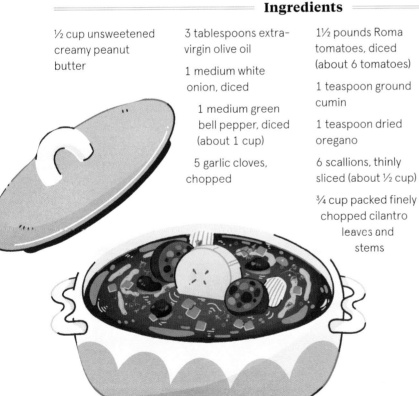

½ cup unsweetened creamy peanut butter

3 tablespoons extra-virgin olive oil

1 medium white onion, diced

1 medium green bell pepper, diced (about 1 cup)

5 garlic cloves, chopped

1½ pounds Roma tomatoes, diced (about 6 tomatoes)

1 teaspoon ground cumin

1 teaspoon dried oregano

6 scallions, thinly sliced (about ½ cup)

¾ cup packed finely chopped cilantro leaves and stems

¼ cup packed finely chopped basil leaves

¼ cup packed finely chopped mint leaves

¼ cup packed finely chopped parsley

1½ tablespoons sazón with achiote

1½ tablespoons kosher salt, plus more to taste

1½ teaspoons freshly cracked black pepper

½ medium head white cabbage, halved

Recipe continues

2 medium carrots, peeled and halved crosswise

2 pounds pig offal (such as hearts, livers, etc.), cleaned, rinsed, and cut into bite-size pieces (see note)

1 pound yuca, peeled and halved (fresh or frozen)

2 large green (unripe) plantains

2 pounds morcilla (also known as blood sausage), cut into 1-inch rounds

2 limes, cut into wedges

Directions

1 Combine 2 cups warm water and the peanut butter in a measuring cup. Mix with a fork until the peanut butter is fully combined and there are no clumps. Set aside.

2 Heat the oil in a large pot over medium-high heat. Once the oil is shimmering, add the onion, bell pepper, and garlic. Cook the sofrito, stirring frequently to avoid browning, until the onion becomes tender and translucent, about 5 minutes.

3 Add the tomatoes, cumin, and oregano. Cook, continuing to stir frequently, until the tomatoes soften, 3 to 5 minutes.

4 Add the scallions, ½ cup of the cilantro, the basil, mint, parsley, sazón, salt, and black pepper. Stir and cook until fragrant, about 1 minute.

5 Add the peanut butter mixture to the pot, along with another 10 cups water. Stir until everything is evenly distributed. Bring to a boil.

6 Once boiling, add the cabbage and carrots. Reduce the heat to low, cover, and cook until the cabbage and carrots are tender, about 20 minutes. Using tongs

or a slotted spoon, remove the cooked cabbage and carrots and set aside to cool.

7 Increase the heat to medium-high. Once boiling, add the offal. Reduce the heat to low and cook uncovered until the meat is tender, 40 minutes to 1 hour. While the soup is simmering, skim off any foam that rises to the top for an extra-clear soup.

8 While the offal is cooking, make the yuca. Bring a medium pot of salted water to a boil. Then add the yuca. Cook until tender, 15 to 20 minutes for fresh yuca or 30 minutes for frozen. Drain and set aside to cool. Once cool enough to handle, remove and discard any hard fibers at the center of each piece. Cut the yuca into 1-inch pieces. Next, cut the cooled cabbage into bite-size pieces and the carrots into ½-inch-thick rounds. Add the cut yuca to the cut cabbage and carrots.

9 Once the offal is tender, cut the plantains. Do not do this ahead of time or the plantains will oxidize, and that's not cute. Cut off and discard the ends of the plantains. Using a paring knife, cut a slit along the length of the plantains, carefully avoiding cutting into the flesh, and then remove the peels.

If the peel is too firm, use a spoon to lift the edges. Slice the plantain crosswise into 1-inch-thick rounds.

10 Add the cut plantains and morcilla to the caldo. Increase the heat to medium. Boil until the plantains are tender and the morcilla is fully cooked through, about 20 minutes. Taste the broth and adjust for salt to your preference.

11 To serve, place some of the cooked yuca, cabbage, and carrots into a bowl. Ladle in the caldo and then sprinkle on some of the remaining cilantro. Serve with the lime wedges on the side so people can add as much or as little as they like. Store the cooked vegetables separately so they don't continue to thicken the caldo.

Note: There are many, many different pig offal cuts out there. For this stew, my grandpa personally prefers a mixture of hearts, livers, and tongue. The more varied the cuts, the more textures and tastes you'll have in the caldo. Many Latin American grocery stores will carry these parts. If not, ask your local butcher and they will hook you up! How you clean each cut varies depending on what it is. For example, you need to soak liver in ½ cup of milk for 30 minutes and then rinse it with cool water until it's clear before you start cooking. But for heart, you can toss it with a couple of generous tablespoons of salt, rub it in, and rinse it with water. Just google how to clean the specific offal cut before you dive into cutting.

YUCA CON MOJO

As a child, I didn't like boiled yuca. I thought it was too starchy and too wet. But that was before I had yuca con mojo. Mojo, pronounced "MO-ho," is a sauce made with lots of garlic, lots of citrus, and lots of spices. While it's eaten throughout the Caribbean, it is an essential part of Cuban cuisine, where it is frequently used as a marinade for various proteins and is also spooned over vegetables. It's traditionally made with a mortar and pestle, but this recipe calls for minced garlic. I also added extra butter instead of oil to slick the surface of the yuca and complement its soft flavors. And the acidity from the lime and orange juice cuts the starchiness completely. Any opinions I had about plain boiled yuca were destroyed and reborn.

Time: 35 minutes • **Serves:** 6

Ingredients

2 pounds yuca, peeled, deveined, and cut into 2-inch pieces (fresh or frozen)

4 tablespoons unsalted butter

1 medium red onion, halved and thinly sliced

10 garlic cloves, minced

1 teaspoon dried oregano

2 teaspoons ground cumin

½ cup fresh lime juice (from 2 to 4 limes)

1 large orange, juiced (about ½ cup)

2 tablespoons white vinegar

2 teaspoons kosher salt, plus more to taste

Directions

1 Fill a large pot with water and 3 generous tablespoons of salt (eyeballing here is OK!). Bring to a boil over high heat. Once it's boiling, add the yuca. Cook until a fork can easily pierce the thickest piece of yuca, about 25 minutes for fresh yuca. If using frozen yuca, cook according to the package instructions. Drain and set aside.

2 While the yuca is cooking, make the mojo. Melt the butter in a deep skillet over medium heat. Add the onion, garlic, oregano, and cumin. Cook, stirring frequently, until the onion is completely soft and tender but not brown, about 7 minutes. Remove from the heat. Add the lime and orange juice, vinegar, and 1½ teaspoons of the salt.

3 Transfer the cooked yuca to a serving dish and pour the mojo evenly over the top. Taste and adjust for salt, if needed. Serve while warm.

A RANDOM BOBA TANGENT

One of my favorite food facts has to do with boba because it connects Latinx and Asian food in a somewhat unexpected way. To start, let's talk about yuca. This root vegetable has a hard, starchy white flesh and a thin, dark brown skin. You might not guess it from the looks of it, but that yuca flesh is the origin of boba pearls. From this root vegetable, tapioca starch is created. And without tapioca starch (the main ingredient in boba!), boba would not exist.

Making tapioca starch is a very involved process. It requires lots of washing and pulping. Once there's finally enough yuca pulp, it's squeezed to extract every last drop of starch. I've watched a few YouTube videos of the process, and it looks like a mini science experiment. As the water settles, the starch falls to the bottom. It's then drained and dried to reveal the powdery substance.

There are countless ways to use tapioca starch, but my favorite is for boba. A common way to make boba pearls is to combine boiling water with the starch and knead it until it becomes a dough. Then you cut, roll, form, and boil these tiny bubble shapes until they're soft and bouncy. In the mid-1980s, Taiwan used them to create bubble tea (a.k.a. boba), and it has since spread into a worldwide craze.

I didn't learn about the yuca-is-boba connection until my twenties. Before then, it was just the yuca of my childhood and the boba I got to love as an adult (there were no bubble tea shops in my town until I moved away for college). Boba itself is a drink that has made me feel proud to be Asian. Although boba is Taiwanese, in the US, it's grown into a celebration of Asian culture in many ways. When I learned how these two seemingly unrelated things were intertwined, it felt like my inner identity crisis began to melt away. Yuca is boba and boba is yuca, and that is a beautiful thing.

TAMARINDO

My grandparents kept their second refrigerator in the garage, and opening it always felt like an adventure. Until I moved in with them, I only ever had one fridge. Neatly lined on the top shelves of the second fridge were rows and rows of off-brand sodas for us kids from Winn-Dixie (shout-out to Chek). On the bottom row, they often stored marinating achiote-stained meats for future family dinners. But the middle is where the aguas frescas lived . . . most notably, the pitchers of tamarindo for Grandpa. When I think back to living with him, I can only imagine him with a big chilled cup of tamarindo in his hand.

Tamarind, the key ingredient in this drink, is a sweet-and-sour fruit that is native to Africa but thrives in tropical climates around the world. Other places like India, Southeast Asia, the Caribbean, and Latin America long ago figured out that underneath the fruit's hard outer shell hides lip-smacking gold.

You can speed up this recipe and boil the peeled tamarind for ten minutes instead of using the overnight soaking method, but Grandma prefers the longer way—and she's always right. If you prefer a mellower version, you can always add more water at the end to taste. One small piece of advice: I've been told since I was a kid that tamarind is a natural laxative, so maybe don't drink a whole pitcher by yourself in one sitting.

Time: 5 minutes, plus shelling and overnight soaking   ●   **Makes:** About 7 cups

Ingredients

8 ounces tamarind pods (about 15)

½ cup sugar

Directions

1 Prepare the tamarind. Using your hands, crack the outer shells and pull off the strings around the fruit. Place the shell-less tamarind into a pitcher or large bowl. Discard the outer shells and strings. (This will take some time to do, so recruit some help or put on a good podcast. I like *Code Switch*.)

2 Cover the pods with 4 cups water, being sure the tamarind is fully submerged. Cover and soak overnight in the refrigerator.

3 The next day, use your hands to squeeze the seeds from the softened fruit, making the seeds as "clean" as possible. Remove and discard the seeds.

4 Transfer the liquid and pulp to a blender. Add the sugar and another 2¼ cups water. Blend until smooth, about 1 minute. Using a fine-mesh strainer, strain the tamarindo back into a pitcher. Serve chilled over ice, making sure to stir before serving because the fruit can settle at the bottom. Store in the refrigerator for up to 5 days.

CHAPTER 3

MY MEXICAN GRANDMA

M y grandma was a grandma before she became a mom.

Technically, we're not related by blood. But when Veronica Ruiz uprooted her life in Mexico and got married to my grandpa, she became my step-grandma legally. And when she immigrated to New York, she became my grandma fully. I was the first child in her life. About two years later, she became a mother herself. Now she holds both titles proudly, and recently she also picked up "great-grandma," too. Throughout my life, Veronica has raised, fed, and guided me more than almost anyone else in my family. When I was a baby, she held me tight in her arms and called me her niña bonita. Today she does the same. Inside my grandparents' small Manhattan apartment is where our relationship started. By all accounts, she is not my step-grandma. She is my full grandma in every sense of the word.

Veronica and I have a normal grandmother-granddaughter food relationship: her knowledge of ingredients and dishes is passed on through our time together in the kitchen. In our family, where normal isn't a given, it's something I cherish deeply. On visits to her house when I was growing up, she would feed us sopes piled high with smooth refried beans, crisp longaniza, shredded lettuce, and homemade salsas. I'd watch her as she fried the thick tortillas in oil and quickly formed them into the proper shape while they were still steaming hot. But when I started living with her in middle school, our food experiences together grew. It wasn't just weekend sopes anymore; now it was easy-to-make meals that she could throw together in thirty minutes on a Monday to feed me, Thor, and George (Veronica's son and my younger half-uncle, who is more like another brother to me). A quickly sautéed meat paired with a big mound of steaming rice and sliced avocado became a weeknight staple, always accompanied by her tub of Jalapeños en Escabeche (page 138). Or Huevos con Weenies (page 113) for a breakfast that would keep us full until well past lunch—and took only five minutes to make.

Most of the foods my grandma passed down to me were not Ecuadorian but Mexican.

Some of my favorite memories with Veronica are of her taking us to the small fruit stand on the corner of their street in Florida. It was operated by a Mexican family who always kept a well-curated selection of candy, sodas, and fresh fruit. The fridge was stocked with a rainbow assortment of Jarritos. I'd usually reach for the pineapple flavor. It was there that Veronica introduced us to some of her favorite Mexican candies. The three of us would snag De la Rosa Mazapán and each do our best to not let the fragile peanut candy crumble in our hands before getting it into our mouths (if you've tried it before, you know it's a very hard thing to do). Veronica would pop off the tops of our Jarritos and we'd drink them on the walk back to her house. I have a number of sad and painful food memories, but with my grandma, each moment was filled with so much warmth and joy, and it still continues.

Though I am not Mexican, Veronica raised me on the Mexican food of her culture. Every time she mashes a salsa together in her molcajete or folds a corn husk over masa to enclose a tamale, the sights, smells, and flavors remind her of where it all started—home.

Veronica was born and raised in Mexico City. She is one of the eldest siblings in a family of seven brothers and two sisters. She grew up in extreme poverty. The walls of the house where she was raised were made from a mixture of wood and cardboard over an exposed clay floor. Already a small space, the area was broken up into even smaller rooms using cardboard dividers. Rain would fall through a hole in the ceiling; her family would cover themselves with whatever plastic was nearby to try to keep dry. She remembers eight to nine people squeezing into one bed every night because that's all they could afford.

I was around five years old the first time I went to Mexico to visit Veronica's family. I don't remember much except for their home. I felt shocked because it was the first time I had seen a house without windows. At such a young age, it was hard for me to understand how so many people could live together and deal with the elements seeping in. But as I grew up, I saw firsthand how my grandma's challenging upbringing did not define her.

At thirteen years old, she moved out and became a stay-at-home caretaker for another family's daughter. While the family wasn't rich, they were able to provide Veronica with a more stable home in exchange for her work. She continued to work and live with them for nearly a decade.

In her midtwenties, she moved to Cancún to join her younger sister and took a job in the accounting department of a hotel. A few years later, she met my grandpa.

After he separated from my biological grandma, my grandpa met Veronica on a vacation. While he was exploring the nearby Isla Mujeres, he met her on the beach. (I've always found it funny that he met her in a place that translates into English as "Island of Women.")

He is twenty-seven years her senior. Some of my grandpa's seven kids are about Veronica's age. It wasn't a typical love story. But after months of keeping in touch by mail and the occasional international call, she decided to give him a chance and went to New York City. Three months later they were married.

While I was interviewing Veronica for this essay, she told me some of what made her want to stay in the US: "You." I was only five months old when she landed in New York. In a way, you could say we were both new to the world. Her, in the bustling setting of Manhattan for the first time (with no English abilities). And me, literally (with zero talking skills). My parents would sometimes leave me with Veronica for weeks at a time, so she raised me as her own. She would put me in a small hammock to rest, then sit by my side as we both learned more and more about our new worlds. When her three-month visit in New York was up, she had to decide whether to go back to Mexico for good. "You looked at me with those beautiful eyes that looked like a scared mouse." She giggled. "You are one of the reasons I decided to stay." My eyes welled up.

Veronica has been a selfless caretaker for most of her life. She's damn good at it. Shortly after my parents moved to Florida, my grandparents followed. Her qualifications in accounting weren't accepted in the US, so she had to look for another career. She soon started working at a day care and was in charge of the three-year-olds—and continued for almost two decades. Every day she would read to them, organize arts and craft projects, make sure they ate their lunch, check on them as they took their afternoon naps, monitor their recess, and teach them early life lessons like the importance of sharing. Eight hours a day, five days a week for seventeen years. I think it takes a special person to choose to work with young children for so long, but it brought her so much joy. She's now a private nanny for families and continues to bring that same care to new kids.

When my brother Thor and I were in foster care (more on this later), Veronica's immediate response was to take us in. Many people would have hesitated to become the guardian of two more kids when they already had their own, but she did everything she could do without a moment's hesitation. After some time (and legally required courses), she became our guardian and got us out of foster care. If it weren't for her, it is very likely I would have spent the rest of my childhood in the system.

> **She is not my step-grandma. She is my full grandma in every sense of the word.**

Working at the day care, she became friends with another woman there who had emigrated from Peru. One day Veronica got a call from her friend saying she was suddenly being deported and her five-year-old son, Benji, had no place to go. Without question, Veronica took Benji in. He lived with George and my grandparents on and off for five years. He's an adult now but still comes to visit for holidays and even volunteered as a taste tester for a lot of the recipes in this cookbook. (Thanks, Benji!)

Aside from me, Veronica has raised so many other children because she has so much love to share. I used to get a little jealous when I heard her call some of these new kids her niña bonita. I thought I was the only one, but now I know it's a sign of just how big her heart is.

This essay about my grandma was the hardest to write. I wasn't sure which facts to include and which to omit. I love her so much, and everything about her is so important to me. How could I accurately capture what a selfless, caring, and wonderful person she is?

There are all the smaller details: In between watching telenovelas, she would sometimes unwind by creating bracelets using Huichol beading techniques, the Indigenous art of beadwork where bright-colored beads are strung together to create geometric patterns. I would stare in wonder at the tiny reflective glass beads and think about how much they looked like candy. At the beginning of the year, she'd go to the Mexican grocery store to buy a sweet bread baked into a wreath shape called rosca de reyes ("wreath of kings" in English); traditionally, it's eaten on Día de los Reyes, Three Kings Day. Hidden underneath the patches of crusted sugar and candied fruit were tiny plastic babies we would search for with delight. After securing the babies, we would eat thick slices of the bread with steaming cups of Mexican hot chocolate, dunking our bread into our cups to soak up even more sweetness.

Even though I was in middle school when I started living with my grandparents, I think back to the food from that time as the flavors of my childhood. Veronica is one of the most influential people in my life, so of course, she has impacted my entire outlook on food.

Beyond the food, she has taught me so much about Mexican culture. On the two trips we took together to Mexico, she showed me her country through her eyes, through her life. She made sure I got to try her favorite aguas frescas (piña with lots of ice), so I could cool off before enduring the summer heat. She took me to Teotihuacán and made sure I made a wish once we climbed to the top of the Pyramid of the Sun. And she carefully eyed every mango before buying the ripest one, which she then promptly doused with lime juice and chile. These little gestures weren't just to give me a fun vacation, but were an outpouring of pride in her culture, which she loves so much. She wanted to pass down her knowledge to me, George, Thor, and Benji. My grandpa taught her how to make Ecuadorian dishes, so I grew up eating a blend of Mexican and Ecuadorian food in their home. But she is the happiest when cooking Mexican dishes, because they remind her of where she comes from.

So much inspires me about my grandma, but what sticks out to me the most is her tremendous spirit of giving. Whether that is making a bubbling pot of pozole to share or dropping everything to become a guardian. She continues to share her culture and love with me, our family, and all the kids in her life. I wouldn't be who I am today if it weren't for my Mexican grandma.

FLAUTAS DE POLLO

There are a few dishes that are impossible to eat and not feel happy—flautas are one of them. It always feels like a party when my grandma makes them. All the toppings sit in their own bowls next to a huge platter of crisp, golden-brown rolled tacos. But the real party starts when you garnish: big spoonfuls of green and red salsas, drizzlings of crema, streamers of lettuce, and a confetti combo of queso, cilantro, and onion that gets sprinkled on like glitter. We don't need any guests for it to get festive—the flautas bring it all on their own. My grandma makes this chicken variation the most often. However, the fillings are endlessly adaptable. (Like, if you have any leftover roasted chicken, that would be excellent for these. Or poblano pepper slices and cheese for a vegetarian version!) Any kind of flauta is guaranteed to make you feel good.

Time: 45 minutes ● **Serves:** 4

Ingredients

1 pound bone-in, skin-on chicken thighs

½ medium white onion (chop half and keep the other half whole)

4 garlic cloves, 2 whole and 2 minced

1 tablespoon chicken bouillon seasoning (such as Malher)

1 teaspoon dried oregano

1 teaspoon dried rosemary (optional)

Vegetable oil, for frying

¼ medium red bell pepper, chopped

Kosher salt

Sixteen 6-inch corn tortillas (see note)

FOR THE TOPPINGS

Sour cream or Mexican crema

½ cup packed finely chopped cilantro leaves

½ cup finely diced white onion

2 cups thinly sliced romaine lettuce

Salsa of choice (such as salsa verde, salsa roja, or both?!)

Crumbled or shredded cheese (such as queso fresco, cheddar, or mozzarella)

Directions

1 Cook the chicken. Bring 2 cups water to a boil in a small pot. Once boiling, add the chicken, the whole onion piece, the 2 whole garlic cloves, the chicken bouillon, oregano, and rosemary (if using). Cover and reduce the heat to medium. Boil until the chicken is fully cooked and tender enough to shred, about 20 minutes. Transfer the cooked chicken to a cutting board or large plate. Discard the liquid. If you wish, you can chop the cooked onion and garlic to add to the chicken mixture later.

2 Shred the chicken. Using two forks or your hands, tear the chicken into small strands, discarding the skin and bones. Taste and adjust for salt. Set aside.

3 Heat 2 tablespoons of oil in a large skillet over medium-high heat. Add the chopped onion, 2 minced garlic cloves, and bell pepper. Cook, stirring frequently to avoid browning, until the onion is translucent and the pepper is tender, about 3 minutes. Add the shredded chicken and remaining cooked vegetables from earlier, if using. Mix and cook until the chicken is warm, about 2 minutes. Season with salt to taste.

4 Warm the tortillas. Place the tortillas on a large plate and microwave until warm, about 1 minute. This will make them easier to roll and less likely to break. Tightly wrap the tortillas with a dry kitchen towel to keep them warm.

5 Prepare your rolling station. Place the skillet of chicken on a trivet and the plate of warm tortillas next to it. Working with one tortilla at a time, place about 2 tablespoons of the chicken filling along the center of the tortilla. Tightly roll up the tortilla, keeping the meat in the center. Keep the closed side of the tortilla on the surface so it doesn't unroll. You may also use two toothpicks on the ends to secure the flauta. Repeat with the remaining tortillas.

6 Heat ¼ inch of oil in a large skillet over medium heat. Once the oil is shimmering, add half the flautas closed side down. Cook until golden brown, about 2 minutes. Using tongs, gently roll each flauta to the other side and continue cooking until they're fully golden brown, about 2 minutes. Transfer to a paper towel–lined plate to drain. Repeat with the remaining half.

7 To serve, place 3 to 4 warm flautas per portion on a plate. Smear sour cream directly on top of the flautas. Sprinkle with the cilantro and onion. Next, place a little pile of lettuce on top. Finally, top with salsa and some cheese.

Note: Use fresh corn tortillas if possible. A lot of Latin American grocery stores will sell fresh ones that are made daily. They just taste better and are easier to work with. But if the shelf-stable ones are the most convenient for you, that's OK, too!

3 Salsas You Must Know How to Make Before You Die

If you didn't read that title with all-cap energy, let's try again. HI HELLO THESE ARE THE THREE SALSAS YOU MUST (YES, *MUST*) KNOW HOW TO MAKE BEFORE YOU DIEEE. Oof. Sorry to yell, but salsa verde, salsa roja, and pico de gallo demand your full attention. There are countless other salsas out there, but these three are essential to Mexican cuisine and a good place to start on your salsa journey. The salsa verde gets its green color from tart tomatillos, roja is red from tomatoes, and pico is a medley of colors from red onions, cilantro, tomatoes, and jalapeño. Each of these salsas has a small kick of spice, but you can amp it up by adding a couple more hot peppers, or reduce the heat by removing the pepper's seeds. For the verde and rojo, you will see two methods to prepare the salsas: boiled and charred. Each creates a flavorful option and is another way to play on your salsa journey.

My grandma always has a salsa (or two or three) tucked away in the fridge. If you want a way to instantly add a zing of brightness to your cooking, keep some stashed in your fridge, too.

SALSA VERDE

Time: 10 minutes • **Makes:** 2 cups

Ingredients

12 ounces tomatillos (about 5 large), husked and rinsed

3 serrano chiles, stemmed

5 garlic cloves, peeled

½ teaspoon kosher salt, plus more to taste

½ cup finely diced white onion

¼ cup packed finely chopped cilantro leaves and stems

Directions

1 If using the boiling method, bring a small saucepan of water to a boil. While the water is heating, cut the tomatillos in half. Add them and the chiles to the boiling water and cook until the tomatillos just begin to soften, about 3 minutes (some color loss is normal).

Remove the tomatillos and chiles from the saucepan to avoid overcooking.

If using the charring method, position a rack at the top of the oven and turn the broiler to high. Once hot, add the whole tomatillos and chiles to a baking sheet and place on the top rack. Broil until the skin is charred, 4 to 5 minutes per side (it's OK for the tomatillos to still be mostly raw inside). Keep a close eye on the broiler to avoid overdoing it with the charring.

2 In a food processor or molcajete, combine the cooked tomatillos and chiles, garlic, and salt. Pulse or smash until mostly smooth, but leave some small chunks for texture. (It should not be totally pulverized like a smoothie.)

3 Place in a serving bowl or storage container. Mix in the onion and cilantro. Taste and adjust for salt. Use immediately or refrigerate for up to a week.

Note: Great with tacos and fish. Or just for dipping into with tortilla chips!

SALSA ROJA

Time: 10 minutes ● **Makes:** 1½ cups

Ingredients

1 pound Roma tomatoes

3 serrano chiles, stemmed

4 garlic cloves, peeled

½ cup roughly chopped white onion

½ cup roughly chopped cilantro leaves and stems

½ teaspoon kosher salt, plus more to taste

Directions

1 If using the boiling method, bring a small saucepan of water to a boil. While the water is heating, cut the tomatoes in half. Add them and the chiles to the boiling water and cook until the tomatoes begin to soften and the skin starts to peel back, about 3 minutes. Remove from the heat and strain.

If using the charring method, position a rack at the top of the oven and turn the broiler to high. Once hot, add the whole tomatoes and chiles to a baking sheet and place on the top rack. Broil until the skin is charred, 4 to 5 minutes per side (it's OK for the tomatoes to still be mostly raw inside). Keep a close eye on the broiler to avoid overdoing it with the charring.

2 In a food processor or molcajete, combine the cooked tomatoes and chiles, garlic, onions, cilantro, and salt. Pulse or smash until mostly smooth, but leave some small chunks for texture.

3 Taste and adjust for salt. Use immediately or refrigerate for up to a week.

PICO DE GALLO

Time: 5 minutes ● **Makes:** 3 cups

Ingredients

1 pound Roma tomatoes, diced (about 2 cups)

½ large red onion, diced (about 1 cup)

1 jalapeño, finely diced (seeds optional)

½ cup packed finely chopped cilantro leaves and stems

1½ limes, juiced

½ teaspoon kosher salt, plus more to taste

Directions

In a large bowl, combine the tomatoes, onion, jalapeño, cilantro, lime juice, and salt. Taste and adjust for salt. Serve immediately because this is when it's at its pico peak.

Note: Toss in diced avocado for added texture. Untraditional but very tasty.

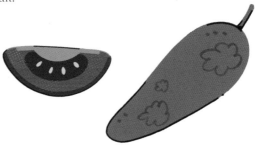

SOPES

Sopes are thick, fried tortillas that are indented in the center to form an edge that acts like a no-splash zone for the fillings. They are believed to have originated around central and southern Mexico. Today there are thousands of variations. My grandma likes to layer hers with refried beans, longaniza sausage, queso fresco, lettuce, and fresh salsa. She would often make them as breakfast or snacks for me, George, and Thor. Because they're so fun to eat, we'd always lose it when she started frying the masa. At the time, though, I didn't know how much she labored over them. The trick to making the tortilla cups the right shape is forming them fresh from the pan, when the dough is the most pliable, which means working while they're still extremely hot. My grandma always uses a clean kitchen towel to protect her hands from the heat, and you should, too.

This recipe is extremely customizable. For an easy vegan version, skip the longaniza and swap vegan cheese for the queso fresco. You can top sopes with whatever your favorite fillings are. There are no limits!

Time: 1 hour 30 minutes   •   **Makes:** 15 sopes

Ingredients

FOR THE SALSA

2 Roma tomatoes

1 jalapeño, stemmed

¼ large white onion, roughly chopped

3 garlic cloves, roughly chopped

Kosher salt

FOR THE LONGANIZA

20 to 24 ounces longaniza

FOR THE TOPPINGS

1 cup crumbled queso fresco

½ large white onion, finely diced

½ cup packed finely chopped cilantro leaves and stems

2 cups packed thinly sliced iceberg lettuce

FOR THE REFRIED BEANS

½ large white onion, diced

Two 15-ounce cans pinto beans, drained and rinsed

Kosher salt

FOR THE SOPES

4 cups masa harina

1 tablespoon kosher salt

1 teaspoon dark brown sugar

1 teaspoon baking powder

½ lime, juiced

Vegetable oil, for frying

Directions

1 Make the salsa. If using the boiling method, bring a small saucepan of water to a boil. While the water is heating, cut the tomatoes in half. Add them and the

Recipe continues

jalapeño to the boiling water and cook until the jalapeño begins to soften and the tomatoes' skin starts to peel back, about 3 minutes. If using the charring method, keep the tomatoes whole. Place them and the jalapeño directly on top of a gas burner over medium-high heat. Cook until the skin is charred and the flesh is tender, about 4 minutes. Or you can broil in an oven until the skin is charred, 4 to 5 minutes per side. Next, in a food processor or molcajete, combine the cooked tomatoes and jalapeño (keep the seeds if you want it spicy; remove them if you don't), onion, and garlic. Pulse or smash until mostly smooth, but leave some small chunks for texture. Season with salt to taste.

2 Cook the longaniza. Heat a large skillet over medium-high heat. While the pan is heating, squeeze the longaniza out of its casing directly into the pan. Discard the casing. Using a wooden spoon, break up the meat into small pieces so the texture resembles ground beef. Cook until it starts to crisp and some parts become dark brown, 7 to 10 minutes. Using a slotted spoon, transfer the meat to a bowl and reserve the skillet with the leftover oil for the beans. Cover the bowl to keep warm.

3 While the longaniza is cooking, prepare the queso fresco mixture. Combine the queso fresco, onion, and cilantro in a medium bowl. Set aside.

4 Make the refried beans. Using the leftover longaniza oil in the reserved skillet, cook the onion over medium heat, stirring

frequently to avoid browning, until tender and translucent, about 5 minutes. Add the beans and ½ cup water. Scrape up any browned bits from the bottom of the pan with a wooden spoon. Once the beans begin to steam, reduce the heat to medium-low and mash with a potato masher or the back of a wooden spoon until they're all crushed. Cook until the beans thicken, 3 to 5 minutes. Season with salt to taste. Turn off the heat and cover the pan.

5 Make the sopes dough. In a large bowl, combine the masa, salt, brown sugar, baking powder, lime juice, and 3 cups warm water. Mix until fully combined using your hands, making sure no dry masa remains. The consistency should be like fresh Play-Doh.

6 Form the sopes. Take about ⅓ cup of dough (about 75 grams for each portion) and roll it into a ball. Then flatten it between your palms into a 3½-inch-wide disc, using your fingertips to gently smooth out any cracks along the edges. Repeat with the remaining dough until you have about 15 sopes.

7 Heat a dry, large nonstick skillet over medium-high heat. To check whether the pan is ready, you can touch the edge of a sope to the pan. If it starts to stick, it is hot enough. If it doesn't stick at all, the pan needs to continue heating. Working in batches, place 4 sopes in the pan, making sure they do not touch. Cook until the surface has some specks of brown, 2 to 3 minutes per side. The sopes will be easy to flip once they are slightly

Recipe continues

browned. If they stick, they are not ready yet. Transfer to a large plate or small baking sheet.

8 Immediately after removing the cooked sopes from the pan, pinch the sides to form a little wall around the circumference and gently flatten the middle using a kitchen towel for some heat protection. They will be very hot, so be careful! The sunken part of the tortilla will hold the fillings, while the raised edges will help prevent them from spilling over (that sopes magic for you!). Repeat with the remaining sopes.

9 Fry the sopes. In the same nonstick skillet, heat ¼ inch of oil over medium-high heat. Once the oil is shimmering, add the pinched sopes, working in batches of 4. Cook until the sopes are a light golden brown, about 2 minutes per side. Transfer to a paper towel-lined plate or serving platter. Repeat with the remaining sopes.

10 Assemble away! Fill the sopes in the following order: refried beans, longaniza, queso fresco mixture, lettuce, and salsa. Eat and feel the happiest you've ever been.

BISTEC EMPANIZADO

My grandma is a busy woman. When I lived with her, she worked full time at a day care managing three-year-olds. After her day job, she would help my grandpa with his handyman work by tiling floors or fixing leaky sinks, including on the weekends. On top of that (if it wasn't already enough), she raised George, Thor, and me, which included making our breakfasts and dinners. We didn't have the money to go out very often, so she cooked most of our meals. My grandma is not just busy; she's a superhero. And one of her powers is making bistec empanizado.

These fried, breaded steaks are rubbed with top-shelf seasonings: sazón, cumin, and garlic powder. But what makes them extra special is the coating of crushed Ritz crackers, which adds extra crunch and butteriness. When she ran out of bread crumbs one day, she used Ritz and has never looked back. As busy as my grandma got, she would regularly make these steaks for us—in part because they take only twenty minutes to cook and we all loved them so much. Eat this recipe with a big pile of rice and sliced avocado for the full Ruiz experience.

While steak is what my grandma usually makes, this recipe would be just as great with chicken, pork, or tofu! Empaniza it all.

Time: 20 minutes ● **Serves:** 4

Ingredients

1½ teaspoons sazón with achiote

1 teaspoon ground cumin

1 teaspoon garlic powder

1 teaspoon kosher salt

½ teaspoon freshly cracked black pepper

1 pound ¼-inch thin top round steaks, cut into 6 equal portions

¾ cup all-purpose flour

4 large eggs, beaten

2½ cups finely crushed Ritz crackers (70 crackers; see note)

Vegetable oil, for frying

1 lime, cut into 6 wedges

Directions

1 In a small bowl, combine the sazón, cumin, garlic powder, salt, and pepper. Then season the steaks on both sides with all of the spice blend.

2 Prepare your dredging station. In three shallow bowls, individually place the flour, eggs, and crushed crackers.

3 Dredge the steaks. Working with one at a time, evenly coat the steak first in flour, then the eggs, and finally the crackers. Repeat with the remaining steaks.

4 Heat ⅛ inch of oil over medium-high heat. (The oil is ready when a pinch of flour sizzles when added to the pan.) Working in batches, add 2 or 3 steaks. Cook until golden brown on both sides, about 5 minutes. Using tongs, transfer them to a paper towel-lined plate to drain. Repeat with the remaining steaks.

Serve immediately with the lime wedges on the side.

Note: You can crush the crackers a few ways. You can place them in a resealable bag and gently pound them with a rolling pin or meat pounder until they're the texture of bread crumbs. You can also use a food processor, which is the fastest method! Or simply use your hands. You won't get that ultrafine texture, but a slightly chunkier consistency also works.

ENSALADA DE NOPALES

Prickly pear cactus thrives best in direct sunlight, where it grows up to three feet tall and six feet wide. Along the cactus's thorn-covered paddles (nopales), tiny magenta fruits (tunas) bloom, both of which are edible once the needles are removed. Native to Mexico, the prickly pear cactus was an integral part of Aztec culture as both food and medicine, and remains significant in Mexican cuisine today for the ingredient's health properties (it's super healthy!), taste, and history. Even the Mexican flag features a drawing of an eagle eating a snake as it perches upon a prickly pear cactus, a reference to a legend that dates back to Aztec times.

Ensalada de nopales is one of the most classic Mexican preparations of the cactus. You can find it nestled in a warm tortilla or simply plated as a side throughout Mexico. My grandma's grandparents who ran a cactus farm taught her this recipe. Nopales that have been cooked have a unique tender texture. (If cooked too long, they can develop a slick film on the surface, so avoid overcooking.) The diced pieces are then tossed with apple cider vinegar, tomatoes, red bell pepper, onion, and cilantro, and finished with a heavy shower of queso fresco for good measure.

Time: 30 minutes ● **Serves:** 6 to 8

Ingredients

1½ pounds nopales (4 to 5 large paddles), cleaned (see note)

3 tablespoons kosher salt, plus more to taste

3 tablespoons apple cider vinegar

1 tablespoon extra-virgin olive oil

1 teaspoon dried oregano

8 ounces Roma tomatoes, halved and cut into ¼-inch slices

½ medium red bell pepper, thinly sliced

½ medium red onion, thinly sliced (about 1 cup)

½ cup packed finely chopped cilantro leaves and stems

Freshly cracked black pepper

½ cup crumbled queso fresco

Directions

1 Prepare the nopales. Dice each nopal into uniform ½-inch pieces. Place them in a colander and rinse with cool water. Bring a medium pot of water with 3 tablespoons salt to a boil. Once boiling, add the diced nopales and cook until tender, about 20 minutes. Drain and rinse with cool water until the cooked nopales reach room temperature.

2 Mix together the vinegar, oil, and oregano in a large bowl. Then add the cooked nopales, tomatoes, bell pepper, red onion, and cilantro. Toss until evenly coated. Season to taste with salt and black pepper.

3 Transfer the salad to a large platter or serve directly from the bowl. Sprinkle the queso fresco evenly over the top. Serve immediately or chilled. Store in the refrigerator for up to 5 days.

Note: Many stores sell nopales already cleaned, which is the easiest, of course. But if your paddles still have spines, here's how to remove them: Carefully hold the paddle by its stem and run a knife along the skin to scrape off the spines. Repeat on the other side. Then trim the edge and remove the stem. The paddle should be smooth.

ALBÓNDIGAS

Meatballs are one of my favorite dishes to cook. From start to finish, I love how hands-on it is: the coolness of the meat when mixing it, the process of forming each meatball by hand. It has always grounded me in the present in a way making other dishes doesn't. And these Mexican albóndigas, or meatballs, are no exception. A good meatball is spiced, tender, and moist. These are all three, *and* are stuffed with a small piece of boiled egg. Fresh mint gives this classic its recognizable taste. The moisture comes from the leftover rice added to the meatball mixture, helping the meatballs soak up the salsa they're cooked in (plus an extra helping of rice on the side when it's time to serve). Another grandma hit.

Time: 45 minutes ● **Serves:** 4 to 5

Ingredients

FOR THE ALBÓNDIGAS

4 large eggs

¼ cup loosely packed mint leaves

3 garlic cloves, peeled

1 teaspoon ground cumin

1 pound ground beef

1 pound ground pork

1 cup leftover cooked white rice

2 teaspoons kosher salt

½ teaspoon freshly cracked black pepper

FOR THE SALSA

1½ pounds Roma tomatoes, halved

1 chipotle pepper from a can (add more if you like it spicier)

¼ large red onion, roughly chopped

¼ large red bell pepper, roughly chopped

4 garlic cloves, peeled

¾ cup packed finely chopped cilantro leaves and stems

¼ cup packed finely chopped parsley leaves and stems

Kosher salt

2 tablespoons extra-virgin olive oil

Directions

1 Hard-boil the eggs. Bring a small saucepan of water to a boil. Once boiling, add the eggs. Cook until fully hard-boiled, 10 to 12 minutes. Strain and rinse in cool water. Peel, and cut each egg into 8 pieces. Set aside.

2 While the eggs are cooking, prepare the albóndiga seasoning. In a molcajete or food processor, combine the mint, garlic, and cumin. Smash or pulse until smooth.

3 Place the beef and pork in a large bowl. Add the rice, 1 egg, the salt, black pepper, and mint mixture. Using your hands, mix until fully combined.

4 Form and stuff the meatballs. Take a generous 2 tablespoons of meat, roll

Recipe continues

it between your palms, and flatten it into a disc about ½ inch thick. Then place about 1 teaspoon of the chopped boiled egg in the center of the flattened meat. Pinch the sides upward to fully enclose the egg. Gently roll the meatball between your palms to form a golf-ball-size round. Transfer to a large plate or baking sheet. Repeat with the remaining meat mixture and chopped eggs until you have about 20 stuffed meatballs. Reserve any extra pieces of egg.

5 Make the salsa. Place the tomatoes in a large pot with water just to cover. Bring to a boil over high heat. Cook until the tomatoes start to soften and the skins begin to peel, about 5 minutes. Reserve 1 cup of the cooking liquid and drain the rest. Transfer the cooked tomatoes to a blender. Reserve the pot for cooking the meatballs.

6 In the same blender, add the 1 cup reserved water, chipotle pepper, onion, bell pepper, garlic, ½ cup of the cilantro,

and the parsley. Blend until smooth, about 2 minutes. Season with salt to taste.

7 Heat the oil in the reserved pot over medium-high heat. Once the oil is shimmering, add the salsa. (It may splash a little, so be prepared.) Bring it to a simmer, skimming off any foam from the top.

8 Reduce the heat to medium-low. Gently add the meatballs, one by one, distributing them evenly in the pot and submerging them in the salsa as much as possible. Cover and cook until the meatballs are cooked through, 10 to 12 minutes, flipping over once about halfway through. (Do not stir the pot before the meatballs are cooked or they may break.)

9 Taste and adjust for salt, if needed. Add any reserved pieces of the chopped eggs. Serve while warm, 3 to 4 meatballs per person. Garnish with the remaining cilantro.

HUEVOS CON WEENIES

. . . Also known as huevos con salchicha, or in English, eggs with hot dogs. When I was a kid, my grandma would fry up hot dog slices until the edges bubbled slightly and crisped. Then she'd bathe them in scrambled eggs until the whole thing became a fluffy blanket dotted with hot dog bites. We would often eat this dish on its own, but folded in a warm tortilla is even better.

This simple meal is a beloved breakfast recipe to many (at least that's what TikTok tells me). Huevos con weenies forever. 🖤

Time: 10 minutes ● **Serves:** 2

Ingredients

4 large eggs

¼ cup whole milk

Pinch of kosher salt, plus more to taste

Freshly cracked black pepper

1½ tablespoons unsalted butter

2 hot dogs, sliced into ¼-inch-thick rounds

Directions

1 Crack the eggs into a small bowl, add the milk, and season with salt and pepper. Beat with a fork until combined. Set aside.

2 Melt ½ tablespoon of the butter in a large nonstick skillet over medium heat. Add the hot dogs and cook until they are slightly crisp along the edges and golden on each side, about 3 minutes.

3 Add the remaining 1 tablespoon butter and reduce the heat to medium-low. Once the butter has melted, add the eggs and cook to your preferred texture, stirring gently with a wooden spoon to incorporate the hot dogs.

HUEVOS CON WEENIES MAX

The alternate title for this was "Huevos con Weenies PLUS ULTRA SUPER MAX" because it does feel like the strongest superhero in a shonen anime. It combines the classic with huevos a la mexicana, making it the deluxe upgrade if you're feeling extra.

Time: 15 minutes ● **Serves:** 2 to 3

Ingredients

5 large eggs

¼ cup whole milk

Pinch of kosher salt, plus more to taste

Freshly cracked black pepper

2 tablespoons unsalted butter

2 hot dogs, sliced into ¼-inch-thick rounds

¼ large yellow onion, diced

1 Roma tomato, diced

1 jalapeño, diced

¼ cup crumbled queso fresco

3 scallions, thinly sliced at an angle (about ¼ packed cup)

Directions

1 Crack the eggs into a small bowl, add the milk, and season with salt and pepper. Beat with a fork until combined. Set aside.

2 Melt ½ tablespoon of the butter in a large nonstick skillet over medium heat. Add the hot dogs and cook until they are slightly crisp along the edges and golden on each side, about 3 minutes.

3 Add another ½ tablespoon of the butter, the onion, tomato, and jalapeño. Cook until the onion is tender and translucent, about 3 minutes.

4 Add the remaining 1 tablespoon butter and reduce the heat to medium-low. Once the butter has melted, add the eggs and cook to your preferred texture, stirring gently with a wooden spoon to incorporate the vegetables and hot dogs. Immediately transfer to a serving plate. Garnish with the queso fresco and scallions. Serve with warm tortillas.

POZOLE ROJO

When I was fifteen, my family and I went to Mexico City to visit my grandma's side. We had been there together once before, but I was too young to really remember much, so this felt like my true first time. After a quick agua fresca break, we arrived at their place. They live in a kind of communal home where some bathrooms and kitchens are accessible to multiple families. In the shared outdoor kitchen, a huge two-foot stockpot was bubbling away with pozole, a Mexican soup made with hominy, chiles, and chicken or pork. Soon after we arrived, we sat down to eat with some of my grandma's family and their neighbors. Each person at the table seemed to be the nicest and most generous person I've ever met—her family is just so lovely and always welcomed me as their family, too. Even though the language barrier made talking difficult, it seemed like the only form of communication we needed was the onion, cilantro, and lime juice we piled into our bowls.

This pozole rojo is my grandma's recipe. It gets its red color from tomatoes and guajillo chiles, giving it a fruity and subtle smoky taste. Whenever her sister and niece visit us from Mexico, my grandma makes this. It has only ever felt like the happiest dish filled with warmth to me. And I hope it feels that way to you, too.

Time: 1 hour ● **Serves:** 8

Ingredients

FOR THE POZOLE

¼ cup extra-virgin olive oil

1 large red onion, diced

9 garlic cloves (4 finely chopped and 5 whole but peeled)

1 teaspoon ground cumin

1 teaspoon dried oregano

2½ pounds bone-in, skin-on chicken thighs

Three 29-ounce cans pozole (hominy), drained and rinsed

1 dried bay leaf

1 tablespoon kosher salt, plus more to taste

3 ounces dried guajillo chiles (about 16 chiles)

1 pound Roma tomatoes, quartered lengthwise

¼ large white onion, roughly chopped (about ½ cup)

2 tablespoons chicken bouillon seasoning (such as Knorr)

Cayenne pepper (optional)

FOR THE TOPPINGS

1 medium white onion, finely diced

½ cup packed finely chopped cilantro leaves and stems

2 cups thinly sliced romaine lettuce

2 limes, quartered

Directions

1 Heat 2 tablespoons of the oil in a large pot over medium-high heat. Once the oil is shimmering, add the red onion, chopped garlic, cumin, and oregano. Cook, stirring frequently to avoid browning, until the onion is tender and translucent, about 3 minutes.

2 Add 12 cups water, the chicken, pozole, bay leaf, and 1½ teaspoons of the salt. Bring to a boil, then cover and reduce the heat to medium. Cook until the chicken is no longer pink, about 20 minutes.

3 While the chicken is cooking, toast the chiles. First, slice the chiles open and remove the seeds. Then add the chiles to a large dry skillet over high heat. Toast, turning frequently to avoid burning, until the chile skins begin to lighten in color and become fragrant, about 3 minutes.

4 Add 4 cups water and the tomatoes to the skillet. Bring to a boil and reduce the heat to medium. Cook until the chiles rehydrate and the tomatoes soften to the point where the skins begin to peel, about 5 minutes. Remove from the heat. Reserve 1 cup cooking liquid and drain the rest. Reserve the skillet.

5 Make the salsa. Transfer the softened chiles, tomatoes (skin intact), and reserved cooking liquid to a blender. Add the white onion and whole garlic cloves. Blend until smooth, about 2 minutes.

6 Heat the remaining 2 tablespoons oil in the reserved skillet over medium-high heat. Once the oil is shimmering, reduce the heat to low and add the salsa. Be careful— it will splash. Cook, stirring frequently, until the oil is fully incorporated and there's a slight golden sheen on the top, about 4 minutes. Turn off the heat.

7 Once the chicken is done, use tongs to transfer it to a cutting board. Carefully cut the chicken into bite-size pieces, discarding the skin and bones. Transfer the chicken back to the pot.

8 Add the salsa to the soup and mix until incorporated. Cover and continue to cook until the chicken is tender, about 20 minutes. Discard the bay leaf. Season with the chicken bouillon and cayenne to taste (if using). Taste and adjust for salt.

9 Place the white onion, cilantro, and lettuce in their own small bowls or in small piles on a large platter so people can add as much or as little of each topping as they want. Serve the pozole in bowls with the limes on the side.

WELCOME TO AMERICA!
¡VAMOS A MEDIEVAL TIMES!

They say Disney World is the happiest place on earth, but I think it's actually a fifteen-minute drive down the road. Located in an unassuming parking lot across the street from a Walmart Supercenter is a large, vine-covered castle that spans more than three city blocks. The building is ornamented with decorative shields, each adorned with its own colorful crest to represent a different knight. A short stroll across the drawbridge and past the iron gates is Medieval Times Dinner & Tournament, a fantastical dinner and show experience that transports diners to the Middle Ages.

We always go here when my grandma's family members visit the US for the first time from Mexico—I don't think there's a more perfect way to experience American culture than from inside a fake European castle in Kissimmee, Florida.

Stepping inside the fortress does feel like entering a time machine. But instead of taking me back to the Middle Ages and greeting me with ornate unicorn tapestries and the plague, it's a gift shop straight out of the '90s selling Nintendo Zelda shields and plastic crowns. As soon as I'm checked in, one of the staff members, who are dressed in medieval-themed outfits (corsets for women and tunics for men), rolls a colorful piece of thick paper into a crown and hands it to me. I promptly place it on top of my head. Everyone in the same party is given the same color crown, each of the six colors representing a specific knight's "royal" court. We all cheer on our assigned knights as they compete to see who's the bravest. It's pretty simple. But before the show starts, the queen of the castle comes out and greets the commoners (us) from her Hall of Arms throne, allowing for photo ops by a not-so-medieval photographer that are available to purchase at the end of the night, next to the $250 swords. Her Majesty waves us commoners goodbye, and then the grand wooden doors open to signal that the show is about to begin.

Stepping inside the dim room, I catch my first peek at the huge sand-covered arena. It's the superdome of theatrical medieval fighting. Three sides of the arena are surrounded with bleacher-like seats. At the head of the area, though, is Her Majesty's seat, high above everyone else to remind all of her status. I shuffle into a row until I'm greeted by my place setting: an iron plate, iron bowl, tall iron mug, and no utensils. It looks like a scene straight out of *Game of Thrones*. The lights darken and Her Majesty welcomes us to her castle. In between the knight jousting, falcon tricks (yes, the animal), sword fights, horse prancing (yes, again: the animal), and overall loose plot, the feast is served.

First comes the tomato bisque, which is poured into the iron bowl. To eat it, I have to hold the handle jutting out at a right angle from the side and sip on it slowly as if it were hot tea. Next, the waiter comes out in rounds bringing tubs of halved roasted chickens, herb potatoes, steamed corn, and buttered garlic toasts. One of each is tossed onto my large iron plate. And then it's time to dig in with my original utensils: my hands. If someone asks for a fork, a server might respond with "What's that?" because we are in the eleventh century, after all. I wash it all down with the unlimited soda refills. My tall mug gets greasier with every sip, as I struggle to grip it with my oily chicken fingers. No feast is complete without dessert, which is a random slice of cake that tastes like it's from Costco. I don't remember feeling good after eating at Medieval Times, but I've never felt more alive.

Out of the ten different Medieval Times locations, I've been to two. While New Jersey's castle and arena has its charm, with slight differences, the Florida one will always be my favorite. (It's also the original castle that started the franchise in 1983.) Although I went only once or twice as a younger kid, the frequency of these trips after I moved in with my grandparents soon made it feel like a regular thing.

I grew up knowing that my grandma's family in Mexico was on a much tighter budget than us. The only times I got to see them were during the two trips we went to Mexico to visit, and they didn't come to visit us in the US for more than a decade. Finally, after years of saving, my grandma's sister and her young daughter were the first to make the journey to Florida, their first trip to America.

The Grand Canyon, Las Vegas, New York City, Yellowstone National Park . . . There's so much to do in the US, a country full of history and natural beauty. How do you boil down an entire country's experience into a week in one city? Besides spending time with my grandma, they wanted to do only one thing—go to Disney World. But while we were in the greater Orlando area, we took them to our favorite place, Medieval Times.

Honestly, Disney shares a lot of the features that make Medieval Times the perfect way to experience the US: the capitalism, the high price, the overindulgence, and of course, the fun. But Disney feels too expected. And while $100-ish allows you all-day access to Disney, Medieval Times costs $67.95 per adult, which only gets you two hours to gawk at knights wielding swords that slightly spark when they hit each other. It's gritty, competitive, very silly, and technically, much more expensive by the hour than Disney. In many ways, Medieval Times just feels more American to me than Mickey—whose polished shoes and tidy bow tie embody a sophistication that the knights do not have—could ever be.

While the dinner and show are *very* loosely based on European history, the extravagance and oily chicken fingers scream red, white, and blue. Cheering for your designated knight throughout the show usually means you're screaming like you're watching the Super Bowl. The mismatching time periods, with the Nintendo Zelda shields and rainbow light-up princess tiaras (both overpriced, by the way), feel similar to how we in the US embellish history to best fit our needs. And the location of every Medieval Times castle—in a sprawling parking lot sandwiched between the drab landmarks of suburbia—offers arguably a more accurate portrayal of what the US looks like than any viewing point around the Grand Canyon. Crammed in a plastic seat gripping a roasted half chicken, wearing a loose-fitting paper crown, and screaming at the top of my lungs for the green knight to win? This *is* America.

We've gone to Medieval Times every time my grandma's sister has come back to the States. And if it's someone else's first time in the US, they tag along, too. It may seem silly to think that someone's only cultural experience of the US is a reenactment of Europe's Middle Ages, but I wouldn't have it any other way.

HORCHATA

There are A LOT of different horchatas out there. In this book alone, there are three kinds. Originating in North Africa, horchata made its way to Spain over one thousand years ago, where tigernuts (also known as chufa nuts) were used to give the drink a creamy consistency. But it was in Latin America where horchata was reimagined into countless variations. In El Salvador, morro beans are a go-to ingredient. For Mexico, it's rice. And in Ecuador, it takes a completely different form as a deep-pink herbal tea. Usually, though, horchata is made by soaking nuts, grains, or both and then mixing them into a sweet beverage.

This version is inspired by Mexican horchata, more specifically, my grandma's recipe (obviously). Soaked rice, almonds, and cinnamon are blended into a cloudy vegan drink. It uses two types of cinnamon to combine the best of both worlds: the subtle floral taste of canela and the stronger notes of ground cassia. If you aren't able to find canela, you can skip it and up the ground cinnamon to 1 tablespoon instead. Serve in a tall glass filled with ice and you'll see for yourself why it's one of the most famous aguas frescas.

Time: 15 minutes, plus overnight soaking   ●   **Serves:** 8

Ingredients

2 cups uncooked long-grain white rice

1 cup whole raw, unsalted almonds

Two 4-inch canela (also called Ceylon) cinnamon sticks

1 cup sugar

1 teaspoon ground cinnamon, plus more for garnish

½ teaspoon vanilla extract

Pinch of kosher salt

Directions

1 Wash the rice. Using a fine-mesh strainer, rinse the rice with tap water several times, using your hand to swirl the grains around. Repeat until the water runs clear.

2 Place the rinsed rice into a large pitcher or bowl. Add the almonds, cinnamon sticks, and 8 cups water. Cover the container and let soak overnight (at least 8 hours) at room temperature.

3 Remove and reserve 4 cups water from the soaked rice. Transfer the remaining liquid, rice, cinnamon sticks, and almonds to a blender, and blend, in batches if necessary, until the solids are finely ground, about 2 minutes.

4 Place a fine-mesh strainer over a large bowl and slowly pour the ground rice mixture into the strainer, working in batches so it doesn't overfill. Use a spoon or small rubber spatula to press out as much liquid from the solids as possible. Discard the solids. Transfer the strained liquid

to a large pitcher. Rinse the strainer and repeat the process. Double straining will make the horchata super smooth. Transfer the double-strained liquid back into the pitcher.

5 Add the reserved 4 cups water, the sugar, ground cinnamon, vanilla, and salt. Whisk well until all the cinnamon is evenly incorporated. Serve over ice and garnish with more ground cinnamon. Store in the refrigerator for up to 5 days. It will separate, so stir well before serving.

HORCHATA DE MELÓN

One of my earliest food memories is face-planting into a juicy honeydew and chowing down until I hit the rind. This is the horchata version of getting a honeydew right to the face. My grandma learned how to make horchata de melón when she was working at a hotel in Cancún. This was the fancy horchata guests could enjoy because it's extra decadent with condensed milk and super-ripe honeydew. Of all the horchatas out there, this one sticks out to me because it uses honeydew seeds to give it texture and bitterness. The seeds balance the sweetness and are a genius way to reduce food waste. But if you really don't like bitterness, you can of course omit the seeds. You will need two ripe honeydews to make this, so be prepared for lots of leftover cut melon, which is just a bonus.

Time: 5 minutes, plus chilling ● **Serves:** 5 to 6

Ingredients

2 cups roughly chopped ripe honeydew

2 cups honeydew seeds (from 2 melons)

Two 4-inch cinnamon sticks (preferably Ceylon)

One 12-ounce can evaporated milk

¾ cup sweetened condensed milk

½ cup whole raw, unsalted almonds

Directions

1 In a blender, combine the honeydew, honeydew seeds, cinnamon sticks, evaporated milk, condensed milk, and almonds. Blend until smooth, about 2 minutes.

2 Strain the horchata through a fine-mesh strainer into a pitcher. You can line the strainer with a cheesecloth if you prefer an extra-smooth texture. If you like your horchata on the thinner side, add water to reach the desired consistency, but it is not necessary. Refrigerate until chilled and serve over ice.

CHILAQUILES VERDES

Few breakfast foods are as perfect as chilaquiles: just-fried cut tortillas bathed in a pool of bright salsa verde and topped with a mixture of scallions, cilantro, and crumbled queso fresco. This recipe is my grandma's version. Chilaquiles are also often made with salsa roja, but she prefers waking up to the brightness of the tomatillos in salsa verde. Serve with crispy sunny-side-up eggs or enjoy on their own. While they are traditionally a Mexican breakfast dish, they're good any time of day.

Time: 30 minutes • **Serves:** 4 to 6

Ingredients

FOR THE GARNISH

1 cup thinly sliced scallions (about 4 whole scallions)

1 cup finely crumbled queso fresco

½ cup packed finely chopped cilantro leaves

FOR THE CHILAQUILES

1 pound tomatillos, husked, rinsed, and halved

1 large jalapeño, halved

¼ large yellow bell pepper, roughly chopped (about ½ cup)

¼ large red onion, roughly chopped (about ½ cup)

¼ cup packed roughly chopped cilantro leaves and stems

¼ cup packed roughly chopped parsley leaves and stems

4 garlic cloves, peeled

2 teaspoons chicken consommé powder (optional)

¼ teaspoon dried oregano

⅛ teaspoon ground cumin

Kosher salt

Vegetable oil, for frying

8 ounces stale corn tortillas, cut into 8 wedges each (see note)

1 tablespoon extra-virgin olive oil

Directions

1 Make the garnish. Mix together the scallions, queso fresco, and cilantro in a small bowl. Set aside.

2 Make the salsa. Bring a small saucepan of water to a boil. Once boiling, add the tomatillos and jalapeño. Cook until the tomatillos begin to soften and the skin starts to peel back, about 5 minutes. Reserve ½ cup water for blending.

3 In a blender, combine the cooked tomatillos and jalapeño, ½ cup reserved water, the bell pepper, onion, cilantro, parsley, garlic, consommé powder (if using),

Recipe continues

oregano, cumin, and salt to taste. Blend until smooth, about 2 minutes.

4 Make the tortilla chips. Heat ½ inch of vegetable oil in a large nonstick skillet over medium–high heat. Once the oil is shimmering, add one-third of the cut tortillas and fry until golden brown and crisp, about 2 minutes. Using a slotted spoon, transfer the chips to a paper towel–lined plate to drain. Repeat with the remaining tortillas, adding more oil if necessary.

5 Cook the chilaquiles. Heat the olive oil in a large skillet over medium–high heat. Add the salsa and sauté until it thickens enough to coat the back of a wooden spoon,

about 4 minutes. Carefully add the chips, doing your best not to break them too much. Toss until evenly coated with the salsa. Cook until they soften a little but still maintain their overall crunchy texture, about 2 minutes.

6 Transfer to a large serving dish and sprinkle with the prepared garnish. Eat immediately.

Note: Stale tortillas are key to avoiding chilaquiles that are too wet or soggy. If you don't have stale tortillas, you can cut them the day before, spread them out on a baking sheet or clean kitchen towel, and leave them uncovered overnight.

Sweet and Savory Tamales

Every Christmas, my grandma makes tamales for the whole family. It's an involved process that she usually spreads over two days: the first is reserved just for soaking the dried corn husks overnight until they're malleable enough to stuff and fold. The second day is when it gets busy. She starts by making the fillings, which can range from chicken to cheese for savory ones, or pineapple to spiced sugar for sweet variations. Then she makes the dough. Getting it just right takes practice, but because my grandma has been making tamales since she was a kid, she can quickly put it together. For her, it's all about the feel and sound the masa makes as you mix the lard (yes, for savory ones it should preferably be lard) into the masa harina. When it doesn't stick to her hands and instead squishes enough to quietly release air like a whisper, that's when she knows she's done. After a quick rest, it's time to fill and fold each tamale. Before the pandemic, my grandma's sister and niece from Cancún would sometimes visit around the holidays, so she would get at least another pair of hands to help assemble.

To be honest, before this book, I had never made tamales with my grandma, only enjoyed them, but making them beside her felt like watching a master at work. There's no need for her to measure anything because she knows exactly how much of the masa needs to be spread across the husk and how much filling is too little or too much from the thousands of tamales she's made in her life. She quickly folds each one, gently adjusting the filling and sides to make them into a uniform shape. By the time I made one tamale, she had finished ten.

Tamales are an essential food in Mexican culture and date back thousands of years. According to historians, the Aztecs invented them to be eaten as a portable food during battle. Since then, cultures around the world have adapted and created their own versions of tamales. I'm not even sure an entire book on tamales alone would do the dish true justice, but what I can say is that these are four tamale variations from my grandma. And she knows good tamales.

Tamales de pollo are made two ways, one with a bright salsa verde and the other with a smoky salsa guajillo. They're a Mexican classic. Tamales de rajas are a vegetarian option that is simply stuffed with cheese, onions, and jalapeños. And finally, tamales dulces de piña are made with anise-spiced masa and stuffed with juicy pieces of pineapple. Some people add raisins, but I omitted them (if raisins are your thing, though, add some!). Each one is wrapped in a little corn husk bow, truly making them feel even more like a present than they already are. The optional drizzle of condensed milk for the tamales dulces isn't how my grandma makes them, but I find it to be the perfect finish and adds to their richness.

A small note about the time: Two hours is the *active* cooking time only. But because of the prep it takes to fill, fold, and arrange all the tamales, I would recommend planning to at least double it. And it's a good chance to ask friends and family to pitch in to help make the process faster and just more fun.

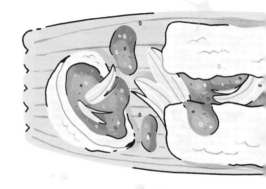

TAMALES DE POLLO, 2 WAYS

Time: 2 hours, plus soaking ● **Makes:** About 30 tamales

Ingredients

40 dried corn husks (from 1 pound)

FOR THE CHICKEN FILLING

1½ pounds bone-in, skin-on chicken thighs

½ medium yellow onion, peeled

4 garlic cloves, peeled

1 tablespoon kosher salt, plus more to taste

1 teaspoon dried oregano

FOR THE SALSA VERDE

1 tablespoon extra-virgin olive oil

1½ cups Salsa Verde (page 96)

FOR THE SALSA GUAJILLO

2 ounces dried guajillo chiles (about 8 large)

2 Roma tomatoes, roughly chopped

½ cup roughly chopped red onion

4 garlic cloves, peeled

Kosher salt

FOR THE TAMALES

5 cups harina de maíz nixtamalizado (such as Maseca)

1½ teaspoons kosher salt

¼ teaspoon baking powder

1¼ cups lard, melted, or vegetable oil

Directions

1 Prepare the corn husks. Place the husks in a large bowl and cover with hot water, using a small plate or bowl to weight them down so they're all fully submerged. Soak for at least 1 hour. You can also soak them the day before by covering the husks with room-temperature water and leaving them overnight.

2 While the husks are soaking, make the chicken filling. Combine 5 cups water, the chicken, yellow onion, garlic, salt, and oregano in a large pot. Bring to a boil over high heat. Once boiling, cover and reduce the heat to medium-low. Cook until the chicken is tender, about 40 minutes.

My Mexican Grandma

●

Recipe continues

3 While the chicken is cooking, prepare the salsa verde. In a blender, combine the olive oil and salsa verde and blend until completely smooth, about 1 minute. Transfer to a bowl and set aside.

4 Make the salsa guajillo. Using your hands or a paring knife, open the guajillo chiles and remove and discard the seeds. Place the guajillos and tomatoes in a small saucepan. Cover with water and bring to a boil over high heat. Cook until the tomatoes begin to soften and the skin starts to peel back, about 3 minutes. Transfer the rehydrated chiles and softened tomatoes to a blender. Add the red onion, garlic, and 3 tablespoons of the water the chiles were cooked in. Blend until smooth, about 2 minutes. Season with salt to taste. Transfer to a bowl and set aside.

5 When the chicken is done, use tongs to transfer it to a cutting board. Let cool for 15 minutes. Strain and reserve the liquid it was cooked in. If you don't want to discard the cooked onion and garlic, you can cut them into small pieces and serve them with the tamales. Once the chicken is cool, use two forks or your hands to shred it into small pieces, discarding the bones and skin. Season to taste with salt.

6 Make the masa. Whisk together the masa, salt, and baking powder in a large bowl. Then add 4¼ cups of the reserved chicken stock (if you run out, you can use warm water) and the lard. Mix with your hands and knead until the consistency is smooth but still slightly tacky to the touch. Cover and let rest for 15 minutes.

7 Fill the tamales. Half of the tamales will have salsa verde and the other half will have salsa guajillo. Take a large corn husk and shake off the excess water. Place the side with more visible ridges on your work surface, with the wide end closest to you. If you look carefully, you will see there's a smooth and rough side to each husk; the smooth side holds the filling. Using the back of a spoon or your hands, evenly spread ¼ cup masa along the center to form a rectangle, leaving about a ½–inch border along the edges of the wide side closest to you and the narrow top portion of the husk completely empty. Next, add the fillings to make the salsa verde half. Place 1 tablespoon of the salsa verde on top of the masa, then add a hefty tablespoon of chicken filling directly on top of that. If you run out of the larger husks, you can slightly overlap two smaller ones.

8 Fold the tamales. Begin by folding the left and right sides to cover the filling, leaving no masa exposed. It should feel snug, like you're tucking someone into bed. Then fold the narrow part toward you with the crease forming where the end of the filling is, leaving the wide top unfolded.

9 Shape the tamales. Using your hands, gently apply pressure on the narrow closed bottom to push the masa toward the exposed top, leaving about ½ inch of space at the end. Do not let the filling fall out. This will lengthen the overall rectangular shape (it should be about twice as long as it is wide to create that iconic tamale look). Then use your hands to gently create a uniform shape along the front and back. The tamale should have a flattish face on the front and back so it doesn't roll around on the plate. (This may take a little practice to get right, but YouTube videos are very helpful here if it's your first time!) Place on a baking sheet with the seam side down so it doesn't pop open. Repeat steps 7 through 9 with the remaining tamales, continuing to use only salsa verde until you have 13 to 15 tamales and then switching to using only salsa guajillo. Reserve any leftover salsa for serving.

10 Steam the tamales. Place a basket insert or a steaming rack into a tamale pot or other large pot. Fill the bottom with water until it's just below the basket. Place a single layer of extra husks on top of the basket to create a little nest for the tamales to sit on. Next, add the tamales vertically, open side up so the filling doesn't fall out, first lining the circumference of the pot and circling your way in. They should be snugly leaning against each other. Take a damp, clean kitchen towel and drape it across the top, gently tucking it between the outermost tamales and the pot itself to trap as much steam as possible. Then cover with

the lid and bring the water to a boil over high heat, making sure the lid is completely closed. Once boiling, reduce the heat to medium-low and simmer for 45 minutes, occasionally adding a little hot water to continue steaming if you don't hear any more bubbling sounds. (Pay close attention to the sound!) To add the hot water, use a small measuring cup, with the tip against the edge of the pot, and carefully pour it into a gap between the tamales so the water falls to the bottom and doesn't get stuck in a husk.

11 To check if the tamales are done, remove one and unwrap it. The masa should come away easily from the husk as you peel it off. Cut it through the center, and if there's no raw masa, you are good to go! If there are some raw bits or the masa is clinging heavily to the husk, rewrap the tamale, place it back into the pot, and continue to steam all the tamales for another 15 minutes. Once cooked, remove the tamales and let cool for 10 minutes. Serve while warm with any leftover salsa. You can also freeze them individually wrapped for up to 3 months. To reheat, thaw and steam them to serve.

TAMALES DE RAJAS

Time: 1 hour 30 minutes, plus soaking ● **Makes:** About 30 tamales

Ingredients

40 dried corn husks (from 1 pound)

FOR THE FILLING

6 jalapeños

1½ large white onions, halved and thinly sliced

1 pound queso fresco, cut into 30 slices

FOR THE TAMALES

5 cups harina de maíz nixtamalizado (such as Maseca)

1½ teaspoons kosher salt

¼ teaspoon baking powder

1¼ cups vegetable oil

Directions

1 Prepare the corn husks. Place the husks in a large bowl and cover with hot water, using a small plate or bowl to weight them down so they're all fully submerged. Soak for at least 1 hour. You can also soak them the day before by covering the husks with room-temperature water and leaving them overnight.

2 Halve the jalapeños lengthwise. Discard the membranes and seeds if you don't like spice. But if you do, keep them! Thinly slice lengthwise to create jalapeño strips.

3 Make the masa. Whisk together the masa, salt, and baking powder in a large bowl. Then add 4¼ cups warm water and the vegetable oil. Mix with your hands and knead until the consistency is smooth but still slightly tacky to the touch. Cover and let rest for 15 minutes.

4 Fill the tamales. Place the sliced jalapeños, onions, and cheese near your filling station. Take a large corn husk and shake off the excess water. Place the side with more visible ridges on your work surface, with the wide end closest to you. If you look carefully, you will see there's a smooth and rough side to each husk; the smooth side holds the filling. Using the back of a spoon or your hands, evenly spread ¼ cup of the masa along the center to form a rectangle, leaving about a ½-inch border along the edges of the wide side closest to you and the narrow top portion of the husk completely empty. Place a slice of cheese on top of the masa, then top with a few slices of jalapeño and onion.

5 Fold the tamales. Begin by folding the left and right sides to cover the filling, leaving no masa exposed. It should feel snug, like you're tucking someone into bed. Then fold the narrow part toward you with the crease forming where the end of the filling is, leaving the wide top unfolded.

6 Shape the tamales. Using your hands, gently apply pressure on the narrow closed bottom to push the masa toward the exposed top, leaving about ½ inch of space at the end. Do not let the filling fall out. This will lengthen the overall rectangular shape (it should be about twice as long as it is wide to create that iconic tamale look). Then use your hands to gently create a uniform shape along the front and back. The tamale should have a flattish face on the front and back so it doesn't roll around on the plate. (This may take a little practice to get right, but YouTube videos are very helpful here if it's your first time!) Place on a baking sheet with the seam side down so it doesn't pop open. Repeat steps 4 through 6 with the remaining tamales.

7 Steam the tamales. Place a basket insert or a steaming rack into a tamale pot or other large pot. Fill the bottom with water until it's just below the basket. Place a single layer of extra husks on top of the basket to create a little nest for the tamales to sit on. Next, add the tamales vertically, open side up, first lining the circumference of the pot and circling your way in. They should be snugly leaning against each other. Take a damp, clean kitchen towel and drape it across the top, gently tucking it between the outermost tamales and the pot itself to trap as much steam as possible. Then cover with the lid and bring the water to a boil over high heat, being sure the lid is completely closed. Once boiling, reduce the heat to medium-low and simmer for 45 minutes, occasionally adding a little hot water to continue steaming if you don't hear any more bubbling sounds. (Pay close attention to the sound!) To add the hot water, use a small measuring cup, with the tip against the edge of the pot, and carefully pour it into a gap between the tamales so the water falls to the bottom and doesn't get stuck in a husk.

8 To check if the tamales are done, remove one and unwrap it. The masa should come away easily from the husk as you peel it off. Cut it through the center, and if there's no raw masa, you are good to go! If there are some raw bits or the masa is clinging heavily to the husk, rewrap the tamale, place it back into the pot, and continue to steam all the tamales for another 15 minutes. Once cooked, remove the tamales and let cool for 10 minutes. Serve while warm. You can also freeze them individually wrapped for up to 3 months. To reheat, thaw and steam them to serve.

TAMALES DULCES DE PIÑA

Time: 2 hours, plus soaking • **Makes:** About 24 tamales

Ingredients

40 dried corn husks (from about 1 pound)

Half of a 4-inch cinnamon stick (preferably Ceylon)

1 teaspoon anise seeds

4 cups harina de maíz nixtamalizado (such as Maseca)

9 tablespoons unsalted butter, melted

1 teaspoon baking powder

1 cup packed light brown sugar

¾ cup shredded dried sweetened coconut

Pinch of kosher salt

2 cups finely chopped pineapple

Sweetened condensed milk, for serving (optional)

Directions

1 Prepare the corn husks. Place the husks in a large bowl and cover with hot water, using a small plate or bowl to weight them down so they're all fully submerged. Soak for at least 1 hour. You can also soak them the day before by covering the husks with room-temperature water and leaving them overnight.

2 Add 3½ cups water, the cinnamon, and anise seeds to a medium pot. Bring to a boil over high heat. Once boiling, reduce the heat to low. Cover and simmer until the water is super fragrant, about 15 minutes. Remove from the heat and strain into a large measuring cup. Let cool for 15 minutes.

3 Make the masa. In a large bowl, mix the masa, butter, baking powder, brown sugar, coconut, salt, and 3 cups of the spiced water with a wooden spoon until well incorporated, switching to your hands once it's cool enough to handle. If the batter looks too dry,

add more water a little at a time as needed. Knead the masa until the consistency is smooth but still feels slightly tacky to the touch. Cover and let rest for 15 minutes.

4 Fill the tamales. Take a large corn husk and shake off the excess water. Place the side with more visible ridges on your work surface, with the wide end closest to you. If you look carefully, you will see there's a smooth and rough side to each husk; the smooth side holds the filling. Using the back of a spoon or your hands, evenly spread ¼ cup masa along the center to form a rectangle, leaving about a ½ inch border along the edges of the wide side closest to you and the narrow top portion of the husk completely empty. Place a hefty tablespoon of pineapple directly on top of the masa. If you run out of the larger husks, you can slightly overlap two smaller ones.

5 Fold the tamales. Begin by folding the left and right sides to cover the filling, leaving no masa exposed.

It should feel snug, like you're tucking someone into bed. Then fold the narrow part toward you with the crease forming where the end of the filling is, leaving the wide top unfolded.

6 Shape the tamales. Using your hands, gently apply pressure on the narrow closed bottom to push the masa toward the exposed top, leaving about ½ inch of space at the end. This will lengthen the overall rectangular shape (it should be about twice as long as it is wide to create that iconic tamale look). Then use your hands to gently create a uniform shape along the front and back. The tamale should have a flattish face on the front and back so it doesn't roll around on the plate. To make a husk ribbon that ties around each tamale (optional step!), take a small husk piece and peel off a ½-inch-wide strip. Next, tie a small knot toward the narrow end. Then tear it in half on the untied end and peel it in half upward toward the knot. Finally, wrap it around the tamale crosswise and tie another knot to secure it. Place on a baking sheet with the seam side down so it doesn't pop open. Repeat steps 4 through 6 with the remaining tamales.

7 Steam the tamales. Place a basket insert or a steaming rack into a tamale pot or other large pot. Fill the bottom with water until it's just below the basket. Place a single layer of extra husks on top of the basket to create a little nest for the tamales to sit on. Next, add the tamales vertically, open side up so the filling doesn't fall out, first lining the circumference of the pot and circling your way in. They should be snugly leaning against each other. Take a damp, clean kitchen towel and drape it across the top, gently tucking it between the outermost tamales and the pot itself to trap as much steam as possible. Then cover with the lid and bring the water to a boil over high heat, making sure the lid is completely closed. Once boiling, reduce the heat to medium-low and simmer for 45 minutes, occasionally adding a little hot water to continue steaming if you don't hear any more bubbling sounds. To add the hot water, use a small measuring cup, with the tip against the edge of the pot, and carefully pour it into a gap between the tamales so the water falls to the bottom and doesn't get stuck in a husk.

8 To check if the tamales are done, remove one and unwrap it. The masa should come away easily from the husk as you peel it off. Cut it through the center, and if there's no raw masa, you are good to go! If there are some raw bits or the masa is clinging heavily to the husk, rewrap the tamale, place it back into the pot, and continue to steam all the tamales for another 15 minutes. Once cooked, remove the tamales and let cool for 10 minutes. Serve while warm with a drizzle of condensed milk, if using. You can also freeze them individually wrapped for up to 3 months. To reheat, thaw and steam them to serve.

How to make TAMALES

WHAT YOU NEED FOR TAMALES DULCES

SPREAD THE MASA EVENLY~

BUT NOT TOO CLOSE TO THE EDGES!

ADD PINEAPPLE ALONG THE CENTER

SNUGLY FOLD THE HUSK OVER THE FILLING & CREASE THE NARROW SIDE UPWARD TO CLOSE THE BOTTOM!

USE YOUR HANDS TO GENTLY SHAPE THE TAMAL

TEAR EXTRA HUSKS AND USE THE PIECES TO MAKE LITTLE BABY HUSK RIBBONS

ADMIRE YOUR TINY TAMAL PRESENTS

CHAMPURRADO

Champurrado is the chocolate variation of Mexican atole, a corn-based drink that's popular throughout Mexico and Central America. It's a warm, soothing beverage made with masa harina, piloncillo, spices, and chocolate. My grandma learned how to make it as a kid, and then she made it for me as a kid. There are tons of flavor variations of atole out there, like coconut, strawberry, and guava, but champurrado is one of the most popular. This version is made with chunks of dark chocolate for extra richness and flavor. Pair with a pan dulce or simply enjoy on its own.

Time: 15 minutes • **Serves:** 4

Ingredients

2 cups whole milk

4 ounces piloncillo, or ½ cup packed dark brown sugar

One 4-inch cinnamon stick (preferably Ceylon)

1 teaspoon vanilla extract

Pinch of kosher salt

½ cup masa harina

3 ounces dark chocolate, roughly chopped (preferably 70% cacao)

Ground cinnamon, for dusting (optional)

Directions

1 Combine the milk, piloncillo, cinnamon stick, vanilla, and salt in a small saucepan. Cook over medium-low heat, stirring occasionally, until the piloncillo is fully dissolved.

2 While the piloncillo is dissolving, slowly whisk together 2 cups warm water and the masa harina in a large measuring cup until lump-free.

3 Gradually whisk the masa mixture into the saucepan and bring to a simmer. Then add the chocolate. Cook the champurrado, whisking frequently to avoid lumps, until the chocolate is fully melted and the consistency is thick enough to evenly coat the back of a wooden spoon, about 5 minutes.

4 Remove from the heat and discard the cinnamon stick. Serve while hot and garnish with ground cinnamon, if desired.

JALAPEÑOS EN ESCABECHE

You can always expect to see a tub of escabeche, or pickled jalapeños, on my grandma's table. In Spanish, escabeche is technically the term for cooking ingredients and letting them soak in vinegar. Fish, chickpeas, garlic . . . if you can think of it, you can escabeche it. Jalapeños en escabeche is one of the most popular variations. It's a mixture of charred jalapeños, onions, carrots, and garlic soaked in a bath of seasoned white vinegar. Its tangy kick cuts the richness of fatty meats, making it a frequent side dish at taquerías. Make a big batch now and your future self will thank you.

Time: 25 minutes, plus cooling ● **Makes:** 2 quarts

Ingredients

1 tablespoon extra-virgin olive oil

1 pound jalapeños with stems

1 large white onion, cut into ½-inch-thick slices

3 carrots, peeled and cut into ¼-inch-thick diagonal slices

12 garlic cloves, peeled

1½ cups white vinegar

2 bay leaves

2 teaspoons kosher salt

1 teaspoon dried oregano

½ teaspoon dried thyme

Directions

1 Heat the oil in a large skillet over medium-high heat. Add the jalapeños and char the outside until some parts become dark brown, about 2 minutes per side. You want some color, but you don't need to fully cook them yet.

2 Add the onion, carrots, and garlic to the pan. Cook until fragrant, stirring frequently to avoid browning, about 2 minutes.

3 Add 1½ cups water, the vinegar, bay leaves, salt, oregano, and thyme. Bring the mixture to a boil. Once boiling, reduce the heat to low and cover. Simmer until the carrots and jalapeños are fork-tender, about 15 minutes. Remove from the heat. Let the escabeche cool completely in the pan with all the cooking liquid. Store in two quart containers (liquid and all) and keep refrigerated for up to 1 month.

TAMALE SOUP

When I miss my grandma, this is what I make. She created this soup using tamale ingredients as the foundation to give the same flavor but in a fraction of the time—about 30 minutes. Masa harina gives the iconic taste and thickens the base, spiced with sazón. Bits of pork speckled throughout add heartiness and give every spoonful a hefty bite. Little piles of extra-crispy pork, neon-fuchsia onions, and fresh cilantro sit on top of every bowl, inviting you in. Born out of heartache and resilience, this is my family's most beloved dish.

My grandma was inspired to make this recipe after eating Cuban tamal en cazuela—a tamale casserole that uses a mixture of blended baby corn as the base. The exact origins of tamal en cazuela are unclear, but some believe it first came from Mexico and was adapted over time to Cuban tastes. Her version replaces the baby corn with masa harina, a finely ground corn flour, which is commonly used in tamales and tortillas today. Although the original dish may have distant Mexican roots, my grandma's version is centered on Mexican flavors.

The garnishes are my favorite part. I mean, what's not to love about mounds of pork, cebollas encurtidas (lime-pickled red onions), and cilantro? Each adds something special that balances that flavor and richness. I like to add the extra lime juice from the red onions for acidity, but you can mix and match until you find your favorite combination.

While my grandma has always used pork, making this vegan would be simple and delicious. Adobo-seasoned oyster mushrooms, enoki "carnitas," or even crumbled tofu spiced with extra sazón would be great replacements. Tamale soup is easy to adapt and make your own.

Time: 30 minutes ● **Serves:** 6 to 8

Ingredients

3 tablespoons extra-virgin olive oil

1¼ pounds leftover Pernil (page 193), shredded

4½ teaspoons kosher salt, plus more to taste

1 large yellow onion, diced

1 medium red bell pepper, diced into ¼-inch pieces

5 garlic cloves, minced

1½ teaspoons dried oregano

1¼ cups masa harina (such as Maseca)

½ teaspoon cayenne pepper (optional)

1 tablespoon sazón with achiote

½ cup packed finely chopped cilantro leaves

Cebollas Encurtidas (page 44)

Directions

1 Heat the oil in a large Dutch oven over high heat. Once the oil is shimmering, add the pernil and 1 teaspoon of the salt. Sauté until the edges crisp and become deep brown, about 7 minutes. Using a slotted spoon, place the pork into a bowl and set aside. You want to leave as much of the rendered fat in the pot as possible.

2 Reduce the heat to medium. Add the onion and bell pepper and cook until softened, about 5 minutes. Add the garlic, oregano, and another ½ teaspoon of the salt. Sauté until fragrant, about 2 minutes.

3 Add 7½ cups water to the Dutch oven and use a wooden spoon to scrape up any browned bits stuck to the bottom of the pot. Increase the heat to medium-high. Once the mixture reaches a gentle boil, slowly add the masa harina while quickly stirring to avoid any clumps. Add half the pork, mix until fully incorporated, and bring to a full boil. Then reduce the heat to medium, stirring to avoid scorching on the bottom. Simmer until the soup thickens enough to coat the back of the wooden spoon, about 15 minutes.

4 Once thickened to a porridge-like consistency, add the remaining 1 tablespoon salt, the cayenne (if using), and sazón. Stir until the spices are evenly incorporated. Taste and adjust for salt. Serve immediately with the remaining crisp pork, cilantro, and cebollas encurtidas as garnishes. Store in the fridge for up to a week or the freezer for 3 months. When reheating, add water to thin out the soup until the desired consistency is reached.

TAMALE SOUP

For three hours once a month, my family looked like any other family—gathered around a table sharing a meal. But this is before I lived with my grandparents. They, George, Thor, and I nestled together in a small booth inside a Miami restaurant, doing our best to act as if things were normal. If it weren't for my brother and me being dropped back off to our respective foster parents, we'd pass as a regular family.

"This tastes like tamales," I said, peering into my steaming, half-empty bowl of yellow soup, fiddling with my spoon to anchor my mind in the present.

"Yes!" Everyone agreed so quickly that it made me wonder if they were doing the same thing.

My brother Thor and I would soon be returned to our foster homes. We wouldn't be able to see each other, or our family, until the next assigned visit. As we finished our soups, the illusion that everything was OK disappeared along with the last spoonfuls.

In 2002, Thor and I were put in foster care after being left alone in a South Beach hotel for three days. I was nine years old, and he was seven. It wasn't the first time we had been left by ourselves, nor was it the longest, but it was the only time we were caught. We had just driven to Miami from New York with my dad. We were living in an art deco hotel along South Beach as "temporary housing," even though there was no clear check-out date. We had no food, which wasn't unusual, but in New York City when my dad left to go on a binge and there wasn't enough to eat, we could call a family friend to bring us supplies. In Florida, we were on our own.

When the first day's hunger crept in, we scraped together whatever change we could find to buy chips and Famous Amos cookies from room service. When someone came to the door, I turned on the shower in the bathroom as a decoy.

"My dad's in there!" I said unprompted and did the biggest hand gesture I could with my small arms. I was sure to let the water run long enough to get steamy before room service arrived just in case they needed visual proof.

At the time I thought I was really smart for coming up with such a believable scheme, but it feels sad now. They didn't ask any questions and handed over the snacks we could afford in exchange for a fistful of quarters from our plastic gallon bag labeled "Life Savings" in scribbled marker. Thor and I cautiously split the snacks. We didn't know how much more food we could afford later. We'd take tiny nibbles from the potato chips and dry cookies and chew as slowly as possible. We wanted to trick our minds into thinking this was a bountiful feast rather than crumbs.

The ironic thing about hunger is that it eventually grows numb. At some point, you no longer want to eat. The sharp pains in my stomach faded on the second day. By the third, I could feel only a hollow sensation. Even the coolest splashes of drinking water were indetectable. I'll never forget what it felt like not to have food. When the police finally found us, my first meal in days was a fast-food burger. I ate it silently out of obligation rather than hunger. The greasiness of it is as vivid as my fear over what would happen next.

Being in the system is weird. There's a uniform process that masks the chaos of everyday life in foster care. My brother and I were together in the first home but soon got separated. We were sent to different homes in different parts of Miami because of "rules." My first assigned social worker did not make the transition of being freshly separated from my sibling any easier. He was cold and treated me more like an item on a to-do list than a person. During my intake, the social worker drove me around to various locations that tested my emotional trauma and cognitive abilities. No one ever explained why, but I think it was to see how much of a potential risk I was or if I needed special care. When my social worker talked to me more seriously about the state of my case, he would raise his voice.

"Why can't I just live with my dad again?" I'd shout at him, confused and frustrated.

"You can't live with him!" he'd shoot back quickly, almost cutting me off. He never offered any further details.

He couldn't grasp why a nine-year-old wouldn't understand the whole situation. I was so young I couldn't begin to get the gravity of it all. During the day, I was a fifth grader who excelled in school. I needed to feel validated before returning to my foster home. Where I felt like nothing. When I look back on my time there, I remember each day repeating in the same mundane sequence, like a skipping record that never gets to the song's chorus. School, food, watch TV, read, sleep, repeat. My foster parents in my second home were both over eighty years old. Keeping up with a kid was not physically possible for them. I get it now, but then I couldn't understand why life was so boring and dull.

Scheduled visits with my grandparents were something I looked forward to. The visits were a brief break from the I'm-in-foster-care cycle. For a couple of hours, we could do normal family things like go to a movie, walk around a mall, or eat at a restaurant. The difficult part was knowing throughout the visit that it would be over soon. The fear would creep in as a thick fog that wouldn't clear— like a relationship you know is going to end, but you do your best to smile through what's left until it hurts.

Most of my grandparents' visits blend together, but one stands out. My grandparents and my uncle took us to a restaurant for lunch near the neighborhood where I was living. It was a Cuban place, but they had some other dishes from Latin America on the menu, too. A sign that all were welcome. We ordered that tamale soup. None of us could remember the exact name. Looking into it now, it was most likely tamal en cazuela, a Cuban tamale casserole made from blended young corn. The soup came out in a large bowl and was more similar to a thick porridge than classic soup. It was dotted with chunks of meat and tasted like the tamales my grandma would spend hours making. The soup's base was pureed corn both sweetened and thickened to the point that it coated the back of my spoon. It was delicious. As we sat next to each other eating quietly, we soaked in the moment as much as the soup.

It hurts to think back to foster care when I eat a bowl, but then I remember my grandma's love and my family's resilience.

After a year and a half in foster care, a judge ruled that I could live with my grandparents, and they became my legal guardians. It's amazing what families will do and sacrifice out of love. I was happy to be back in a *real* home with a *real* family, not a state-appointed one. We quickly got into the rhythm of everyday life. My grandpa was a handyman, so George, Thor, and I would tag along on his summer jobs. He worked while we waited and button-mashed on Game Boys. The boys would play pretend WWE on the outdoor trampoline or practice skateboarding while I watched, sitting in the humid air. My grandma worked in a day care with three-year-olds for years, but no matter how tired she was from convincing children to nap, she always made sure to feed us a good but quick meal.

Tamales were the opposite. Tender masa stuffed with various juicy meats that would take at least two days to make. They were almost exclusively reserved for the best of days. Christmas, birthdays, or when my grandmother's family visited from Mexico for the first time. If Grandma was going to spend the time making tamales, it had to be worth it. But tamale soup was a shortcut—summoning the taste without the hours of labor. She had her own version of tamale soup, inspired by the memories and flavors of that soup we ate together in Miami.

My grandmother would cook up leftover pork and use the remaining fat in the hot pan to fry onions, bell peppers, and garlic until the scent filled the kitchen. Then she would add yellow Maseca and water until it formed the same thick consistency as that first time. She seasoned it with sazón con culantro y achiote, oregano, and salt. Each bowl was served with a pile of crispy pork in the center and pickled red onions scattered on top. Grandma used the Mexican ingredients of tamales with the original Cuban dish to create a soup that was ours.

Digging into a steaming bowl of tamale soup makes me feel the same way as hearing my grandma call me her niña bonita. Whatever weight I am carrying on my shoulders before I start eating instantly melts away. The thick-but-still-runny-enough-to-fall-off-a-spoon masa mixture coats the mouth with the flavors of tamales and home. It's light and rich at the same time. And always comforting and soothing. The garnishes are my favorite part. Pork gets crispy edges like chicharrón. Red onion slices transform into electric-pink strands after being soaked in lime juice. The color pops against the yellow soup as much as the onions pop in my mouth from the acid.

The first time I made tamale soup at home, I followed my grandma's loose directions. "Use 1 cup of Maseca, add water. If it's too thick, add more water." *OK, Grandma, but how much water exactly?* "Whenever it's the right texture, add the seasonings." *Um, how much seasoning?* Like so many great home cooks, my grandma lets instinct guide her to the final dish. I stumbled making it on my own at first. It tasted vaguely like hers and provided some feeling of comfort, but it's taken some time and tinkering to get it just right. Now whenever I'm homesick, I can make it with the same ease as picking up the phone to call her.

Tamale soup has become a symbol of home for my family and reminds me of our past. It hurts to think back to foster care when I eat a bowl, but then I remember my grandma's love and my family's resilience. I don't go home enough these days. When I do make the trip, though, I'm always greeted with a big pot of hot tamale soup. It wouldn't be a family visit without it.

CHAPTER 4

MY CUBAN
FOSTER MOTHER

When I started writing this book, I felt nervous about how to approach this chapter.

Should I try to find my foster parents?

Can I even remember their full names?

Or my old address?

If I do contact them, would they want to speak with me?

I'm not big into the supernatural, but digging through my memories from over twenty years ago felt like chasing a ghost. I started the only way I could think of—requesting public records.

It took two and a half months to get my foster care file from the Department of Children and Families. When I finally got the email, I waited a week to open it. And when I did, eighteen pages of social worker reports from my year and a half in foster care stared back at me. The detailed account of the day the police found Thor and me in the South Beach hotel after being left alone by my father, the he-said, she-said arguments that led to our prolonged release from foster care, and notes about how this was far from the first case of negligence. As I read the sad details, the memories I prefer to keep tucked away in the old box labeled "Hard Times" in my mind burst open and flooded the floor. At first, I felt like these reports were about another person. Who I am now is almost unrecognizable from that girl in the hotel room, but as I sat there staring at the open file, those feelings from that day creeped back a little. Therapy and time have helped me so much, but some of the fear and sadness from that time felt vivid as I scrolled through the document and relived the moments. I remembered that those eighteen pages were really about me, not someone else. Once the dust settled and I had some time to process my emotions, I saw it: my foster parents' full names, their then phone numbers, and a Miami home address. *Now what?*

A lot of my memories from that time are hazy. Some are even gone forever, like when a roll of film is suddenly exposed to a flash of light. Others are half-clear, with only gentle light leaks seeping in. I can't exactly recall meeting my foster parents, but I remember thinking they were really old. I always picture my foster mom in a muumuu, her frown accentuated by her heavy jowls, and silver shoulder-length hair revealing just the faintest traces of platinum blonde lingering at the tips. My foster dad had thick-rimmed metal glasses and short, wavy white hair, with a thick walrus-like mustache to match. I'm sure he had other clothes, but I really only think back to his loose-fitting tan trousers and wrinkleless guayaberas, a button-up shirt with two vertical pleats running parallel to the opening, classic Cuban men's attire. While my recollection of our introduction is fuzzy, how I felt the first night isn't.

It was dusk and I was alone in this unfamiliar house in a part of Miami I had never been to before. Each smell, sound, and sight was new, but not in an exciting way. As I crawled under scratchy covers into the twin bed, all I could feel was loneliness.

In the morning light, I was able to explore my new home. There was a cream-colored couch near the entrance that we would almost never use except to meet with different social workers when they came to visit over the year-plus that I lived there. Delicate wooden furniture was scattered throughout the various rooms, and I can still vividly smell the lemon-scented Pledge I used to clean them every weekend. A tall, fragile porcelain lamp with people who looked like Marie Antoinette on it perched on a table; I was afraid to go near it in case I accidentally broke it. It felt like an old home, one not meant for children. Sepia-toned photos of my foster parents from their heyday were mounted on the walls near the kitchen. They looked young, glamorous, and happy. There were pictures of them riding camels together in Egypt and portraits in which they resembled old Hollywood movie stars. As I looked at my foster parents in person, I wondered when they had stopped laughing.

We had a very difficult time communicating. They spoke only Spanish with the occasional "No, stop!" in English, words they would yell at me when I'd touch something by accident that I wasn't supposed to. And I didn't speak Spanish then, and understood way less of it than I do now. So, we just didn't talk much. I knew they were from Cuba, but I don't know when or why they immigrated to the US. I don't know what they did before they retired. And I don't know what inspired them to accept unknown children of any age into their home.

In Florida, with the weather being the same warm temperature every day, it can make it hard to feel like time is passing. It was the same in foster care; each day was the same as the last. I would usually start my mornings eating leftovers for breakfast in front of the TV as I binged Cartoon Network for hours. Then I'd tiptoe from room to room, worried about being too loud in the otherwise very quiet house, the mixed result of their old age and our language barrier. But dinners were when this routine stopped. Dinners meant it was time to cook.

My foster mom always made big batches of food to last a few meals, enough to feed me, her husband, and whomever else they were fostering at the same time (other kids would frequently rotate through). And there were plenty of leftovers to spare in case someone got hungry again later. The Cuban flavors cut through the monotony of my everyday life. Citrusy and garlicky mojo reached out to me and shook me awake. Cumin-spiced black beans soothed my pain in its warmth. And picadillo with its bright tomato base and plump raisins jolted me back to the present.

The TV I used was next to the kitchen, so once I heard the sizzling from the stove start, I would scurry over to the counter and quietly watch my foster mom cook. Even though we rarely spoke to each other, I felt like I got to know her more through every dish she made. I'd watch in silence as she eyeballed the seasonings for her golden arroz con pollo and topped off the pot of rice with a can of beer.

It's dedicated to all the food I loved most from one of the hardest times of my life.

Someone she trusted taught her this recipe, and she has never made it another way since. Without measurements, it always came out the same every time. *Because she's cooked this for years and this is how her family likes it, she never needed to change it.* The chicken became so tender it slid off the bone, the rice golden and fluffy from drinking up the beer, with specks of bright vegetables dotted throughout like rainbow sprinkles. *Maybe cooking this reminds her of her past life with past people.*

She relied on simple classic Cuban dishes for the main meals, but she would also make an occasional treat. It was unclear whom it was for—the kids, her, or my foster dad—but I liked it all the same. She would stuff any leftover picadillo into balls of mashed potatoes and fry them to make papas rellenas that would release tiny billows of steam when I'd eat them fresh. In the evenings, she would blend Honey Smacks with milk and ice to make batido de trigo. But the simplest treat of them all was saltine crackers slathered with thick layers of cream cheese and slices of guava paste. My foster mom didn't express a lot of outward love or perform acts of comfort, but dishes like these spoke loudly and provided me with joy at a time when I needed it most.

When I looked back on my eighteen-page foster care file, I was really tempted to give their old number a call. Or try one of the other ways to contact them I found from those sketchy people-search websites that seem like they might give your computer a virus if you click around too much. Ultimately, I decided not to reach out to them for this book. My memories from that period of my life are stained with heartache, and my interactions with my foster parents were often unhappy. I didn't think it was worth the potential risk of a poor encounter to find only the same arroz con pollo recipe. But despite that, I wanted to preserve the recipes from that time because the food, her food, nourished my body and then broken spirit. It offered me solace, and still does even now. When I think back to that home, the sad memories flood in almost as quickly as the food ones.

It has been a strange experience to try to re-create the exact flavors of dishes I ate over twenty years ago, but that is what this chapter is all about. It's dedicated to all the food I loved most from one of the hardest times of my life. For each recipe I have had to relive the flavors, textures, and experiences that led me back to those first bites over and over again.

When I was re-creating a lot of these recipes at my grandparents' house, I asked them their thoughts on my foster parents for the first time. My grandparents went through so many court appearances and so much paperwork to eventually become guardians for my brother and me. They regularly visited us then, and they became acquainted with my foster parents. My grandma told me that my social workers were planning on shoving me deeper into the system by moving me into a group home, but my foster mom protested.

"She has a family who cares about her," my foster mom said to the social workers, my grandma recalled.

She's the reason I wasn't placed there. She's part of the reason I was able to leave. For that, I'll be forever grateful.

PICADILLO

Because of its ease and quantity, picadillo was my foster mom's go-to weekday meal. On Monday, she'd make a big batch for dinners throughout the week, and on the weekend it became the filling for papas rellenas. It's perfect when eaten fresh with a heaping pile of rice and golden maduros, and equally as perfect stuffed into other dishes like empanadas.

I grew up thinking of picadillo as a strictly Cuban dish, although its popularity spans Latin America and the Philippines. The exact recipe varies from person to person; the base usually includes a mixture of ground beef and tomato. My version is inspired by taking my favorite parts of all the picadillos I've eaten: golden potato chunks for extra heartiness, white wine for added flavor, briny capers for a sodium kick, and sweet raisins that grow plump in the beef and tomato sauce.

Not to seem biased, but this is the only picadillo recipe you need.

Time: 30 minutes ● **Serves:** 4

Ingredients

2 tablespoons extra-virgin olive oil

1 large Yukon Gold potato, peeled and diced into ¼-inch cubes

½ large yellow onion, diced

½ large green bell pepper, diced

½ large red bell pepper, diced

5 garlic cloves, finely chopped

1 pound ground beef

1 tablespoon ground cumin

2 teaspoons dried oregano

2 teaspoons kosher salt, plus more as needed

½ teaspoon cayenne pepper (optional)

½ teaspoon freshly cracked black pepper

1 dried bay leaf

½ cup dry white wine

One 14.5-ounce can diced tomatoes

⅓ cup raisins (golden or dark, dealer's choice!)

2 tablespoons capers, drained

⅓ cup pimiento-stuffed Manzanilla olives, drained and halved crosswise

½ cup packed finely chopped cilantro leaves and stems

Directions

1 Heat the oil in a large skillet over medium-high heat. Once the oil is shimmering, add the potato and cook until it begins to turn golden brown, about 5 minutes. Remove the potato and set aside.

2 In the same skillet, cook the sofrito. Add the onion, both bell peppers, and the garlic and cook until tender and fragrant, about 3 minutes.

Recipe continues

3 Add the ground beef, cumin, oregano, salt, cayenne (if using), black pepper, and bay leaf. Cook, breaking up the beef with a wooden spoon, until it starts to brown, about 4 minutes. Once it's broken up, the more you leave the beef alone, the more it will crisp.

4 Return the potatoes to the pan along with the wine, tomatoes, raisins, capers, and olives. Fill the tomato can with water and empty it into the skillet. Using a wooden spoon, scrape up any browned bits from the bottom of the skillet. Increase the heat to high and bring to a boil. Once boiling, reduce the heat to medium and cook until the potatoes are fork-tender and most of the liquid has evaporated, about 10 minutes. Discard the bay leaf. Garnish with the cilantro and serve with white rice.

PAPAS RELLENAS

A lot of countries have their own take on papas rellenas. There are different variations in Peru, Colombia, Ecuador, Cuba, and Puerto Rico, just to name a few. The basics are usually the same, though: fried mashed potato croquettes stuffed with filling and coated in a crunchy bread crumb layer. I grew up eating the variety found in Cuban cafés scattered across South Florida. But it wasn't until foster care that I started making them myself. My foster mom would cook enough picadillo to last a couple of meals, but she would always make a bit extra to stuff papas rellenas. I didn't cook a lot then, so this is one of the only dishes I remember helping her make. I'd try to carefully smush the stuffed mashed potato ball closed while she instructed me in Spanish. I couldn't understand everything she told me, but somehow we always ended up with a fresh batch. I'm not sure whether it's because she took over in frustration or I magically understood her Spanish—my memory is fuzzy on the details.

Time: 40 minutes   ●   **Makes:** 10 balls

Ingredients

2 pounds Yukon Gold potatoes, peeled and diced into equal-size pieces

1½ teaspoons kosher salt

3 large eggs, beaten

½ cup all-purpose flour

2 cups panko bread crumbs (see note)

Scant 1 cup leftover Picadillo (page 152)

Vegetable oil, for frying

Directions

1 Place the potatoes in a medium pot with water to cover. Bring to a boil over high heat. Once boiling, cover the pot and reduce the heat to a simmer. Cook until the potatoes are tender, about 15 minutes.

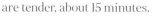

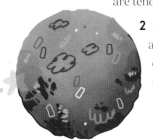

2 Drain the potatoes and run cool water over them until they're mostly room temperature. Place the drained, cooled potatoes back into the same pot. Then, using a potato masher or fork, mash until smooth. Season with the salt and set aside.

3 Prepare your dredging station. Individually place the eggs, flour, and panko in three shallow bowls. Set aside.

4 Assemble the papas rellenas. Divide the mashed potatoes into 10 equal portions.

My Cuban Foster Mother   ●

Recipe continues   **155**

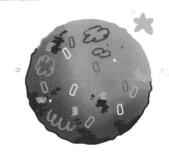

Using your hands, take one portion of the potatoes, roll it into a ball, and flatten it into a disc about ½ inch thick. Next, take about a hearty tablespoon's worth of picadillo and place it into the flattened center. Then enclose the filling by folding the potato edges toward the center so no filling is showing. If necessary, you can gently shift some of the mashed potato on the exterior toward any thinner areas. Repeat to make the remaining papas rellenas.

5 Dredge the papas rellenas. Working with one at a time, first gently roll the papa rellena in the flour so it's evenly coated. Next, dip it into the eggs. Then finish by covering it with bread crumbs. You can carefully press the panko onto the surface to ensure an even, thick coating. Place on a plate and repeat with the remaining papas rellenas.

6 Heat ¼ inch of oil in a large skillet over medium-high heat. (The oil is ready when a pinch of flour sizzles when added to the pan.) Transfer half the papas rellenas to the pan and fry, turning frequently, until golden brown all over, 4 to 5 minutes. Using a slotted spoon, transfer them to a paper towel–lined plate to drain. Repeat with the remaining papas rellenas and serve while warm.

Note: Panko bread crumb sizes can vary greatly. If your panko is on the finer side, start with 1 cup and add ¼ cup as needed. If it's on the coarser side, 2 cups is the right amount.

ARROZ CON POLLO

Arroz con pollo has always felt like a magic trick to me. Raw chicken and dried white rice go in. A lid covers the pot to conceal what's happening inside. Then, when the lid is removed, a small puff of steam—like the smoke from a magician's wand—reveals tender chicken and warm golden rice. "How did she do it?!" I thought every time my foster mom made it.

I definitely ate arroz con pollo before foster care, but I don't really remember it. To me, arroz con pollo starts with my foster mom's version. Unlike papas rellenas, I never helped her make this, only watched. The trick to her recipe is adding strips of roasted red pepper and a can of beer, which gives everything depth and earthiness. My version is inspired by her technique, complete with the same bright specks of green peas and olives.

Time: 1 hour 30 minutes ● **Serves:** 6

Ingredients

2 pounds chicken legs

5 teaspoons kosher salt

1 teaspoon freshly cracked black pepper

2 tablespoons extra-virgin olive oil

½ large red bell pepper, diced (about 1 cup)

½ large green bell pepper, diced (about 1 cup)

½ large yellow onion, diced (about 1 cup)

5 garlic cloves, minced

One 12-ounce can lager beer

1 cup tomato sauce

½ cup packed finely chopped cilantro leaves and stems

2 dried bay leaves

1 tablespoon sazón with achiote

½ teaspoon dried oregano

2 cups medium-grain white rice

½ cup pimiento-stuffed Manzanilla olives, drained and halved crosswise

2 tablespoons capers, drained (optional)

1½ cups frozen peas

1 tablespoon white vinegar

1 jarred roasted red pepper, sliced into thin strips

Directions

1 Pat the chicken dry, then season with 3 teaspoons of the salt and the black pepper. Heat the oil in a large Dutch oven or large pot over medium-high heat. Once the oil is shimmering, add the chicken in a single layer and cook for 8 to 10 minutes, turning several times to brown evenly. Transfer the chicken to a plate and set aside.

2 In the same pot, reduce the heat to medium and cook the sofrito. Add both

Recipe continues

bell peppers, the onion, and garlic. Cook until the onion is translucent and the mixture is fragrant, about 5 minutes.

3 Add the beer, tomato sauce, ¼ cup of the cilantro, the bay leaves, sazón, oregano, and reserved chicken. Increase the heat to high and bring to a boil. Once boiling, reduce the heat to medium-low, cover, and cook until the chicken is tender, about 30 minutes, stirring occasionally.

4 When the chicken is just about done, rinse the rice in a fine-mesh strainer with cool water until the water runs clear. Then put the rinsed rice directly into the pot along with the remaining 2 teaspoons salt, the olives, and capers (if using). Give the pot a small shake to level out the rice.

Then, increase the heat to high and bring to a boil. Once boiling, reduce the heat to low and cover.

5 After 20 minutes, sprinkle the peas on top and cover. Turn off the heat and leave covered for 15 to 20 minutes. The rice will be al dente at first but will continue to cook while covered even with the heat off.

6 Just before serving, add the vinegar and gently fluff the rice. Some parts on the bottom will be crisped. When fluffing, mix in the bottom parts with the top. Discard the bay leaves. Leave the pot uncovered and let the steam release for 5 minutes. Garnish with the roasted red pepper slices and the remaining ¼ cup cilantro. Serve while warm or refrigerate for up to 5 days.

CAFECITO

Cafecito means "little coffee" because it is, literally, a little coffee, but don't let the size fool you. It's a very, very strong, tiny cup of dark-roasted espresso that is packed with so much sugar that even the sweetest coffee drinkers will admit that it tastes candied.

I love how putting an *-ito* or *-ita* at the end of anything in Spanish automatically makes it cute. Kiera becomes Kier*ita*, perro becomes per*rito*, café becomes cafe*cito*. I could just say, "Every morning, Kiera drinks coffee with her dog." But doesn't "Every mañanita, Kierita drinks her cafecito con her perrito" sound so much cuter?

What makes cafecito extra special is the crema foam that sits on top of every cup. Making it requires you to vigorously mix the very first drops of coffee (it has the most concentrated taste) with a hefty amount of sugar to create a light-tan paste. The lighter the color, the foamier the top. Usually, there's no cinnamon in cafecito, but my version calls for a pinch. And there's never milk in it, but sometimes I like to top my cup off with it. So if you add some, just be low-key about it.

The following directions are for a single cup; multiply the ingredients as needed for additional servings. And adjust the sugar amount to your liking. If you're making it for a crowd, you can mix the crema in a mixing cup instead to save some time and an arm workout.

Time: 5 minutes ● **Serves:** Varies based on your moka pot

SPECIAL EQUIPMENT Moka pot

Ingredients

Finely ground dark roast coffee, preferably Café Bustelo

1¼ tablespoons sugar per cup

Pinch of kosher salt

Pinch of ground cinnamon (optional)

Directions

1 Prepare the moka pot. Fill the bottom chamber of the moka pot with water until it just touches the bottom of the steam valve. Next, using a spoon, add coffee until the filter is completely full and level it off with the back of the spoon. Place the filter into the bottom chamber and secure the top.

2 Place the moka pot over medium heat with the lid open so you can look out for the first drops of coffee to appear, which are the strongest. It will take only about 2 minutes to start brewing, so keep a close eye on it! If you miss the first drops, you can use the fully brewed coffee if necessary. While the pot is heating, add the sugar, salt, and cinnamon (if using) to a cup.

3 Once the coffee begins brewing, pour the first few drops (about ½ teaspoon) into the cup with the sugar and begin to mix with the back of a spoon. The texture should be like a paste at first and not too liquidy. If it's not mixing easily, add a few more drops of coffee. Mix vigorously until it becomes a light-tan color and has a creamy texture. Once it falls gently off the spoon, the crema is ready.

4 By the time you're done mixing, your coffee should be brewed. Check on it to make sure it doesn't burn the coffee grounds. Once the moka pot stops making brewing sounds, remove it from the heat.

5 Pour the coffee directly into the cup and gently use the spoon to incorporate the crema. The top should be evenly light and frothy. Sip immediately and pretend like you're in South Florida.

Maduros (page 15)

Cuban Black Beans
(page 179)

Ropa Vieja
(opposite)

ROPA VIEJA

Literally "old clothes" in Spanish, ropa vieja is a Cuban classic made from shredded beef and bell peppers that are stewed slowly in a tomato-spiked sauce until tender. It gets the name from the long, raggedy texture of the flank steak, which resembles clothing that has been ripped apart. My favorite part about this dish is the leftovers. Like many tomato-based dishes, the flavors only intensify as they settle in the fridge, making the ropa vieja even better the next day. Serve with white rice and maduros. But a side of beans won't hurt either.

Time: 1 hour 45 minutes ● **Serves:** 4

Ingredients

1 pound flank steak

1½ teaspoons kosher salt, plus more to taste

1½ teaspoons freshly cracked black pepper

3 tablespoons extra-virgin olive oil

1 large yellow bell pepper, sliced into ¼-inch pieces

1 large red bell pepper, sliced into ¼-inch pieces

1 large green bell pepper, sliced into ¼-inch pieces

1 large yellow onion, sliced into ¼-inch pieces

6 garlic cloves, chopped

3 ounces tomato paste

1 cup dry white wine

4 cups unsalted beef stock

2 dried bay leaves

2 teaspoons ground cumin

1½ teaspoons dried oregano

⅓ cup pimiento-stuffed Manzanilla olives, drained and halved crosswise

½ teaspoon sugar

1½ teaspoons white vinegar

Directions

1 Prepare the steak. Pat the steak dry with a paper towel. Season both sides with the salt and black pepper.

2 Heat 2 tablespoons of the oil in a Dutch oven over medium-high heat. Once the oil is shimmering, add the steak and brown on both sides, about 3 minutes per side. Remove the steak and set aside.

3 In the same Dutch oven, add the remaining 1 tablespoon oil, the bell peppers, onion, and garlic. Cook, stirring frequently to avoid browning, until the onion is translucent and the mixture is fragrant, about 5 minutes.

4 Add the tomato paste and cook until the color darkens to a brick red, about 2 minutes.

Recipe continues

5 Add the wine, beef stock, bay leaves, cumin, and oregano. Mix until combined, scraping up any browned bits from the bottom. Then add the steak, making sure it is covered by the liquid. Bring to a boil. Once boiling, reduce the heat to low, cover, and simmer until the steak is fork-tender and soft enough to be shredded, about 1 hour 15 minutes, stirring occasionally to make sure the meat is still submerged as much as possible as the liquid reduces.

6 Transfer the steak to a cutting board or large plate and let it cool until it's comfortable enough to handle, 10 to 15 minutes. Using two forks, shred the meat. While the steak is cooling, increase the heat under the Dutch oven to medium and cook the remaining liquid uncovered until it reduces to a thick, sauce-like consistency, about 15 minutes. If the liquid is already at a consistency you are happy with when you remove the steak, just turn off the heat and cover to keep warm.

7 Once the liquid has reduced, add the shredded steak back into the pot and mix to combine. The meat should be saucy but not soupy. If it's still too liquidy, increase the heat to high and continue reducing it uncovered, stirring frequently, until it reaches the desired texture. Discard the bay leaves. Add the olives, sugar, and vinegar. Taste and adjust for salt. Serve immediately or store in the refrigerator for up to a week. The taste and texture will only get better.

PASTA DE BOCADITOS (CUBAN! HAM! SPREAD!)

I don't have many photos of myself from when I was in foster care. I mean, it feels pretty obvious, but I didn't have a lot of let's-snap-a-pic-to-remember-this-time-forever sort of moments. One of the few photos I do have, though, is from my tenth birthday. I'm not sure how, but my foster parents allowed almost all my immediate family to come over to celebrate the day with me: my grandparents, George, Thor, and my dad. And they did not skimp on the food. The photo captures my ten-year-old self standing at the head of the table with my mouth half-open laughing and a sea of Cuban finger food laid out in front of me. Most prominent is a huge tray of pasta de bocaditos, Cuban ham spread on sweet rolls, a personal favorite.

In Miami, you can buy huge platters of these tiny sandwiches for events. To make the filling, you blend ham, cream cheese, olives, roasted red peppers, and little pickles together until it becomes a sunset-orange spread. It's equal parts tangy, creamy, savory, and rich. You can eat it as a dip with crackers, but you will see it most commonly on sweet, slider-size buns that balance the saltiness.

More than twenty years after that photo was taken, I finally asked my grandparents what they thought about my foster parents. "They were nice to let us come to your birthday," my grandma said. *Were you not allowed to come?* They weren't supposed to have them over because it was against the rules, but my foster parents wanted them to come for my birthday. My feelings toward them remain complicated, but I will never forget that party.

Time: 10 minutes ● **Makes:** 24 finger sandwiches

Ingredients

8 ounces cooked ham (such as SPAM, deviled ham, or leftovers from a whole ham), roughly chopped

8 ounces cream cheese, room temperature

1 large roasted red pepper (jarred works perfectly)

½ cup pimiento-stuffed Manzanilla olives, drained

1 teaspoon yellow mustard

½ teaspoon kosher salt

¼ cup finely chopped cornichon or dill pickle

24 Hawaiian rolls (preferably King's Hawaiian)

Recipe continues

Directions

1 In a food processor, combine the ham, cream cheese, red pepper, olives, mustard, and salt. Blend until completely smooth and an even orange color, stopping occasionally to scrape down the sides, about 2 minutes.

2 Transfer to a large bowl and mix in the pickles. If eating right away, cut the rolls in half and spread the mixture evenly across the the bottom halves, then cover with the top halves. If using later, store the spread in an airtight container in the refrigerator for up to 1 week.

CUBAN PASTELITO DREAMS

Sprinkled throughout South Florida are Cuban eateries offering a huge array of shiny, flaky treats. Each baked (and sometimes fried) good seemingly shines brighter than the next. Every pastry is licked with a reflective gloss that's amplified inside glass cabinets and looks like it's spewing tiny rainbows as the light hits it. They all look beautiful and perfect. Pastelitos in all flavors make up a large majority of the inventory, but ham croquettes, empanadas, sandwiches, and fresh chicharrón are also up for grabs. My favorite thing about many of these places is that they often have a window counter, or ventanita, that's open twenty-four hours.

Ventanita means "little window" in Spanish, and this type of cafe was invented by Felipe Valls Sr., the founder of the institutional Versailles Restaurant Cuban Cuisine and, apparently, about thirty other restaurants. He wanted to bring Cuban coffee culture to Miami, so the ventanita was born.

No matter what time it is, I can always get a glittery pastelito and hot cafecito. Ventanitas have been a cherished place for me since I was a kid. In elementary school, my parents would drive up to snag a papa rellena for me, but as I got older, I'd drive myself to meet up with friends for coffee after a late night out. At those windows, the warm humidity of Florida wraps around me, and with a snack and coffee in each hand, it feels like anything is possible. These are a couple of my favorites you can easily make with frozen puff pastry, but for the real thing, you have to go to South Florida and experience the ventanita magic firsthand.

HOT HONEY PASTELITOS DE CARNE

Pastelitos de carne are a glossy treat that shines on the counters of Cuban bakeries. This super-flaky pastry is stuffed with picadillo and brushed with a sweet glaze that makes the outside glisten like gold. I downed these by the handful when I was living in foster care (and still do) because I love the balance of sweet and salty flavors. Instead of the usually equal sugar-to-water ratio for the glaze, I've swapped hot honey to enhance the shine and add a little heat. The cayenne pepper is to taste, but feel free to be generous with it. Only a little gets added when you brush it onto the pastries, so you can be pretty heavy with the spice.

Time: 35 minutes ● **Makes:** 12 pieces

Ingredients

FOR THE PASTELITOS

1 large egg

¾ cup leftover Picadillo (page 152)

2 sheets frozen puff pastry (about 8 ounces each), thawed and refrigerated

All-purpose flour, for rolling

FOR THE HOT HONEY GLAZE

¼ cup honey

2 teaspoons cayenne pepper, plus more to taste

Pinch of kosher salt

Directions

1 Preheat the oven to 375°F. Line a baking sheet with parchment paper.

2 Prepare the egg wash. Beat the egg in a small bowl and set aside.

3 On a lightly floured surface, unroll one sheet of puff pastry. (Keep the other sheet in the refrigerator until it's time to cut.) Using the rim of a glass cup that is 3 inches wide or a 3-inch biscuit cutter, cut out 9 pieces and transfer to the prepared baking sheet. Next, combine the dough scraps into a ball and roll it out to cut out an additional 3 pieces, then transfer them to the baking sheet. Repeat with the remaining puff pastry sheet to make 24 total pieces, but do not place this half on the baking sheet yet. If you have any dough scraps remaining, bake them off and enjoy as a snack, because you deserve it.

4 Using a teaspoon, evenly fill the 12 halves on the baking sheet with picadillo, about a hearty teaspoon per serving. Using a pastry brush, paint the edges of the dough on the baking sheet with the egg wash. Then take the remaining 12 halves and place them on top. Using your fingertips, press to close the edges of each pastelito. Brush the tops with egg wash.

Recipe continues

5 Bake until golden brown, about 25 minutes. Let cool on the baking sheet for at least 5 minutes before transferring to a serving plate for another 15 minutes. They should be warm but not burning hot to the touch.

6 While the pastelitos are baking, make the hot honey glaze. Heat 2 tablespoons water, the honey, cayenne, and salt in a small saucepan over medium-high heat. Bring to a boil, then reduce the heat to medium-low and let simmer for 5 minutes. Remove from the heat.

7 After the pastelitos have cooled, brush with the hot honey glaze. Serve immediately or store in the refrigerator for up to 1 week. Bring to room temperature before serving.

QUESITOS

Equal parts creamy and flaky, quesitos are a staple pastelito at many Latin American bakeries. In the windows of Cuban cafés, you can see mounds of quesitos glistening from their sweet glaze. This recipe is my tribute to them. Orange isn't a typical quesito ingredient. Instead, it's a nod to all my favorite pastelitos from South Florida (hence the citrus) and adds even more shine.

Time: 30 minutes ● **Makes:** 18 pieces

Ingredients

FOR THE QUESITOS

1 large egg

8 ounces cream cheese, room temperature

¼ cup granulated sugar

½ teaspoon vanilla extract

Pinch of kosher salt

Zest of 1 orange

2 sheets frozen puff pastry (about 8 ounces each), thawed and refrigerated

All-purpose flour, for rolling

Turbinado sugar, for sprinkling

FOR THE GLAZE (OPTIONAL)

½ large orange, juiced (about ¼ cup)

¼ cup granulated sugar

Pinch of kosher salt

Directions

1 Preheat the oven to 375°F. Line a baking sheet with parchment paper.

2 Prepare the egg wash. Beat the egg in a small bowl and set aside.

3 Combine the cream cheese, granulated sugar, vanilla, salt, and orange zest in a medium bowl. Mix with a spoon until fully incorporated. Set aside.

4 On a lightly floured surface, unroll one sheet of puff pastry and cut into 9 equal squares. (Keep the other sheet in the refrigerator until it's time to cut.) Put

1 heaping teaspoon of filling in the center of each puff pastry square. To close, take one corner, fold it over the filling, and gently press the middle down to spread the filling slightly out toward the opposite corners. Using your finger or a pastry brush, dab a little bit of egg wash along the edges of the corner facing you, opposite the corner you just folded; this will act as "glue." Next pick up the quesito, then take the freshly egg-washed corner and pull it across the filling to fully close it snugly on the other side. Gently pinch the tip to the pastry body

Recipe continues

to ensure it doesn't open during baking. You should have two points with some filling exposed, and the cream cheese will look like you just tucked it in for a long sleep. Finally, place the quesito on the prepared baking sheet. Repeat until you have 18 quesitos, including cutting and filling the second sheet of chilled puff pastry.

5 Using a pastry brush, paint the tops of each quesito with egg wash. Sprinkle with turbinado sugar. Bake until golden brown, about 25 minutes. Remove from the oven and let cool on the baking sheet for at least 5 minutes before transferring to a serving plate for another 15 minutes. The quesitos

should be warm but not burning hot to the touch.

6 While the quesitos are baking, prepare the glaze, if using. Combine the orange juice and granulated sugar in a small saucepan over medium-high heat. Bring to a boil. Cook until the sugar fully dissolves and the mixture has the consistency of a light syrup, about 3 minutes. Remove from the heat and set aside. As it cools, the glaze will thicken.

7 Using a pastry brush, paint glaze onto the cooled quesitos until they're shiny. Serve immediately or store in the refrigerator for up to 5 days. Bring to room temperature before serving.

PASTELILLOS DE GUAYABA Y QUESO

Inside Cuban bakeries, so many pastries sparkle, but pastelillos de guayaba y queso feel like they shine the brightest. Layers of buttery dough are stuffed with rich cream cheese and a sweet, deep-magenta paste made of guava, a tropical fruit that's beloved all over Latin America. After the pastelillos finish baking, a sweet glaze is brushed on, giving them that razzle-dazzle look. My version follows a lot of the classic steps but with the addition of fresh orange in the glaze and a sprinkle of turbinado sugar before baking, which clings to the pastry surface and looks like glitter. There are a few different ways to fold the dough, but my shape is based on the version from the grocery chain Publix, whose pastries and subs always inspire me.

Time: 30 minutes ● **Makes:** 8 pieces

Ingredients

FOR THE PASTELILLOS

1 large egg

2 sheets frozen puff pastry (about 8 ounces each), thawed and refrigerated

All-purpose flour, for rolling

4 ounces cream cheese, chilled, cut into 8 equal pieces

8 ounces guava paste, cut into 8 equal pieces

Turbinado sugar, for sprinkling

FOR THE ORANGE GLAZE (OPTIONAL)

½ large orange, juiced (about ¼ cup)

¼ cup granulated sugar

Zest of 1 orange

Pinch of kosher salt

Directions

1 Preheat the oven to 375°F. Line a baking sheet with parchment paper.

2 Prepare the egg wash. Beat the egg in a small bowl and set aside.

3 On a lightly floured surface, unroll one sheet of puff pastry and cut it into 4 equal pieces. (Keep the other sheet in the refrigerator until it's time to cut.) Stack one piece of cream cheese and one piece of guava paste and place in the center of each puff pastry rectangle, gently pushing down on the guava paste to flatten it a little so you can fold the pastry. Using a pastry brush, paint the edges of each square with egg wash. To close the pastillos, take one corner of the dough and fold it diagonally across the filling to create a triangle, adjusting the filling if necessary. Then use a fork to crimp the edge closed. Repeat with the remaining puff

Recipe continues

Hot Honey Pastelillos
de Carne (page 168)

Pastelillos de Guayaba y Queso (page 173)

Quesitos
(page 171)

pastry squares and transfer, using a bench scraper if necessary, to the prepared baking sheet. Repeat the entire process with the second sheet of chilled puff pastry to create 8 pastelillos total.

4 Using a pastry brush, paint the tops of each pastelillo with the egg wash. Next, use kitchen scissors to cut three small slits on top of each pastelillo. Then, sprinkle the surface with turbinado sugar. Bake until golden brown, about 25 minutes. Remove from the oven and let cool on the baking sheet for at least 5 minutes before transferring to a serving plate for another 15 minutes. They should be warm but not burning hot to the touch.

5 While the pastelillos are baking, prepare the glaze, if using. Combine the orange juice and granulated sugar in a small saucepan over medium-high heat. Bring to a boil. Cook until the sugar fully dissolves and the mixture has the consistency of a light syrup, about 3 minutes. Remove from the heat and set aside. Stir in the orange zest and salt. As it cools, the glaze will thicken.

6 Using a pastry brush, paint the glaze onto the cooled pastelillos until they're shiny. Serve immediately or store in the refrigerator for up to 5 days. Bring to room temperature before serving.

WAITING ROOM

You know that scene in *Mean Girls* where Regina George gets hit by a bus? She manages to walk away still looking hot with only a metal back brace. Later, it even gets decorated with pastel-colored flowers to accompany her shiny prom-queen crown. In the movie, it's quirky and cute. But in real life, it's the opposite.

Late one night, my foster mom went to lie down in her bed—but instead of hitting the mattress, she crashed onto the floor. The next time I saw her, she was in a back brace just like Regina George's (minus the flowers). My foster mom's upper body was enclosed in a metal frame like an animal trapped inside a cage. A dark halo crowned her head; screws were drilled into her skin to keep her from moving her neck. It looked like a torture device, and I felt scared to see her in such an unfamiliar way. At that time *Mean Girls* didn't yet exist, so I had no reference for the intense contraption swallowing my foster mom up whole.

The time inside the house before and after the accident blurs together, but things grew even quieter once it happened. I'm certain she still continued to cook, but the only times I can actually recall are from before the back brace. Without meals to break up the monotony of life, my days mushed together more. Shortly after, though, a new activity began—lots of doctors' appointments.

I have lived in Miami only twice: when I was two years old and during that year and a half in foster care, so I cannot confirm that the following claim is true of every doctor's office in the city that serves older people. But this is what it was like for my foster mom (to the best of my recollection): inside every waiting room is a full, unlimited spread of Cuban treats. Huge sheet-pan-size trays of bocaditos cover the table. Each fluffy, overstuffed finger sandwich oozes orange filling; the mixture of cream cheese, ham, and roasted red pepper (where it gets its color) bursts from the edge of the bread like cotton stuffing from an open teddy bear. Stacks of shiny pastelitos de carne sticky with glaze are packed on plates, leaving no negative space. Little fried ham croquettes are hastily placed together in random corners after being plundered by the other older folks waiting for their appointments. If I was lucky, I would find the occasional pastelillo de guayaba y queso. Digging my teeth into the flaky pastry and getting to that guava and cream cheese center felt like striking gold.

My Cuban Foster Mother

177

In the past, some of my doctors would give me a piece of hard, old candy for bravely making it through a shot, but this was on another level. I had never been to a doctor's office like this. If the circumstances hadn't been so sad, my foster mom's doctor's office would have been my favorite place on earth.

Any time she went to an appointment, I had to tag along. I'm not sure how many times we went together, but in my memory, it feels like we were there at least once a week. That waiting room soon became an extension of their home. As soon as we arrived, I would start snacking. I knew where every kind of treat was and which ones were the most sought after among the other guests. I'd wash everything down with cups and cups of the Cuban coffee that flowed freely for whoever needed a caffeinated boost.

Even if one of the other, ever-rotating foster kids was also at the appointment, I always felt alone. But the routine of going to the doctor's, eating every Cuban treat I could, and finishing with sugary cups of Café Bustelo created a sense of normalcy and much-needed joy in a very abnormal, bleak time. Outside the waiting rooms, I was an isolated foster kid grappling with the extreme challenges of being trapped in the system. But inside those waiting rooms, I could happily escape into the dazzling world of glazed pastelitos with rivers of sweet, milky coffee that never ran dry. In many ways, it was the closest I felt to being a regular ten-year-old then.

CUBAN BLACK BEANS

Did you know that rice and beans make a complete protein? Eaten separately, they lack certain amino acids. But eaten together, they fill in what the other is missing. In many Latin America countries, rice and beans are a big part of the food culture. (And it has been since way before the US-based health food trend. I like to revel in how ahead of the curve they were.)

Cuban-style black beans is one of my all-time favorite ways to eat beans in general. My foster mom would make a big batch so we could eat them throughout the week. While she knew they were good right out of the pot, she would wait for them to get even more delicious as they slowly thickened with each passing day. Around the two-day mark is when I usually like them best.

The trick to a good pot of beans is layering flavors. First, the soaked beans simmer with red bell pepper and bay leaves to infuse each bean. Once softened, white wine is added for depth. Forty-five minutes later, sofrito and cumin. But it's the final addition of white vinegar that really ties everything together and makes these vegan black beans sing.

This recipe does start with dried black beans because it's the classic way to make them, and I think the texture is better (more structure!). But if you're looking for a fast but also tasty version, please refer to my breakfast tostadas (page 243), which use canned black beans. It's not an exact dupe for these Cuban black beans but will help in a pinch.

Eat these as a side or pair with white or yellow rice and maduros. I also really like making veg-loaded bowls with this recipe. Usually, I sauté sliced bell peppers and onions until they're tender and a little caramelized and place them snugly into a bowl of rice and beans. Then I tuck in some avocado slices along the side and shower the top with fresh cilantro, lime juice, and hot sauce. These bowls have saved me many, many times.

Time: 1 hour 20 minutes, plus overnight soaking ● **Serves:** 4 to 6

Ingredients

1 pound dried black beans, picked over and rinsed

2 tablespoons extra-virgin olive oil

½ large white onion, finely diced (about 1 cup)

½ large green bell pepper, finely diced (about 1 cup)

10 garlic cloves, finely chopped

¼ large red bell pepper

2 dried bay leaves

1 tablespoon kosher salt, plus more to taste

¼ cup dry white wine

1½ teaspoons dried oregano

2 teaspoons ground cumin

½ teaspoon sugar

1½ tablespoons white vinegar

Recipe continues

Directions

1 Place the beans in a large bowl and cover them with water by 2 inches. Let soak for at least 4 hours or preferably overnight. Drain and rinse before using.

2 Make the sofrito. Heat the oil in a large pot over medium-high heat. Once the oil is shimmering, add the onion, green bell pepper, and garlic. Cook, stirring frequently to avoid browning, until the onion is translucent and the sofrito is fragrant, 3 to 5 minutes. Transfer the sofrito to a bowl and set aside.

3 In the same large pot, place the soaked beans and cover them again with water by 2 inches. Add the red bell pepper, bay leaves, and salt. Bring to a boil over high heat. Once boiling, cover and reduce the heat to medium-low. Simmer until the beans are tender, stirring occasionally, about 1 hour.

4 After the beans have cooked for 30 minutes, add the wine and oregano. Cover and continue to cook.

5 After the beans have cooked for 45 minutes, gently mash a generous 1 cup of beans (eyeballing this is OK!) and the red bell pepper directly in the pot using a potato masher or the back of a wooden spoon. The mashed beans will help thicken the liquid. Cover and continue to cook until the beans are tender.

6 Once the beans are tender, mix in the reserved sofrito, the cumin, and sugar. Increase the heat to medium-high and let the liquid reduce, stirring frequently to avoid scorching, until it's thick enough that a wooden spoon leaves a trail after you drag it across the top of the beans, 15 to 20 minutes.

7 Before serving, turn off the heat and mix in the vinegar. Discard the bay leaves. Taste for salt and adjust to your preference. Serve while warm or store in the refrigerator for up to a week. The beautiful thing about beans is they taste even better the next day.

MY PERFECT CUBAN BREAKFAST

When I was in foster care, the only time I remember going out to a restaurant with both my foster parents was for the occasional weekend breakfast. Their adult son and his wife would join us. I don't remember either of their names, but I can fuzzily recall that he had salt-and-pepper hair and a big smile. It was one of the few times during that year when I felt normal, as if it were the before times. To someone walking by, we could even probably pass as a family.

I took their son's lead when it came to ordering. He spoke English fluently and filled in any language gaps. Soon, big plates of scrambled eggs speckled with ham, long pieces of buttered Cuban bread, seasoned potatoes, and cafés con leche filled the table. He showed me that the best way to enjoy a tostada cubana was to dunk it into the piping hot café con leche. A little sweet, a little savory, and it would melt away in a bite. This recipe is my take on those special breakfasts.

Though it's composed of four parts, you only need instructions for two. Tostada cubana is toasted Cuban bread with lots of butter. Because it's commonly served at restaurants toasted in a sandwich press, the bread doesn't pick up a lot of color. Since I assume most people don't own this specific press (but more power if you do!), the instructions below use an oven. There is no true substitution for Cuban bread. It is traditionally made with lard, which gives it a subtle savory flavor and makes it extra, extra crunchy. And the sazón breakfast potatoes are my own take, inspired by those breakfast memories. I split up the recipes below in case you want to make them at different times. But if you eat them together (which is my preference), start the tostada and cook the potatoes while the bread toasts to save time.

The only two additions you'll need to supply yourself are your choice of coffee and eggs. I recommend scrambled eggs with tiny chunks of ham and café con leche for dunking.

TOSTADA CUBANA

Time: 15 minutes ● **Serves:** 2

Ingredients

6-inch piece Cuban bread, sliced in half lengthwise

4 tablespoons unsalted butter, room temperature

Directions

Preheat the oven to 400°F. Place the bread on a baking sheet and smear the cut sides with the butter. Bake until the bread is toasty but not brown, about 12 minutes. Serve while warm.

SAZÓN BREAKFAST POTATOES

Time: 15 minutes ● **Serves:** 2

Ingredients

2 tablespoons extra-virgin olive oil

8 ounces Yukon Gold potatoes, peeled and diced into ¼-inch cubes

1 teaspoon sazón with achiote

¼ teaspoon ground cumin

2 tablespoons diced yellow onion

2 tablespoons diced green bell pepper

2 garlic cloves, finely chopped

Cayenne pepper (optional)

Kosher salt and freshly cracked black pepper

Directions

1 Heat the oil in a large nonstick skillet over medium-high heat. Once the oil is shimmering, add the potatoes, sazón, and cumin. Mix until the potatoes are the same even orange shade. Cook, stirring occasionally, until they are crisp, about 7 minutes.

2 Reduce the heat to medium. Then add the onion, bell pepper, and garlic. Cook, stirring frequently to keep the garlic from burning, until the onion is tender and translucent, about 2 minutes. Season with cayenne (if using), salt, and black pepper to taste. Transfer the potatoes to plates to serve.

BATIDO DE TRIGO

This classic Cuban milkshake is made with puffed wheat cereal, which is how it gets the name batido de trigo, or wheat shake. My foster mom would always make these for my foster dad as a sweet finish to the night, but they can be enjoyed at breakfast as well. I started drinking them, too, and she would make a little extra for me, always topping off each glass with a sprinkle of cereal. The wheat adds a toasted nuttiness that I can't find in any other milkshake. I don't remember a lot of sweets from my time in foster care, but this one I can't shake.

Time: 5 minutes ● **Serves:** 2

Ingredients

2 cups whole milk

2½ cups ice cubes

⅓ cup sweetened condensed milk

2¼ cups puffed wheat cereal (such as Honey Smacks or Golden Crisp), plus more for garnish

½ teaspoon ground cinnamon, plus more for garnish

¼ teaspoon freshly grated nutmeg

½ teaspoon vanilla extract

Pinch of kosher salt

Directions

1 Put all the ingredients in a blender and mix until smooth.

2 Garnish with puffed cereal and ground cinnamon. Serve immediately.

CHAPTER 5

AUNT TT IS A KITCHEN GOD

If you're my good friend and *really* like good food, I will always try to convince you to get dinner at the best place to eat in New York City, my aunt TT's house. Aunt TT's real name is Pilar, and she's the third oldest of my grandpa's eight kids. I call her Aunt TT because when I was a kid, I couldn't get the subtle rolling *r* sound in Pilar just right and could muster only a sound like *tt* instead. It's been my nickname for her ever since. But Pili is what she goes by to most people. And in our family, she is also known as the best cook.

After a couple of years living and working in California, I decided I wanted to move back to New York to pursue my dream of becoming a food writer. As a kid, I saw my aunt TT at family events since we lived within driving distance of each other in Florida. If we were visiting her in her then Miami home, she would always prepare tables and tables of glistening foods. Even as a child, I was in awe. But she moved, I moved, and we fell out of touch. A few years before my New York adult move, though, Aunt TT had also found herself back in the city. I reached out to her and started visiting her in her new neighborhood of Jackson Heights, Queens—and I really wanted to eat.

Whenever I step into her home, my body is immediately engulfed in the sweet smell of whatever meat she has spent the last three days cooking and the warmth of energy bursting inside. Aunt TT gives me a quick kiss on the cheek to say hello before rushing off to the kitchen to check on the plethora of bubbling pots on the stove. Mario, my uncle, gives me a big hug. And my grandma Patricia (my grandpa's first wife, who is related to me by blood) quietly shuffles over and squeezes me before returning to her seat on the couch, where she hums along to the Spanish lyrics of the music playing from YouTube on the TV.

From the moment you enter to the second you leave, you will be fed the best food you've ever tasted. Various appetizers like savory bites of soft cheese and smoked meats are already waiting on the table, laid out over ornate plates that match the delicate porcelain figurines peeking out from shelves all over their home. But before I'm halfway through my first round of appetizers, my uncle always asks my friend if they'd like to try the "Mario Special," a fruity cocktail he's picked up from his time working in bars that never fails to impress with its only distinguishable taste, peach schnapps. Aunt TT buzzes around: telling jokes, checking on the kitchen, refilling glasses, and clearing plates, a remnant from her restaurant days. By the time the second Mario Special starts to hit, the food is already coming out. It feels like the real-life version of the "Be Our Guest" montage from *Beauty and the Beast*. Each plate is more dazzling than the last. But instead of French food, it's dishes from all over Latin America. And instead of the Disney soundtrack, it's Marc Anthony.

Platters appear on the table: lustrous rabo encendido, with oxtail so tender you barely have to chew, and posta negra cartagenera, where each thick slice of carrot-stuffed beef is cloaked in a caramelized sauce of panela, Coca-Cola, and cloves. Nestled between the mains are a sea of side dishes ranging from arroz con coco to homemade lasagna (just because!). And at the center of the table is always Aunt TT's signature dish, a huge lettuce-lined bowl filled to the brim with Peruvian ceviche complete with white leche de tigre.

Although Pili learned to cook after she immigrated to the US, her interest in food started when she watched her next-door neighbor prepare meals in Guayaquil, Ecuador. She stared in wonder as the woman carefully cut and seasoned meats. Pili still remembers the alluring scents of sizzling beef wafting from that woman's home and smiles as she recalls the memory to me.

I consider Pili to be my fun aunt. She loves to throw a party and dance into the night. After immigrating to New York at around thirteen years old, she grew up in the disco era of the city. Over the years, she's told me briefly about her nights out—including one time at Studio 54 during its heyday. I can clearly envision her large curly hair bouncing up and down to disco beats with a light-up rainbow floor underneath her. If there's a perfect setting for Aunt TT, it's on a dance floor under a silver disco ball.

In her late teens, she met a Colombian man who became her first husband and father to her only son, my cousin Brian. To teach Pili to cook, her then mother-in-law gifted her her first cookbook: *Old Spain Cooking in Latin America* by Teresita Roman de Zurek, the English translation of *Cartagena de Indias en la Olla*. Pili owns both versions, of course. The 542-page book of over 1,300 recipes is an encyclopedia of Latin American recipes and other dishes that were popular in the 1970s, ranging from Colombian arepas to a dessert called strawberry excelsior made with gelatin and a can of fruit cocktail (I'm still unclear what it's supposed to look like, even after reading the description a few times). The once cream-colored pages have faded into a warm yellow stained from age and heavy use.

"If you had to bring one cookbook with you on a desert island, which one would it be?" I asked her. *"Cartagena de Indias en la Olla,"* she responded without any hesitation, almost cutting me off with her speed.

This cookbook inspired her to get into the kitchen and eventually start a cookbook collection. Now she has forty-five cookbooks that span different cuisines stacked in neat piles in her office, and the Colombian, Ecuadorian, and Peruvian ones are her favorites. Whenever she travels, she always adds a new one to her collection. She's currently trying to master the tagine recipes from her Moroccan cookbook so she can put the two tagines she owns to good use.

After splitting from her first husband, she met my now-uncle Mario while they were working together in a Miami restaurant. Mario immigrated to the US from Costa Rica in 1987 and has been mostly working in restaurants since. What started as a friendship bloomed into a twenty-year-plus marriage. He's her life partner, especially so when it comes to dinner parties. Without saying a word to each other, they already know their duties for the evening. Mario is on cleaning, table setting, bartending, and cinnamon-cappuccino-making (with dessert) duty. And Pili is on cooking, which is the biggest lift. Their home is filled with the same energy you feel stepping inside the busiest and most well-established restaurant on a Saturday night. They're the best tag team, quietly supporting each other and doing what the other needs help with before even being asked. It's always frictionless so the guests can do what they're there to do—eat all the food. They have become experts at hosting because they've been doing it for over two decades, both professionally and just for fun, and their experience shows.

Early into their relationship together, Pili opened her first and only restaurant that specialized in Peruvian cuisine in Miami. It was called Pilares. The menu had many Peruvian classics: ceviche, tallarines verdes, and chaufa de mariscos. While she was responsible for managing the restaurant, she sometimes cooked a daily special from whatever ingredients they had in excess, creating dishes that were distinctly Pili, like Ecuadorian seco de chivo. But her chefs took the lead and taught Pili how to make the many Peruvian dishes she loves so deeply. On the weekends, the restaurant

But not everything needs to be made on a Tuesday night in under twenty-five minutes with four ingredients. It's the difference between cooking for survival versus relishing it.

was packed, with people filling every one of the green and off-white chairs. There were musical performances by a regular piano player or an occasional traveling musician from Peru. Some of the waiters happened to know classic Peruvian dances and would perform to entertain the customers. I was too young to remember much firsthand, but when my parents did drive me down to visit, I have fuzzy memories of a kind waiter who let me stand on her shoes as we walked together. We wove between the decorative pillars of the restaurant while I giggled the whole way. After a two-year run, Pilares closed.

From a home cook perspective, it's clear that the habits Pili picked up running a restaurant are forever a part of her approach in the kitchen. The neat cabinets, clean-as-you-go lifestyle, and all-around fearless approach to cooking are qualities that separate her from others who "just cook for fun." (Once Pili told me she cooked for a dinner party of seventy-five at her house, and I was like, "Yeah . . . normal people can't do that.") To learn her recipes, I went back to the US and stayed with her for a week. I was fresh off the flight, but we were already in the kitchen together cooking for what soon felt like a marathon I had not trained for. One day we cooked side by side for about ten hours straight, a new record for me. It wasn't until I looked at the clock that I realized it was midnight and asked Pili if we could call it a day due to my jet lag. "Are you tired already? I can keep going," she said, looking as bright-eyed as ever.

A couple of years ago, she moved into a bigger place in Jersey City. My grandma Patricia moved along with Pili and Mario; she has lived with them for over a decade. As Patricia has gotten older, Pili has stepped up to become her caretaker. In addition to her day job, Pili makes sure Patricia is groomed, fed, entertained, and generally taken care of. I don't have a close relationship with Patricia. Before she moved in with Pili, I had only met her once as a kid. But my visits with Pili have given me a chance to get to know her better.

On that trip, we cooked and cooked and cooked together for seven days straight. At the end of it, we had made more food than I had ever made in my life. So, we did the only logical thing—throw a party. I invited as many friends as I could to feast on our hard work. Almost every dish in this chapter was on the table: pernil, menestra de lentejas, tallarín con atún, guacau, olla de carne, arroz chaufa, cazuela de mariscos, and, of course, ceviche in the center. By the time everyone had their third helping, it still looked like almost no one had touched anything, though. It was easily enough food for forty people. But Pili packed all the leftovers in tidy, organized containers for people to take home like school day goodie bags. We ended the night with the biggest Carvel ice cream cake I could find that said

"My (Half) Latinx Kitchen" scribbled on it in sky-blue icing. Another perfect Pili dinner party.

Right before I left Aunt TT's place, we sat together at her table and chatted while I sipped on one of Mario's iconic cinnamon cappuccinos. "I want you to have my first cookbook," Pili said to me. How could I take something that means so much to her? I refused, but she insisted. "I want you to have it because I know you will enjoy it as much as me," she rebutted. After a few more back-and-forths, I gently wrapped it in a few layers of soft clothing like a swaddled baby to keep it safe on my journey back to Japan. *Old Spain Cooking in Latin America* now sits on my bookshelf as my most prized cookbook.

Many of the recipes in this chapter are different from the others in this book. Like Pili's parties themselves, they're full of life, have more than enough good vibes (a.k.a. food) to go around, and take a long time. When you enter Pili's house, you will likely not reemerge for at least five hours. These days, it feels like there's an obsession with getting meals cooked in as little time as possible and with the fewest ingredients. But not everything needs to be made on a Tuesday night in under twenty-five minutes with four ingredients. It's the difference between cooking for survival versus relishing it. Aunt TT's recipes often force you to slow down, both to prep ingredients and to cook, sometimes for hours. And along the way, you can throw the best dinner party of your life with these recipes. Take her olla de carne; it has over twenty ingredients and takes about four hours to cook. But within that process, you find peace and stillness as you watch the stew bubble like a jacuzzi until the meat softens and the broth thickens. You'll be guaranteed to make friends for life after your guests try a bite. Pili's food is all about the joy in cooking, the masterful technique of building flavors, sharing food with the people who matter most, and what happens when you're willing to spend more time on yourself. The results are always worth it.

PERNIL

On Thanksgiving and Christmas, my family never had turkey or ham on the table. Instead they had a big roasted pernil (pork shoulder), complete with skin so crunchy that the whole room could hear it crackle as we munched away. It is one of Puerto Rico's most beloved dishes. But there are many different versions found throughout Latin America. This recipe is a mix of Puerto Rican, Ecuadorian, Aunt TT's, and my techniques: Puerto Rican with the heavy garlic and acidic kick from white vinegar, Ecuadorian with the accompaniment of fuchsia cebollas encurtidas, Aunt TT's addition of beer, and my method for getting the crispiest skin possible—always the best part.

The key to a super-flavorful pernil is getting the marinade in the pork itself and leaving it to soak at least overnight or, even better, for 2 days. Not going to lie, I always feel a bit like Hannibal Lecter when I prepare the meat. You have to literally hold the knife serial-killer style and stab the pork shoulder over and over again. Playing angry metal music helps during this step. Also, a quick note about roasting: Your pan will get burnt bits on the bottom, especially if you're trying to achieve the maximum skin crispiness. So use a pan you don't mind dirtying up because it will char in the process. You can also line it with aluminum foil if you prefer, but you'll still have a bit of mess to clean up at the end.

Pernil is one of those dishes that just keeps on giving. Make it on a weekend and eat well for a week (or months if you freeze some leftovers). Fry it with rice, make sandwiches with it, throw it in soup, add it to pasta, or toss it in a quesadilla.

When I finally cooked for Pili the first time, I made pernil—and she was very impressed. Of course I am biased, but this is the best version of pernil that I've had. Make it for anyone you want to impress, yourself included.

Time: 7 hours, plus overnight marinating   •   **Serves:** 8 to 10

Ingredients

¼ cup white vinegar

12 garlic cloves, peeled

6 teaspoons kosher salt

1 tablespoon freshly cracked black pepper

1 tablespoon dried oregano

1 tablespoon ground cumin

1 tablespoon sazón with achiote

One 12-ounce lager beer

One 7- to 9-pound bone-in, skin-on pork shoulder with skin covering the entire top layer (see note)

Cebollas Encurtidas (page 44)

Recipe continues

Directions

1 Prepare the marinade. In a food processor, combine the vinegar, garlic, salt, pepper, oregano, cumin, sazón, and about half the beer. Pulse until the garlic is finely minced and the seasonings are well combined. Set aside.

2 Prepare the pork. Rinse the meat and dry with a paper towel, then transfer it to a cutting board. With the skin side up, carefully separate part of the skin from the meat, leaving about 3 inches of the edge still connected so you can easily move the skin up and down but not fully remove it. With the skin lifted up, pierce 1-inch holes all over the meat's surface and sides. The more holes the better! Then flip the pork skin side down and make even more holes. You may feel like you're in *Friday the 13th*, but that's OK. Transfer the pork skin side up to a casserole dish or deep roasting pan.

3 With the skin lifted, spoon half the marinade over the top, using your fingers to push it into the holes in the meat. Your hands will get lightly stained from the sazón, so wear gloves if that bothers you. Gently flip the pork skin side down and repeat with the remaining marinade. Then pour the remaining beer into the dish. Cover and marinate in the fridge overnight or up to 2 days, flipping the pork halfway through.

4 Take the pork out of the refrigerator 1 hour before roasting and let it rest at room temperature. Preheat the oven to 325°F.

While the oven is preheating, loosely cover the pork with aluminum foil. Then transfer to the center of the oven. If your pork shoulder is around 7 pounds, roast for 5 hours, basting it with its own juices once every hour. (If it's 9 pounds, roast for 7 hours.) Once the juices evaporate, add a little water to the pan to avoid burning the pan too much.

5 Remove the foil and increase the heat to 400°F. Roast uncovered for another 1 hour 30 minutes, basting once more about halfway through. Continue to add a little water as needed when the liquid gets low. The meat should be tender and easy to pull apart. The skin should be mostly crispy and make an audible crack when you tap it with the back of a knife. If you want the skin to be extra, extra crispy, continue to roast at 400°F for another 30 minutes, but keep a close eye on it to make sure it doesn't burn. It's a fine line between crispy skin and good charred bits versus bad ones.

6 Remove from the oven and let rest for 10 minutes. Transfer to a serving dish. Using a long knife or kitchen shears, separate the skin from the meat and then use the kitchen shears to cut the crispy bits into portions for serving. If desired, discard any excess fat that did not crisp up. Cut up the rest of the pork, which will be very tender and easy to portion. Eat with yellow or white rice and cebollas encurtidas.

Note: Depending on where you live, the size of the pork may vary. Feel free to adjust the cooking time as needed to match the pork shoulder size you get. The general rule is about 1 hour of roasting for every 1 pound of pork. The easiest way to adjust this is to add more roasting time while it's covered. Do not add more time when it's uncovered because the pernil could burn more easily.

I have made pernil without a bone before, so it is possible to cook it that way, too. But the bone gives more flavor throughout the roasting process. If you can get bone-in pork, do it, but this recipe works with boneless pork shoulder as well.

MENESTRA DE LENTEJAS

I hate playing favorites, but this is another one of my favorite recipes in this book because of taste alone. Pili's menestra de lentejas is a gift to the world. This vegan lentil stew can be found throughout Ecuador, but the country's coastal region is often credited with creating the dish. Brown lentils cook in a mixture of sofrito, cumin, adobo, and sazón until tender. In the last few minutes of cooking, a grated green plantain is added, which thickens the stew, giving every bite an earthiness. There are variations out there that use tomato paste instead to help thicken the texture, but plantains give it that extra depth of flavor. It is typically eaten with carne asada, but I like it just on its own with some fresh rice, sweet maduros, and sliced avocado. If Pili has extra the next day, she'll often reheat it in a pan with leftover rice and a splash of water so the excess lentil liquid softens the rice. So good.

Time: 45 minutes   •   **Serves:** 8 to 10

Ingredients

- ¼ cup extra-virgin olive oil
- ½ cup diced red onion
- ½ cup diced white onion
- ½ cup diced green bell pepper
- ½ cup diced red bell pepper
- 1 cup diced Roma tomatoes (about 2 small tomatoes)
- 4 scallions, chopped (about ½ cup)
- 4 garlic cloves, chopped
- 1 tablespoon ground cumin
- 1 tablespoon adobo seasoning
- 1½ teaspoons sazón with achiote
- ½ teaspoon freshly cracked black pepper
- 1 pound dried brown lentils, picked over and rinsed
- ½ cup packed finely chopped cilantro leaves and stems
- 1 teaspoon kosher salt, plus more to taste
- 1 green (unripe) plantain

Directions

1 Heat the oil in a large Dutch oven or large pot over medium-high heat. Once the oil is shimmering, add the onion and bell peppers. Cook, stirring frequently to avoid browning, until the onion is translucent and the bell peppers are crisp-tender, 3 to 5 minutes.

2 Add the tomatoes, scallions, garlic, cumin, adobo, 1 teaspoon of the sazón, and the black pepper. Cook, stirring frequently, until the white parts of the scallions and garlic are tender, about 3 minutes.

3 Add 7 cups water, the lentils, cilantro, and salt. Increase the heat to high and bring to a boil. Once boiling, reduce the heat to low. Cook uncovered until the lentils are mostly tender, about 15 minutes, stirring occasionally.

4 Around the 15-minute mark, prepare the plantain. First, fill a large measuring cup with 2 cups hot tap water and mix in the remaining ½ teaspoon sazón. (This will prevent the plantain from oxidizing and darkening in color.) Cut off and discard the ends of the plantain. Using a paring knife, cut a slit along the length to remove the peel. If the peel is too firm, use a spoon to lift the edges, then discard the peel. Then using the medium holes of a box grater, grate the plantain into the sazón water, stirring occasionally to avoid clumping. Stir well to combine and break up any clumps.

5 While stirring the lentils with a wooden spoon, pour the plantain mixture into the pot. Continue to stir quickly to keep the grated plantain from forming clumps. Increase the heat to medium-high and keep stirring until the plantain starts to cook and the lentils thicken, about 3 minutes. Once boiling, reduce the heat to low. Simmer, stirring occasionally, until the plantain is cooked and the lentils are fully tender, about 10 minutes. If you prefer a thicker consistency, continue to simmer until the desired texture is reached. Taste and adjust for salt. Serve while warm. Store in the refrigerator for up to a week, thinning with a small amount of water if desired. You can also freeze any leftovers for up to 3 months.

CAZUELA DE MARISCOS

Along the Ecuadorian coast, cazuelas reign. Blended green plantains layered with seafood (a.k.a. mariscos) are baked inside a clay pot (a.k.a. cazuela) until the top is bubbling and crisp at the edges. Aunt TT's version is of course bigger and feeds a crowd. In her recipe, she uses a casserole dish instead of the traditional smaller cazuela, but the result is the same. Her choice of seafood is shrimp and tilapia, which can be substituted with snapper or striped bass. The seafood is baked while it's raw so it cooks slowly, making each bite tender and delicious.

Time: 1 hour 30 minutes ● **Serves:** 8 to 10

Ingredients

- 7 green (unripe) plantains
- ¼ cup creamy unsweetened peanut butter
- 1½ teaspoons sazón with achiote
- ¼ cup extra-virgin olive oil, plus more for brushing
- ½ large red onion, finely diced (about ¾ cup)
- ½ medium green bell pepper, finely diced (about ½ cup)
- 3 scallions, thinly sliced (about ⅓ cup)
- 4 garlic cloves, minced
- 2 teaspoons adobo seasoning
- 1 tablespoon ground cumin
- 1½ teaspoons dried oregano
- 1 medium tomato, diced
- ¾ cup whole milk
- 1 cup packed finely chopped cilantro leaves and stems
- 1 chicken bouillon cube (optional)
- ¼ teaspoon cayenne pepper (optional)
- 1 pound medium to large shrimp, peeled and deveined
- 1 pound tilapia, cut into 1½-inch pieces
- 1 teaspoon white pepper
- Kosher salt
- Nonstick cooking spray
- 2 limes, quartered

Directions

1 Peel the plantains. Cut off and discard the ends. Using a paring knife, cut a slit along the length of the plantains, carefully avoiding cutting into the flesh, and then remove the peels. If the peel is too firm, use a spoon to lift the edges, then discard the peel. Roughly cut each plantain into 1-inch-thick rounds.

2 In a blender, add the cut plantains, peanut butter, and ¾ teaspoon of the sazón. Add water, ½ cup at a time, until the plantains blend easily, but be careful not to add too much liquid. Blend until the plantain mixture is fully smooth and has the consistency of an extra-thick smoothie, about 3 minutes. Set aside.

3 Heat the oil in a large Dutch oven or large pot over medium-high heat. Once the oil is shimmering, add the onion, bell pepper, scallions, garlic, 1 teaspoon of the adobo, the cumin, and oregano. Cook, stirring frequently to avoid browning, until the onion is tender and translucent, about 3 minutes. Then add the tomato. Cook, continuing to stir, for an additional 3 minutes.

4 Add 3½ cups water, the milk, remaining ¾ teaspoon sazón, the cilantro (reserve about 2 tablespoons for garnish), chicken bouillon (if using), and cayenne (if using). Stir to combine. Then bring to a boil.

5 Once boiling, reduce the heat to medium-low, add the plantain mixture, and immediately stir well with a wooden spoon to prevent clumps from forming. Cook, stirring often to keep the cazuela smooth, until the plantains are fully cooked and the consistency is like oatmeal, 10 to 15 minutes. If it is too runny, increase the heat to medium-high and continue cooking until it is thick enough to pick up with the spoon and hold its shape a bit, but still able to very slowly fall off the spoon. Taste and adjust for salt.

6 While the cazuela is cooking, prepare the seafood and preheat the oven. In a bowl, season the shrimp with ½ teaspoon of the white pepper and ½ teaspoon of the adobo. Remove and set aside about one-third of the shrimp for the cazuela top. In the same bowl with the majority of the shrimp, add the tilapia, remaining

½ teaspoon white pepper, and remaining ½ teaspoon adobo. Mix until the seasonings have evenly coated the seafood. Next, preheat the oven to 350°F with the rack in the center.

7 Lightly grease a 9 × 13-inch pan with cooking spray. Add half the cazuela mixture, using a spoon or rubber spatula to spread it to the edges. Next, add the shrimp and tilapia mixture (saving the reserved one-third shrimp for later), evenly placing it across the top. Then add the rest of the cazuela mixture evenly over the seafood so it's fully coated and brush the top with oil. Finally, add the reserved shrimp, which double as part of the garnish, neatly over the top. Bake until the seafood is cooked through and a thin crust forms over the top, about 30 minutes. For a darker crust, broil for a few minutes. Garnish with the reserved cilantro. Serve hot with the lime wedges on the side.

ARROZ CHAUFA ESPECIAL

The first big wave of Asian immigrants settled in North and South America in the nineteenth century. Like the immigrant communities that came before and after, many arrived in hope of a better life. But they were soon faced with extreme hardships: After slavery was abolished, the Americas searched for new sources of labor. Some countries used indentured workers, often an inhumane way to entrap people in contracts that they could not escape from.

In Peru, more than ninety thousand Chinese indentured laborers arrived by the end of the late 1800s. While in the beginning everyday life was extremely challenging, over time the Chinese population integrated more and more into Peruvian culture. As a result, Chifa cuisine – a mix of Chinese and Peruvian cooking techniques and ingredients—was born.

Arroz chaufa is a key dish of Chifa cuisine. It is essentially Peruvian Chinese fried rice that merges the flavors and styles of the two cultures into one delicious dish. This is Aunt TT's special version, with a little bit of chicken, beef, pork, and shrimp all in one. But if you want to make it with only one or a couple of the options, you can easily do that, too. Just adjust the amounts to your serving and taste preferences.

This recipe has a good number of ingredients, so allow for extra prep time.

Time: 45 minutes   ●   **Serves:** 6

Ingredients

8 ounces chicken breast, cut into bite-size pieces (¾ to 1 inch)

8 ounces boneless beef cut of choice, cut into bite-size pieces

8 ounces medium shrimp, peeled and deveined

4 ounces boneless pork cut of choice, cut into bite-size pieces

3 large eggs, beaten

1½ teaspoons sazón with achiote

1 teaspoon plus 2 dashes adobo seasoning

1 teaspoon ground cumin

¼ teaspoon white pepper

1½-inch piece ginger, grated

¼ cup soy sauce

1 tablespoon oyster sauce

¼ cup extra-virgin olive oil, plus more as needed

1 bunch scallions, thinly sliced at an angle, white and green parts divided

½ cup diced green bell pepper

½ cup diced red bell pepper

½ cup diced red onion

2 tablespoons sesame oil

6 cups cooked white rice

Recipe continues

Directions

1 Season the proteins. Place the chicken, beef, shrimp, pork, and eggs in individual bowls. To the chicken, add ¾ teaspoon of the sazón, ¼ teaspoon of the adobo, and ¼ teaspoon of the cumin. To the beef, add the remaining ¾ teaspoon sazón, ¼ teaspoon of the adobo, and ½ teaspoon of the cumin. To the shrimp, add the white pepper, a dash of the adobo, and the grated ginger. To the pork, add ¼ teaspoon of the adobo and the remaining ¼ teaspoon cumin. Finally, to the eggs, add a dash of the adobo. Toss or mix until the seasonings are well combined with their respective protein. Set aside.

2 Combine the soy sauce and oyster sauce in a small bowl or measuring cup.

3 Heat the oil in a large nonstick skillet or preferably a seasoned wok over medium–high heat. Once the oil is shimmering, add the chicken. Cook, stirring frequently, until lightly browned and fully cooked through, 4 to 5 minutes. Set aside in a large bowl. This bowl will be used for all the cooked proteins.

4 In the same wok, add the beef. Cook until lightly browned and the desired doneness is reached, 2 to 4 minutes. Transfer the cooked beef to the bowl with the chicken.

5 In the wok, add the pork and more oil, if needed. Cook until lightly browned and fully cooked through, 2 to 4 minutes. Transfer the cooked pork to the large bowl.

6 In the wok, add the shrimp. Cook until pink all the way through, about 2 minutes. Transfer the cooked shrimp to the large bowl.

7 To the wok, add the scallion whites, both bell peppers, and the onion, adding more oil if the pan seems dry. Cook, stirring frequently to avoid browning, until the onion is translucent and tender, about 5 minutes.

8 Reduce the heat to medium. Add the sesame oil, rice, and soy sauce mixture. Cook, stirring occasionally, until well combined and the rice starts to crisp, about 7 minutes. Taste and adjust with more soy sauce as needed.

9 Push the rice to one side of the pan. Add the eggs and stir vigorously to scramble. Cook until the eggs are just set, 1 to 2 minutes. Mix the scrambled eggs into the rice. Then add the reserved meats and remaining scallion greens. Mix until well combined. Serve while hot.

TALLARÍN CON ATÚN

When I asked Pili where she learned how to make this, she turned to me and looked as intense as she did excited. "From a captain," she said. "On a boat." It's not every day you learn an incredible pasta recipe from a boat captain, at least not for me, but maybe it is for Aunt TT.

This tallarín con atún is ♪espectacular♪, as my uncle Mario would say. It's a Latin American take on tomato tuna pasta but is spiked with sofrito, sazón, adobo seasoning, lime, and briny capers. The sauce is so good that it's hard not to eat it as just soup.

Dear mysterious boat captain—wherever you are—thank you so much for one of the best and simplest pastas I have ever eaten.

Time: 30 minutes ● **Serves:** 4 to 6

Ingredients

3 tablespoons extra-virgin olive oil

¼ large red onion, diced

¼ large white onion, diced

¼ large green bell pepper, diced

¼ large red bell pepper, diced

6 garlic cloves, minced

2 scallions, chopped (about ¼ cup)

½ cup packed finely chopped cilantro leaves and stems

2 Roma tomatoes, diced (about 1 cup)

1 tablespoon dried oregano

1 tablespoon adobo seasoning

1½ teaspoons sazón with achiote

1½ teaspoons ground cumin

½ teaspoon freshly cracked black pepper

¼ teaspoon cayenne (optional)

One 6-ounce can tomato paste

2 dried bay leaves

Three 5-ounce cans solid white albacore, drained

2 tablespoons capers, undrained

1 pound linguine

Kosher salt

½ lime

Grated Parmesan, for serving

Directions

1 Heat the oil in a large Dutch oven over medium-high heat. Add the onions, bell peppers, and garlic. Cook, stirring frequently to avoid browning, until the onions are tender and translucent, about 5 minutes.

2 Add the scallions, cilantro, tomatoes, oregano, adobo, sazón, cumin, black pepper, and cayenne (if using). Cook, continuing to stir frequently, until the white parts of the scallions are tender, about 2 minutes.

Recipe continues

3 Add the tomato paste and cook until it darkens, about 2 minutes. Then add 2½ cups water, the bay leaves, tuna, and capers. Bring to a boil and then reduce the heat to low. Simmer the sauce uncovered for 15 minutes, or until it reaches the desired thickness.

4 While the sauce is simmering, make the pasta. Add the pasta to a large pot of salted boiling water and cook according to the package instructions until a little under al dente.

5 Using tongs, transfer the pasta directly from the pot to the sauce and toss. Increase the heat to medium-high and cook until the pasta is al dente, stirring frequently. Discard the bay leaves. Squeeze in the lime and season to taste with salt. Serve with Parmesan.

LOMO SALTADO

In this recipe, tender slices of beef, sliced red onions, and softened tomatoes are licked with umami-rich soy sauce. Just before serving, everything gets tossed with crispy french fries that act as tiny sponges that soak up all the tangy juices.

"A plate of lomo saltado tells a story of Peru's creole cuisine," says Peruvian chef and food writer Nico Vera of Pisco Trail in an email interview. "Indigenous native ingredients like hot peppers, potatoes, and tomatoes . . . are sautéed with strips of beef introduced by colonial foodways, and seasoned with soy sauce and ginger introduced by indentured workers from Canton."

Many food historians point to Lima's Barrio Chino, Peru's most famous Chinatown, as the birthplace of the dish. A classic lomo saltado usually includes steak, onion, scallions, ají amarillo, soy sauce, and fries. But like many culturally significant recipes, the dish can vary from kitchen to kitchen. Aunt TT's version here uses a slightly different technique and seasonings, omitting the scallions and ají, and adding adobo and sazón. She first learned the recipe from a chef while running her Peruvian restaurant in Miami and has since put her own spin on it. Nico, who is vegan now, sometimes substitutes mushrooms for the beef, giving it a similar meatiness and umami flavor. And while fries are usually tossed with the lomo and sauce, some people like to eat them on the side so they stay crispy.

According to Nico, a good lomo saltado is all about balance among the ingredients, shapes, flavors, textures, and colors. And this one checks off those boxes and then some.

Time: 25 minutes • **Serves:** 4

Ingredients

1 pound beef tenderloin, skirt steak, or other tender steak

½ teaspoon adobo seasoning

¼ cup soy sauce

1½ tablespoons white vinegar

¼ lime, juiced

1½ teaspoons oyster sauce

¼ cup finely chopped cilantro leaves

1½ teaspoons ground cumin

½ teaspoon sazón with achiote

½ teaspoon dried oregano

½ teaspoon freshly cracked black pepper

¼ teaspoon dried parsley (optional)

8 ounces store-bought frozen thick-cut french fries

2 tablespoons extra-virgin olive oil

½ large red onion, cut into ½-inch slices

1½ medium tomatoes, cut into ¾-inch wedges

1-inch piece ginger, peeled and grated

Recipe continues

My (Half) Latinx Kitchen

Directions

1 Preheat the oven to temperature stated on the frozen fries package instructions.

2 Prepare the beef. Cut the beef against the grain into ¼-inch strips. Season with the adobo and set aside.

3 Combine the soy sauce, vinegar, lime juice, oyster sauce, I tablespoon of the cilantro, the cumin, sazón, oregano, pepper, and parsley (if using). Mix until fully combined and set aside.

4 Bake the fries according to the package instructions. Set aside.

5 While the fries are baking, make the lomo saltado. Heat the oil in a large nonstick skillet or preferably a seasoned wok over medium-high heat. Once the oil is shimmering, add the beef. Sear until some parts have become dark brown and almost no pink color remains, about 5 minutes.

6 Add the soy sauce mixture. Cook until it starts to boil, about 3 minutes. Then add the onion, tomatoes, and ginger. Reduce the heat to medium-low and cover. Let the lomo saltado simmer until the onion starts to soften but the tomatoes are still red and intact, about 3 minutes.

7 To serve, mix an individual french fry portion with a lomo saltado portion and garnish with the remaining cilantro. Eat with a side of white rice. To store, keep the fries and lomo separated to avoid soggy fries.

PERUVIAN CEVICHE
WITH LECHE DE TIGRE

As with many nationally treasured dishes, there are many variations from all over the world out there (heyyy, Ecuadorian ceviche on page 7 . . .), but Peru's is globally renowned for its special combination of raw seafood soaked in lime juice. Even though this approach is simple, it lets each ingredient shine its brightest. The ceviche is soaked in a unique citrus marinade called leche de tigre, or tiger's milk, named for its white color and the boost of energy you feel after drinking it. Like, you are a tiger, get it?

Many restaurants and home cooks serve leche de tigre in shot glasses to enjoy on its own. Some claim it's a hangover cure and aphrodisiac. There are even cocktails made with it! This is the way Pili makes signature ceviche, and there have never been any complaints. Ever.

Time: 25 minutes, plus chilling ● **Serves:** 10 to 12

Ingredients

2½ cups lime juice (from 14 to 16 limes)

10 garlic cloves, minced

¼ habanero pepper, seeded and minced (optional)

1 tablespoon kosher salt, plus more to taste

½ teaspoon ground white pepper

Dash of MSG (optional)

2 pounds tilapia (or tender white fish such as grouper, bass, or corvina), cut into 1-inch pieces

1 pound medium shrimp, peeled, deveined, and halved

1 celery stalk, peeled and finely diced

½ teaspoon ají amarillo paste (such as Inca's Food), plus more to taste

½ cup whole milk or coconut milk

1 cup packed finely chopped cilantro leaves

½ small iceberg lettuce, for garnish (optional)

Directions

1 Combine the lime juice, garlic, habanero (if using), salt, white pepper, and MSG (if using) in a large bowl. Once mixed, add the tilapia. Set aside.

2 While the fish is marinating, cook the shrimp. Fill a medium pot with water about halfway and bring to a boil. Once boiling, add the shrimp. Cook until just pink, about 30 seconds. Remove the shrimp and set aside. Reserve 1 cup of the shrimp water for later, letting it cool at room temperature.

Recipe continues

3 Once the fish begins to appear white and firmer, about 15 minutes, add the 1 cup reserved shrimp water (it's OK if it's still warm, but it should not be hot enough to cook the fish), celery, ají amarillo, cooked shrimp, milk, and cilantro. Mix until fully incorporated. Taste and season with salt and ají amarillo as needed. If you use too much ají amarillo, the color will change, so add in very small amounts if you want more spice. Cover and refrigerate until chilled, about 30 minutes.

4 To serve, place lettuce leaves, if using, in a large serving bowl, being sure to lay out the prettier leaves around the edges. Pour in the ceviche with the leche de tigre. Serve while chilled.

ARROZ CON COCO

Pili fell in love with arroz con coco on a visit to Cartagena along the coast of Colombia. The sweet perfume of coconut paired with the nutty aroma of toasted rice made it a dish she knew she'd have to master. It's become one of her go-to recipes, especially when paired with Posta Negra Cartagenera (page 220). To really bring out the coconut flavor, you will need to reduce a can of full-fat coconut milk. It takes some time to transform into only a couple of tablespoons, but be patient and trust the process. If you want to speed up the panela process, you can microwave it in 10-second increments until it's soft enough to break into smaller pieces. This is made to Pili's taste, but if you want it more or less sweet, it's easy to adjust the panela to your liking.

Time: 1 hour 15 minutes • **Serves:** 6

Ingredients

One 13.5-ounce can full-fat coconut milk

3 ounces panela (also called piloncillo), or 2 tablespoons dark brown sugar

2½ cups long- or medium-grain white rice, rinsed until the water runs clear

½ cup raisins (optional)

1½ teaspoons kosher salt

Toasted coconut flakes, for garnish (optional)

Directions

1 Heat the coconut milk in a medium pot over high heat. Once simmering, reduce the heat to medium-low and cook, stirring frequently with a wooden spoon, until it reduces to a couple of tablespoons and the coconut solids separate from the oil and start to become a rich brown color, about 30 minutes.

2 Add the panela. Cook, continuing to stir frequently, until the panela is melted, about 7 minutes. If you're using brown sugar, it will only take 1 or 2 minutes.

3 Add the rinsed rice and mix until the sugar is well incorporated. Increase the heat to medium and cook, stirring constantly and scraping the bottom of the pot, until the rice begins to toast in some areas, about 8 minutes. Add the raisins, if using, and stir to combine.

4 Add 3 cups water and the salt. Using a wooden spoon, scrape the bottom of the pot to get all the remaining sugar. Increase the heat to high. Once boiling, reduce the heat to medium-low, cover, and cook for 15 minutes. Remove from the heat and leave covered for another 15 minutes. Fluff with a fork or wooden spoon before serving, evenly incorporating the crispy bottom rice. Garnish with toasted coconut, if using.

RABO ENCENDIDO
a.k.a. What to Eat to Feel $uper Extra Rich

When I imagine being rich—like dumb-stacks-of-bills-around-me rich—I see myself holding oxtails in both hands and slurping up tender bites of meat and softened fat. These aren't just any oxtails in my hands. They are rabo encendido.

Rabo encendido is a dish of luxury, and no one makes it better than my aunt TT. It's made by slowly simmering tough oxtail in a mixture of tomato paste and wine until the meat glides off the bone. It's a staple Cuban dish that can be found throughout South Florida. All versions are subpar to Aunt TT's.

Her oxtail is something of legend. Unlike the common versions of rabo encendido out there, Aunt TT's adds briny capers and olives, which cut through the richness of the meat. Rabo encendido translates as "tail on fire," so Aunt TT insists on some heat from cayenne. This dish needs to be a little bit picante. Whole cloves add more spice and depth. But her ultimate secret is raisins, which I know may be triggering to some people. (I get it; I usually don't like raisins either.) These raisins are different. They rehydrate throughout the slow cooking process and grow plump and sweet—little bombs creating perfect harmony in the dish. This rabo encendido is a little sweet, a little salty, and a whole lot of savory. Eat with a pile of steaming rice and maduros, and you'll feel like you're dumb-stacks-of-bills-around-me rich, too.

Time: 3 hours 30 minutes ● **Serves:** 6 to 8

Ingredients

4 pounds oxtail, rinsed and trimmed

½ cup all-purpose flour

3 teaspoons kosher salt, plus more to taste

¼ cup extra-virgin olive oil, plus more as needed

2 medium yellow onions, diced into ¼-inch pieces

1 large green bell pepper, diced into ¼-inch pieces

1 large red bell pepper, diced into ¼-inch pieces

6 garlic cloves, peeled and minced

One 6-ounce can tomato paste

2½ cups unsalted beef stock

2 cups dry white wine

½ cup raisins

¼ cup pimiento-stuffed Manzanilla olives, drained and halved crosswise

¼ cup capers, drained

3 dried bay leaves

½ teaspoon whole cloves

1½ teaspoons sazón with achiote

1 teaspoon dried oregano

½ teaspoon ground cumin

1 teaspoon freshly cracked black pepper

1 teaspoon cayenne pepper, plus more to taste (optional)

Recipe continues

Directions

1 Pat the oxtail dry with paper towels. Season with the flour and 1½ teaspoons of the salt. Gently toss until evenly coated.

2 Heat 3 tablespoons of the oil in a large Dutch oven or large pot over medium-high heat. Once the oil is shimmering, add about one-third of the oxtail, making sure to shake off excess flour before adding. Do not overcrowd the pan or the oxtail won't color as easily. Cook until the oxtail is browned on both sides, 3 to 4 minutes per side. Continue to cook in batches, adding more oil with each batch if the pan gets dry, until all the oxtail is browned, adjusting the heat as needed. Set aside.

3 Position a rack in the middle of the oven, then preheat to 325°F. While the oven is preheating, make the sofrito. Using the same Dutch oven, heat the remaining 1 tablespoon oil over medium heat. Add the onions, bell peppers, and garlic. Cook, stirring regularly to avoid browning, until the peppers have softened and the onions have become translucent, about 7 minutes.

4 Increase the heat to medium-high and add the tomato paste. Cook until it darkens in color, about 2 minutes, while using a wooden spoon to break it up and more evenly distribute it throughout the pot.

5 Add the beef stock, wine, raisins, olives, capers, bay leaves, cloves, sazón, oregano, cumin, black pepper, cayenne (if using), and remaining 1½ teaspoons salt to the pot. Stir, scraping up any browned bits stuck to the bottom of the pot, until everything is combined. Then add the oxtail. Bring to a boil, cover, and turn off the heat. Transfer the pot to the oven and cook until the oxtails are tender and the meat can easily slide off the bone, about 3 hours.

6 Return the Dutch oven to the stovetop, uncover, and cook over medium heat, stirring frequently to avoid scorching, until the sauce reduces, about 10 minutes. The sauce should be thick enough to coat the back of a spoon.

7 Taste and adjust for salt and cayenne, if needed. Discard the bay leaves. Serve while hot. Refrigerate for up to 1 week or freeze in an airtight container for up to 3 months.

JACKSON HEIGHTS

Jackson Heights is a special neighborhood in Queens, New York. Walking down the street, you won't just pass a multitude of diverse people, but miniature countries. Indian bakeries displaying neat arrangements of colorful cham chams, silver leaf–topped kaju katli, and syrup-soaked gulab jamun lure in anyone lucky enough to catch the scent of cardamom wafting out to the sidewalk. Tibetan food carts serve plump momos, which release puffs of steam as you bite through the tender dumpling skin to the meaty center. Ecuadorian restaurants serve huge bowls of stews to hungry customers looking for a taste of comfort. And it's home to a growing LGBTQIA+ community and the Queens Pride Parade, the second largest in the city. Among the 180,000 people who live in the neighborhood, about 60 percent of them were born outside the US, bringing over 160 different languages to the area alone.

My aunt Pili lived in an apartment in the heart of Jackson Heights from 2013 to 2019. In 2016, I had just moved back to New York, my first time living in the city since I was a kid. Being new again, I was looking to build a community, so reconnecting with my aunt TT seemed like a perfect place to start. We began seeing each other regularly at her epic dinner parties. I loved having the excuse to make the trek out to Queens from Brooklyn to explore the neighborhood, my favorite part of visiting her (after her food and catching up, of course). In a crowd, I could fully blend into the sea of diversity around me. There aren't too many places I've been to where I can do that. When the opportunity arises, I relish in the bliss of utterly and completely not sticking out in any way.

It wasn't until a couple of years in that I learned how many Ecuadorians lived in the neighborhood. When my grandparents and I would return to visit New York from Florida, we would sometimes have dinner at an Ecuadorian restaurant in Jackson Heights. A quick Google Maps search shows just how many options there are, reflecting the large population there. In my hometown as a kid, though, there wasn't even one Ecuadorian restaurant.

Queens is the most ethnically diverse borough in New York City (and probably one of the most diverse in the world). But Jackson Heights is the most mixed neighborhood within it, according to the *New York Times*. About 50 percent of Jackson Heights's population identifies as Hispanic, compared to 28 percent in Queens as a whole or 29 percent in New York City as a whole. According to a 2017 report by the New York State Comptroller, the top three immigrant groups from Jackson Heights are: Mexican (11 percent), Dominican (14 percent), and Ecuadorian (20 percent), who alone represent one-fifth of the entire immigrant population there. In 2021, the Ecuadorian population grew to 22 percent and still represents the largest immigrant population in the neighborhood. Outside of Ecuador, the biggest population of Ecuadorians is found in New York City, with Queens having the most concentration.

A lot of New Yorkers know how good the food in Jackson Heights is. They talk about the Indian curries and Nepalese food trucks but often leave out Ecuadorian cuisine completely. It's why I wanted to write this piece. As the largest immigrant population in Jackson Heights, Ecuadorians deserve more recognition.

In his book *Kitchen Confidential: Adventures in the Culinary Underbelly*, Anthony Bourdain wrote this: "No one understands and appreciates the American Dream of hard work leading to material rewards better than a non-American. The Ecuadorian, Mexican, Dominican and Salvadorian cooks I've worked with over the years make most CIA-educated white boys look like clumsy, sniveling little punks." It was the first time I had read anything about Ecuador in food writing, and I felt proud to know Bourdain recognized some of our contributions to the culinary world, even if it was a small mention. I still think about it often.

Most of the times when I went to Jackson Heights it was to visit Pili, but occasionally when I wasn't full beyond measure from an Aunt TT dinner party, I would dine at Ecuadorian restaurants. Before this, the only Ecuadorian restaurants I had ever seen were around Miami and they were scarce. There's something beautiful about seeing the food you grew up with elevated in a restaurant setting. The flavors are grounded in the same sofrito and achiote taste, but the presentation is so different. The sauces are spooned over with more care, and the cilantro garnish gives a new luster. It's similar to how I felt the first time I saw an Ecuadorian artist in a modern art museum in the city. I saw myself and my history represented in a way I had never seen before, and it made me feel proud to be Ecuadorian.

I'm not sure whether I'll move back to New York again. But if I do, I know I'd want to live in Jackson Heights.

POSTA NEGRA CARTAGENERA

If you're looking to make something for the winter holidays—or to *feel* like it's the holidays—this is it. Posta negra cartagenera is carrot-stuffed roasted beef seared in caramelized panela and braised in a sauce made with Coca-Cola, wine, beer, cinnamon, and cloves. As it cooks, your kitchen fills with the sweet smell of spices, a scent that only grows stronger over time. It gets its name three ways. Posta, the Colombian name of the specific cut of meat. Negra, or black, for the dark color of the caramelized beef and the rich sauce from the reduced liquids that accompany it. And Cartagena, from Cartagena, the popular coastal city in Colombia, where this dish is famous. This is a more involved recipe, but each step is worth it for the flavorful slices of beef, the pop of orange from the carrot, and the sauce spooned over the top that's so good I could eat it on its own. Serve with a big mound of Arroz con Coco (page 214); you won't regret it.

Time: 4½ hours   ●   **Serves: 6**

Ingredients

2 tablespoons Worcestershire sauce

1 tablespoon Maggi Jugo seasoning sauce (optional)

3 garlic cloves, minced

1 tablespoon adobo seasoning

1 tablespoon freshly cracked black pepper

1 tablespoon ground cumin

1½ teaspoons dried thyme

1½ teaspoons sazón with achiote

2½ to 3 pounds beef round eye roast

4 large carrots, 3 carrots cut into 2-inch pieces and 1 whole peeled carrot (see notes)

4 ounces panela (also called piloncillo)

¼ cup extra-virgin olive oil

4 scallions, thinly sliced (about ½ cup)

1 Roma tomato, diced

½ large white onion, diced (about 1 cup)

¼ medium red onion, diced (about ½ cup)

½ cup finely chopped parsley leaves and stems

½ cup packed finely chopped cilantro leaves and stems

¼ medium green bell pepper, diced (about ½ cup)

1 cup dry red wine

1 cup lager beer

One 12-ounce can Coca-Cola

1 cinnamon stick

6 whole cloves

1½ teaspoons kosher salt, plus more to taste

8 ounces whole button mushrooms, rinsed

1 pound papas criollas or fingerling potatoes (see notes)

Directions

1 Make the marinade. In a large bowl, combine the Worcestershire, Maggi Jugo (if using), garlic, adobo, black pepper, cumin, thyme, and sazón. Set aside.

2 Prepare the beef. Using a boning knife, pierce the center of the tenderloin lengthwise; you want to go mostly but not all the way through. Remove the knife, turn the tenderloin 180 degrees, and repierce the center, creating a hole wide enough for the carrot. Insert the whole carrot into the hole (sorry, there's no way to write that and keep it from sounding like a raunchy novel!). Then use the tip of the knife to pierce ½-inch slits all over the meat's surface. Next, use butcher twine to secure the exposed carrot end so the carrot doesn't fall out during the cooking process. Finally, place the meat into the bowl with the marinade and fully coat it.

3 Microwave the panela in a heatproof bowl in 5- to 10-second increments until it is soft enough to break into smaller chunks but not melted. Be sure to rotate it occasionally to evenly distribute the heat.

4 Add the oil and panela to a large Dutch oven. Cook over medium-low heat, stirring occasionally, until the panela is fully melted and begins to darken in color, 5 to 10 minutes depending on how soft your panela is. The key is to darken it but not burn the sugar, so keep a close eye on it and adjust the heat accordingly.

5 Once the panela has melted and darkened in color, add the marinated beef along with any excess marinade. Increase the heat to medium. Sear the beef until each side has formed a thin crust and is caramelized, about 3 minutes per side. It's OK for the sugar to darken in color, but watch it carefully so it doesn't burn. Remove the seared meat and set aside.

6 Keeping the heat at medium, add the scallions, tomato, onions, parsley, cilantro, and green bell pepper. Cook, stirring frequently, until the vegetables have softened, about 5 minutes. Return the meat to the pan.

7 Add 1 cup water, the red wine, beer, Coca-Cola, cinnamon, cloves, and salt. Bring to a boil and then reduce the heat to medium-low. Cover and simmer for about 10 minutes.

8 While the meat is simmering, preheat the oven to 225°F and set a rack in the middle position. Once the oven is preheated and the meat has simmered for 10 minutes, add the mushrooms and remaining carrots to the pan. Cover and transfer it to the oven. Cook for 2 hours. Remove the pan, rotate the meat, scatter the potatoes along the sides, and spoon some of the braising juices directly on top. Continue to cook until the tenderloin is tender and gives a little when you squeeze it with tongs, about another 1 hour 30 minutes.

9 Transfer the Dutch oven to the stove. Transfer the tenderloin to a cutting board, remove the butcher twine, and let rest for

Recipe continues

at least 15 minutes. While the meat is resting, reduce the cooking liquid to make a sauce. Turn the heat to medium and bring to a boil. Cook uncovered until the liquid reduces by about a fourth and is thick enough to coat the back of a spoon, about 15 minutes. Taste and adjust for salt. Remove from the heat.

10 Once the cooking liquid has reduced and the tenderloin has rested, cut the meat into ½ inch slices. Neatly place the slices back into the center of the Dutch oven (if using it to serve in; if not, just place the meat back in gently) and spoon some of its braising juices directly on top, letting the residual heat warm the meat through. Serve in the Dutch oven or arrange the meat in the center of a platter with the vegetables placed around and extra sauce spooned on top.

Notes: The peeled carrot is for the center of the tenderloin, which means it should be roughly the same length. If your carrot is too long, just cut it to size. If it's too short, add part of another one so it's the same size as the beef. Easy peasy!

Papas criollas are a specific variety of small yellow potatoes from Colombia.

They are Aunt TT's go-to potato for this dish, because the centers are extra creamy and tender—perfect for soaking up all that flavorful sauce! You can buy them frozen from many Latin American grocery stores. But if you can't track them down, don't worry. Fingerling potatoes, which have a similar small size, can work in their place.

OLLA DE CARNE

Hunger, a hangover, or even a broken heart—olla de carne is the Costa Rican stew that cures it all. Similar to sancocho, a hearty dish that's popular in places like the Dominican Republic, Puerto Rico, and Colombia, olla de carne only gets better the longer it cooks. The base of the stew starts with short ribs, oxtails, and a mix of sofrito. As the first layer slowly cooks and becomes tender, a medley of vegetables is added. Cabbage, carrots, corn, yuca, calabaza, plantains, potatoes, and chayote (a light-green pear-shaped squash from Central America) give the stew so much texture, flavor, and depth that it feels like you're diving headfirst into a warm beef-flavored ocean with no bottom in sight. But cabbage is the secret star that melts into the broth, giving it thickness.

Salsa Lizano is what separates a true olla de carne from the wannabes. It's the prized sauce of Costa Rica and is used in countless recipes, including the national dish, gallo pinto (Costa Rican rice and beans). In 1920, it was first created to accompany foods like encurtido (pickled vegetables), but its popularity spread, and it has now become an essential part of Costa Rican cuisine. Salsa Lizano is made from a blend of onions, carrots, cauliflower, cucumber, and spices; a few tablespoons of this brown sauce adds tang and acidity to anything it touches.

Pili's original recipe also uses about 1 pound of beef neck bones, which add depth of flavor. But she uses a HUGE restaurant-size stockpot. Since most people don't own a pot that large, I've omitted the neck bones, but if you happen to have a pot that big, I would recommend throwing some in. And she's a fan of using Maggi rib-flavored soup mix, which adds a punch of MSG and a little sprinkle of thin, bite-size noodles. It's optional, but if you don't use it, heads-up that you will need to add more salt at the end to tie all the flavors together. Last, don't forget to serve with a side of white rice and sliced ripe avocado.

Time: 3 hours ● **Serves:** 10

Ingredients

2 pounds bone-in short ribs, preferably cut into 2-inch pieces (see note)

1½ pounds oxtail, rinsed and trimmed

1 tablespoon kosher salt, plus more to taste

¼ cup extra-virgin olive oil, plus more as needed

1 small green bell pepper, diced (about 1 cup)

½ cup diced white onion

½ cup diced red onion

½ cup packed finely chopped cilantro leaves and stems, plus more for garnish

2 scallions, chopped (about ¼ cup)

2 Roma tomatoes, diced (about 1 cup)

Recipe continues

12 cloves of garlic, minced (about ¼ cup)

1 tablespoon adobo seasoning

8 ounces white cabbage, cored and roughly chopped into ½-inch pieces

2 large carrots, peeled and cut into 1-inch pieces

2 celery stalks, peeled and cut into 1-inch pieces (see note)

2 tablespoons Salsa Lizano, plus more for serving

8 ounces frozen peeled yuca

2 green (unripe) plantains

½ teaspoon sazón with achiote

2 ears corn, shucked and cut into 1-inch pieces

8 ounces calabaza or kabocha squash, seeded and cut into 2-inch pieces

8 ounces Yukon Gold potatoes, peeled and cut into 1-inch pieces

8 ounces green chayote, peeled, seeded, and cut into 1-inch pieces

One 2.05-ounce package Maggi rib-flavored soup mix (optional)

Directions

1 Sear the beef. Pat the short ribs and oxtail dry with a paper towel and season with the salt. Heat 2 tablespoons of the oil in a 12-quart stockpot over medium heat. Once the oil is shimmering, add the short ribs. Cook, flipping occasionally, until most of the meat is seared with some dark brown crust, about 7 minutes. Transfer to a plate. Add the remaining 2 tablespoons oil and the oxtail. Repeat until seared and transfer to the plate.

2 Reduce the heat to medium. If the pot is looking a little dry, add a bit more oil. Then add the bell pepper, onions, cilantro, scallions, tomatoes, garlic, and adobo. Cook, stirring frequently, until the onions are translucent, about 7 minutes.

3 Add the cabbage, carrots, celery, and reserved meat. Next, fill the pot with enough water to fully submerge the meat, 8 to 10 cups. Bring to a boil, reduce the heat

to medium-low, and cover. Cook, stirring occasionally, until the meat begins to soften, about 1 hour.

4 After 1 hour, skim off any fat or foam that has risen to the top. Next, add 1 cup water, the Salsa Lizano, and yuca. Increase the heat to high and bring to a boil. Once boiling, reduce the heat to low and cover. Cook for another hour, adding more water as necessary to keep the meat submerged so it cooks evenly.

5 After the yuca is completely fork-tender, about 30 minutes, use tongs to remove it from the pot. On a cutting board or plate, cut each piece of yuca in half and remove the center thread. Then cut it into about 1-inch pieces (doesn't have to be perfect!). Set aside.

6 Around the end of the second hour, prepare the plantains. Cut off and discard the ends. Using a paring knife, cut a slit along the length of the plantains, carefully avoiding cutting into the flesh, and then remove the peels. If the peel is too firm, use a spoon to lift the edges, then discard the peel. Cut one plantain in half crosswise. Place the halved plantain in a blender along with ½ cup water and ¼ teaspoon of the sazón. Blend until smooth. Slice the remaining plantain into 1-inch-thick rounds and set aside.

7 Using a wooden spoon, quickly stir the blended plantain mixture into the hot stew to keep it from forming clumps. Next, add the sliced plantain, corn, calabaza, potatoes, chayote, and remaining ¼ teaspoon sazón. Increase the heat to medium and cook uncovered, stirring occasionally, until the vegetables are tender and the stew has thickened slightly, about 30 minutes.

8 During the last 10 minutes of cooking, add the cut yuca and Maggi soup mix (if using). Taste and adjust for salt. Enjoy hot in bowls and garnish with chopped cilantro. Keep the Salsa Lizano nearby for the optional dash.

Notes: Do not cut the short ribs at home or your knife will suffer. Ask your butcher to do it. And if you can't, whole short ribs will work just fine.

I know peeling celery seems a little awkward, but you only need to peel the stringy, curved side. As the celery cooks, it will melt into the soup. To keep the consistency string-free, you have to remove that part from the celery from the beginning. No one wants a stringy soup.

CHILEAN PEBRE

Spooned over grilled meat, drizzled on top of empanadas, or slathered on bread, pebre is a staple condiment in Chile. It's typically made from a mixture of tomatoes, onions, garlic, herbs, and a light-yellow-green pepper called ají cristal that's native to the country. When Aunt TT has a dinner party, you can bet a big bowl of pebre will make an appearance on the table. Each ingredient is finely diced into a uniform shape and mixed with a bit of oil, lime, chile-garlic sauce, and wine (or vinegar, if you don't drink). And it sparkles like a bowl of glitter confetti when it catches the light. Although pebre takes only a couple of minutes to toss together, it is important to spend time carefully prepping every ingredient. The smaller and more uniform your dice, the better your pebre will be. Slather it on bread, empanadas, or meat, or spoon over salad . . . the options are endless!

Time: 5 minutes, plus marinating   ●   **Makes:** About 3 cups

Ingredients

2 Roma tomatoes, finely diced

1 medium red onion, finely diced

1 ají cristal or jalapeño, finely diced (seeds optional)

2 garlic cloves, minced

¼ cup packed finely chopped parsley leaves and stems

¼ cup packed finely chopped cilantro leaves and stems

2 tablespoons extra-virgin olive oil

1½ tablespoons dry white wine or white wine vinegar

1 teaspoon chile-garlic sauce (such as Huy Fong)

½ lime, juiced

Kosher salt and freshly cracked black pepper

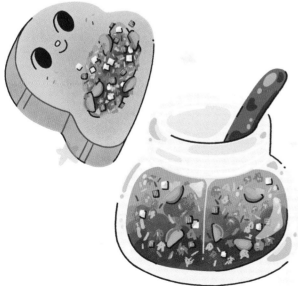

Directions

1 Combine all the ingredients in a large bowl. Mix until well combined. Season to taste with salt and pepper.

2 Refrigerate for 2 hours to let the flavors blend.

GUACAU

If it isn't clear already that Aunt TT is a culinary genius, this should prove it. Guacau is a true Pili original! It combines the Peruvian cau cau, a golden African-influenced tripe stew that's spiked with turmeric and mint, and Ecuadorian guatita, also a tripe stew but made with peanut butter (hence the name: gua~~tita~~ + cau ~~cau~~). Peru and Ecuador have a long—and sometimes not so peaceful—history together. One of the few things I know about my great-grandfather is that he fought in the Ecuadorian-Peruvian War of 1941, one of several conflicts between the two countries in the twentieth century. Pili likes to think of guacau as a dish of peace by combining two of the countries' most beloved recipes. Also, the combination of tender honeycomb tripe with the velvety turmeric and peanut butter sauce doesn't hurt. Serve with hot white rice to soak up all that turmeric-gold goodness.

Time: 1 hour 15 minutes ● **Serves:** 8 to 10

Ingredients

2 pounds beef honeycomb tripe, washed and cleaned

½ bunch cilantro, tied with butcher twine or wrapped in a cheesecloth

8 garlic cloves (4 whole and 4 minced)

2 teaspoons kosher salt, plus more to taste

⅓ cup creamy unsweetened peanut butter

¼ cup extra-virgin olive oil

½ large white onion, finely chopped

½ large red onion, finely chopped

½ medium green bell pepper, finely chopped

2 scallions, thinly sliced

1½ pounds Yukon Gold potatoes, peeled and cut into 1-inch pieces (about 7 medium potatoes)

1 Roma tomato, chopped into ½-inch pieces

2 tablespoons adobo seasoning

2 tablespoons turmeric

1½ cups whole milk

1 chicken bouillon cube

¼ teaspoon cayenne pepper (optional)

¾ cup packed chopped mint, plus more for garnish (see note)

Directions

1 Cook the tripe. Bring a large pot of water to a boil. Once boiling, add the tripe, cilantro bundle, whole garlic cloves, and salt. Reduce the heat to medium and cook uncovered until the tripe is completely tender and soft enough to cut with a fork, about 40 minutes.

Remove and discard the cilantro bundle. Reserve 4 cups of the cooking liquid. Drain and set the tripe aside to cool. Once it's cool enough to handle, cut it into 1-inch pieces. You can prepare the tripe a day or two ahead if you'd like.

Recipe continues

2 Add 1½ cups hot tap water and the peanut butter to a large measuring cup. Mix with a spoon or fork until there are no clumps. Set aside.

3 Heat the olive oil in a large Dutch oven or pot over medium-high heat. Once the oil is shimmering, add the onions, bell pepper, scallions, and minced garlic. Cook, stirring frequently to avoid browning, until the onions are tender and translucent, about 5 minutes.

4 Add the potatoes, tomato, adobo, and turmeric. Mix until everything is coated and has the same golden hue. Cook until the tomato starts to soften, about 2 minutes.

5 Add the reserved 4 cups cooking liquid, cut tripe, peanut butter mixture, milk, bouillon cube, and cayenne (if using).

Mix until everything is incorporated. Bring to a boil and then reduce the heat to medium. Maintain a steady rolling boil, adjusting the heat as necessary if it starts splashing. Cook uncovered until the guacau thickens enough to coat the back of a wooden spoon and the tripe has a velvety texture, about 30 minutes, stirring occasionally to avoid scorching. Once thickened, turn off the heat, stir in the mint, and taste and adjust for salt. Serve while hot and garnish with more mint.

Note: If you prefer using dried mint, you can swap ¼ cup dried mint for the fresh. Instead of adding it at the end, mix it in when you add the turmeric. Dried herbs need more time to release their full flavor, but with enough time, they can be as bright as their fresh counterpart.

CREMA DE AJÍ AMARILLO

Ají amarillo is a golden pepper grown throughout Peru and is considered to be one of the most culturally important ingredients in Peruvian cuisine. It's a slender hot pepper with fruity flavor notes and vibrant orange-yellow skin that resembles a sunrise. I have never eaten it fresh because it can be difficult to find just harvested in the US. But you can easily buy them frozen or as a paste from most Latin American grocery stores or online. This crema de ají amarillo is a staple sauce for Aunt TT. The recipe makes a larger batch that can be enjoyed with multiple meals, but you can easily scale it down for a smaller portion. And if you want it hotter, just add more ají. Spoon it over chicken, potatoes, or anything else to add a spicy, tangy kick.

Time: 5 minutes • **Makes:** 3 cups

Ingredients

¾ cup mayonnaise

½ cup sour cream

¾ cup ricotta cheese

½ cup plus
2 tablespoons ají
amarillo paste,
(such as Inca's Food),
plus more to taste

1 teaspoon ketchup

Dash of ground
achiote or sazón
with achiote

4 limes, juiced (about
½ cup)

4 scallions, trimmed
and cut into 3-inch
pieces

Kosher salt and
freshly cracked
black pepper

Directions

1 In a blender, combine mayonnaise, sour cream, ricotta, ají amarillo paste, ketchup, achiote, lime juice, and scallions and blend until smooth, about 3 minutes. Scrape down the sides to ensure the sauce is an even orange-yellow color. Taste and adjust with more ají amarillo if you want the crema to be spicier.

2 Season with salt and black pepper to taste. Serve in a small bowl or store in the refrigerator for up to a week.

CHAPTER 6

ALL GROWN UP!
KINDA

All the previous chapters and stories walk you through different times of my childhood and young adulthood. But here we are at the last chapter: the present. I'm currently writing this from the Tokyo immigration office. Whenever I come here, it takes at least four hours until I see sunshine again, and it's sometimes as long as six hours. The bleak, off-white space is lit with the same fluorescent glow as a doctor's office. Thousands of people from around the world crowd together on benches and other makeshift seats, each hoping they correctly filled out their paperwork and remembered to bring the right documents (otherwise they'll have to take the bus out to the middle of Shinagawa again to repeat the painfully mundane process). Cell service barely works. There's no Wi-Fi. Or vending machines. And when it's finally my turn to talk to someone, I speak in the baby-level, broken Japanese I've been able to learn so far and inevitably embarrass myself.

Coming here makes me wonder what my family's experience in US immigration offices was like. Not the happy-ending part, where they eventually became citizens and took photos in front of the American flag, but the gritty details that came before. Did the immigration office in New York have the same off-putting lighting as Tokyo's? When their number was finally called, how much did they struggle in broken English to try to get their point across? How many times did they think they had filled out the correct form, only to discover later that they had to come back the next day because they misunderstood something and left feeling defeated?

There are so many reasons why I wanted to leave the US and move to Japan, but the short answer is the same as my family's when they immigrated: to pursue a better life. Not to imply that my life in the US was bad at all. In fact, at times I was thriving (and I may even return one day)! But I wanted something more. Since I was a teenager, I had dreamed about living abroad. And now having finally achieved this lifelong goal, I know none of it would have been possible without my family's sacrifice and initial leap into the unknown. Trust me when I say it is not a leap of faith but a big ol' plunge into something that's completely unfamiliar and uncomfortable in every way.

My move has made me reflect a lot more than I ever have on how absurdly difficult my family's journey to the US must have been. I can't even begin to imagine having seven kids, on top of everything else. I never thought it was easy, but experiencing the process of learning firsthand about every aspect of life in another country has made me realize that, in some ways, I'm walking in their footsteps—along the same route by a different path. When I tell my friends about how difficult it is to navigate the post office in Japan with very little language ability, I usually get a response like, "Wow, that's crazy!" But when I told my grandma Veronica, she was like, "It sucks, right?" When I told her about the difficulty I had learning a new trash system, she said, "Oh yeah. I remember that when I came to the US." Nothing was shocking to her because she's lived it all before. But of course she and the rest of my family had it much harder, with fewer initial job prospects and way more kids to manage (I just have my one dog).

The slight cold sweat I feel when I see an important document addressed to me in my mailbox, and I have no idea where to start. The time I got rejected for a credit card because I have no credit history in the country I moved to. The awkward moments of trying to say "good morning" but blurting out "good night" in the new language I'm trying to learn. Through these many, many uncomfortable encounters, I have found a raw vulnerability. And because of it I feel closer to my family. I can't think of a better time in my life to write this book than now, especially when I'm the farthest I've ever been from home.

Latinx, Asian, and American, no part is more or less. I am all three cultures, and I've never felt more proud.

I was really hoping that after a year of writing this book (and the years leading up to it), I would have been left with a deep, profound conclusion about cultural identity that nicely wraps up everything in a big bow—it didn't. But it did leave me with this feeling of knowing my family on a deeper, more personal level. I've been able to stand alongside them and cook the food of their childhood for hours. I got to dive through their pantries and listen to new stories because I asked different, more informed questions. It left me with a better understanding of my new home in Tokyo because I now know where to get fresh tamarind and, on rare occasion, plantains. It left me with new information about my past, like the eighteen-page document about my time in foster care and my new favorite cookbook (that's actually very old) from my aunt TT.

Sometimes the path to understanding one's cultural identity isn't linear. It can be zigzag, up and down, diagonal, at a complete standstill, in seemingly nonsensical circles, or a combination of all the above. I was always on the path regardless of what direction I went in. No one, not even myself, can take away the fact that I am Ecuadorian. Because it simply is. There is not a specific thing I have to do in order to finally be recognized as Latinx. I just am.

So much of my life I've felt plagued by the question "What are you?" And now I rarely think about it because I know who I am. And that's someone who is still figuring it out. There is so much more I want to learn.

This essay is shorter than the others because it is still being lived, still being written. While much of the book covers my childhood, this chapter is centered on what's been happening in my life as an adult. Since growing up, I've had the immense privilege to move around the world on my own terms. In the last decade, I've lived in Gainesville (Florida), Orange County (California), Los Angeles, San Francisco, Brooklyn, Honolulu, and now Tokyo. The recipes and stories are inspired by my time in those places, people I've met along the way, and the overall life I've lived so far. They're a look into the kinds of flavors I love while always remembering where I've come from but not letting it define me.

When I moved to Hawai'i, I couldn't find plantains in my neighborhood grocery store for the first time. I knew then that I was a long way from home. I didn't realize how much comfort I found overhearing conversations in Spanish on the sidewalks of New York until I was gone. Now in Japan, I realize the culture I looked for has always been a part of me. And through cooking, I reinforce it.

In some ways, it's ironic that I've titled this book *My (Half) Latinx Kitchen,* because the truth is that there's no clear line of division within myself. There's not a line that separates the Latinx from my Asian and American side. They're all mixed up together like a woven fabric. Latinx, Asian, and American, no part is more or less. I am all three cultures, and I've never felt more proud.

In the process of being half, I've found out I've been whole this entire time.

ELOTE TAQUITOS

When I was thinking of original recipes for this chapter, I focused on two things: the foods I love eating the most and what makes me feel the happiest. So elote and taquitos (or little tacos) just made sense. Mexican street corn dressed in all its rainbow toppings fills me with as much joy as golden taquitos do. These elote taquitos combine the best of both worlds in one dish. The result is even more happiness. The filling includes sweet corn, Tajín, lime zest, cheese, and mashed potatoes (to make it all stick together). After some time in the oven, the crisp taquitos are garnished with all the classic Mexican street corn toppings: crema, crumbled cheese, cilantro, lime, and more Tajín. You can also fry these, but I found the corn kernels popped too much in the oil. If you're feeling brave and have a splatter guard, you can follow the frying steps in the Flautas de Pollo recipe (page 93).

My grandma tasted my first batch and said, "Mi niña, it tastes just like elotes. How did you do that?!"

About the differences between taquitos and flautas: Flautas *sometimes* use larger tortillas, and taquitos *always* use small tortillas. But they are the same dish! My grandma refers to her version as flautas, regardless of the small corn tortilla size. Since this was an original spin of mine, I wanted to call them taquitos; however, both names are OK to use, as they're often used interchangeably depending on the region.

Time: 45 minutes • **Serves:** 4

Ingredients

1¼ pounds Yukon Gold potatoes, peeled and diced into equal pieces

1 tablespoon kosher salt, plus more to taste

4 tablespoons unsalted butter

2 teaspoons Tajín, plus more for garnish

1 teaspoon cornstarch or potato starch

Zest of 2 limes

3 cups corn kernels (preferably fresh from 4 ears)

1 cup shredded cheddar

Sixteen 6-inch corn tortillas (preferably as fresh as possible for maximum rollability)

¾ cup extra-virgin olive oil

Mexican crema, for garnish

Crumbled cotija or queso fresco, for garnish

¼ cup packed finely chopped cilantro leaves

1 lime, cut into 6 wedges (optional)

Recipe continues

Directions

1 Place the potatoes and salt in a medium pot with water to cover. Bring to a boil over high heat. Once boiling, cover and reduce to a simmer. Cook until the potatoes are tender, about 15 minutes.

2 Drain the potatoes. Place the drained potatoes back into the same pot. Then, using a potato masher or a fork, mash until smooth, adding the butter, Tajín, cornstarch, and lime zest about halfway through. Next, add the corn and cheddar. Mix until evenly distributed. Taste and adjust for salt. Set aside.

3 Preheat the oven to 425°F.

4 While the oven is preheating, place the tortillas on a heatproof plate and loosely cover with a damp paper towel. Microwave in 15-second increments until warm.

5 Roll the taquitos. Working with one tortilla at a time, rub about 2 teaspoons of olive on the tortilla (roughly 1 teaspoon per side) to lightly coat it. Next, place about a scant ¼ cup of filling along the center of the tortilla. Tightly roll up the tortilla and tap the filling at the ends a little toward the center to keep it from spilling out. Place the rolled taquitos seam side down onto a baking sheet. Repeat with the remaining tortillas. Pour any remaining oil directly onto the tray.

6 Bake for 10 minutes, or until the taquitos begin to crisp and hold their shape. Remove from the oven and flip the taquitos. Transfer back to the oven and bake for another 8 to 10 minutes, until the tortillas are fully crisp and golden, but stay close by so they don't burn.

7 To serve, place 4 warm taquitos per portion on a plate. Drizzle crema on top. Sprinkle with the crumbled cotija, Tajín, and cilantro. Eat while hot and serve with the lime wedges on the side.

MEXICAN HOT CHOCOLATE COOKIES

Homemade hot chocolate was one of the first dishes I made that impressed people. I was around twelve years old and was cooking (or at least trying my very best) for my family. I ladled out the piping hot chocolate into cups, handing one to each guest. On the surface, it looked like any other cup of cocoa. But when you took a sip, the warmth of cinnamon and sweetness of vanilla washed over you like a huge wave. It tasted like I did something special, but really I just used Abuelita, the store-bought chocolate disc that's a staple for making Mexican hot chocolate. *My* abuelita would use Abuelita, so I did the same.

The original Mexican hot chocolate dates back over three thousand years, to when the Olmec, Maya, Toltec, and Aztec people began cultivating cacao. It is believed that the Olmecs were the first to ferment and roast cocoa beans, the most important step to bringing out their complex richness. But it wasn't until the sugar was added in the 1800s that chocolate got the familiar sweet taste we know today. Sugarcane originated in the islands of the South Pacific and then was spread around the world through exploration, trade, and colonization. For years, sugar was used only as a luxury product, but the enslavement of Black and Brown people in places like the Caribbean and Latin America made it possible to produce in bulk and it became more accessible to the masses, leading to Europeans adding it to chocolate in 1847.

These cookies are not a drink (surprise!), and you might be thinking, "Why are you telling me so much about chocolate history?" But it's good to know where the flavors originated, especially when it's as important to a culture as chocolate is to Mexico. This recipe is inspired by the spiced chocolate of Abuelita and will hopefully spark the same cozy feeling as sipping on a cup of cocoa. But instead of warm cocoa, it's warm cookies . . . which I think might be even better.

Time: 35 minutes, plus resting and cooling   •   **Makes:** About 30 cookies

Recipe continues

Ingredients

1 cup (2 sticks) unsalted butter

1¾ cups all-purpose flour

¼ cup Dutch-processed cocoa powder

1 tablespoon plus ¾ teaspoon ground cinnamon

1 teaspoon kosher salt

1 teaspoon baking soda

⅛ teaspoon ground nutmeg (preferably freshly grated)

1 cup packed light brown sugar

¾ cup granulated sugar

2 large eggs, room temperature

1 tablespoon vanilla extract

¼ teaspoon almond extract

10 ounces dark chocolate, coarsely chopped, or 1½ cups dark chocolate chunks (preferably 70% cacao)

Flaky sea salt, for sprinkling (optional)

Directions

1 Place the butter in a small saucepan and cook over medium heat, stirring often, until it foams, then browns, about 5 minutes. Remove from the heat and let cool for at least 10 minutes.

2 Whisk together the flour, cocoa, cinnamon, salt, baking soda, and nutmeg in a medium bowl. Set aside.

3 In a stand mixer fitted with a paddle attachment or in a large bowl with an electric hand mixer, combine the brown butter, brown sugar, and granulated sugar and mix together on medium speed until fully combined, about 1 minute. Scrape down the sides with a rubber spatula. Then add the eggs, vanilla, and almond extract. Mix on medium speed until the mixture falls in shiny ribbons when you stop and lift up the beaters, about 1 minute.

4 Using the spatula, gradually fold the dry ingredients into the wet ones until just incorporated. Add the chopped chocolate and mix to incorporate. The cookie dough will look a little wet at first but will thicken. Place in the refrigerator to chill for 30 minutes.

5 About 10 minutes before the dough is finished chilling, preheat the oven to 350°F. Line two baking sheets with parchment paper.

6 Once the dough has chilled, form the cookies. Working in batches, use a tablespoon to generously scoop out cookie dough; each ball of dough should be around the size of a ping-pong ball. Place the cookies 3 inches apart on the prepared baking sheets to avoid crowding. Do not flatten. Bake for about 10 minutes, until the edges are just set and your kitchen smells very chocolaty.

7 Remove from the oven. Gently tap the baking sheets on a counter to even out the cookie surfaces. Sprinkle the tops with flaky salt, if using. Let the cookies cool on the pans for 10 minutes, then transfer to a wire rack to cool completely. Repeat with the remaining dough. Serve while warm or store in an airtight container for up to 3 days. You can also freeze the cookie dough balls for up to 3 months.

BREAKFAST TOSTADAS
WITH LAZYYY BEANS

When I enter a truly lazyyy (not lazy, but lazyyy) state, it means one or all of the following things: (1) For whatever reason, I have not been feeling good for days/weeks/months. (2) I have not been nourishing my body well and probably desperately need to make a change. (3) I'm just tired and don't want to cook anything. If I feel lazyyy, *this* is what I make.

Although these breakfast tostadas take a bit more work than pouring a bowl of cereal, cooking them jolts me back to feeling like my normal self, even just for a moment. To start, I add a bunch of aromatics to the canned beans to, well, make them not taste like canned beans. But the act of sautéing onions, garlic, and spices together grounds me in the present, and the smells take me back home. The crisp, lacy egg and extra splashes of hot sauce remind me that I won't feel lazyyy forever.

Time: 20 minutes ● **Serves:** 4

Ingredients

1 tablespoon extra-virgin olive oil

½ medium yellow onion, diced

3 garlic cloves, minced

1½ teaspoons ground cumin

½ teaspoon crushed red pepper flakes

One 15-ounce can black beans, drained and rinsed

½ teaspoon kosher salt

¼ teaspoon MSG (optional)

¼ cup vegetable oil

Four 6-inch corn tortillas

4 large eggs

1 cup crumbled queso fresco

2 ripe avocados, thinly sliced

Flaky sea salt and freshly cracked black pepper, for serving

Hot sauce (preferably Cholula or Valentina), for serving

Directions

1 Heat the olive oil in a small pot over medium-low heat. Once the oil is shimmering, add the onion and cook, stirring frequently to avoid browning, until just softened, about 2 minutes.

2 Add the garlic, cumin, and red pepper flakes. Cook until fragrant, about 1 minute.

3 Add the beans, salt, and MSG (if using) and stir until combined with a wooden spoon. Using the back of the spoon, press the beans against the side of the pot to gently crush about half of them. Then add 1 cup water. Increase the heat to medium and continue to cook, stirring frequently

All Grown Up! Kinda

●

Recipe continues

to keep any bits from burning on the bottom of the pot, until the beans thicken, about 5 minutes. Remove from the heat, cover, and set aside.

4 Heat the vegetable oil in a large nonstick skillet over medium–high heat. Once the oil is shimmering, add the tortillas one at a time and cook until crispy and golden brown, about 30 seconds on each side. Remove and let cool on a paper towel–lined plate to drain.

5 In the same skillet, reheat the oil over high heat. Once the oil is shimmering, cook the eggs sunny-side up until the edges

bubble up and become golden brown, about 2 minutes. Remove from the heat. You can cook them all at once and separate them with the tip of your spatula, or make them two at a time for a cleaner look.

6 To assemble, place a crisp tortilla on a serving plate. Spoon about one-quarter of the beans directly on top. Sprinkle with one-quarter of the queso fresco. Spread one-quarter of the avocado slices over the cheese. Top with 1 egg, flaky salt, and fresh cracked pepper. Repeat for the remaining tostadas. Serve immediately with lots of hot sauce.

SOFRITO BOLOGNESE

I have a lot of memories with this one particularly terrible ex-boyfriend that I don't like to think about, but eating this sofrito pasta that his mom used to make is not one of them. She emigrated from Colombia and adapted American dishes to her taste, but her meat sauce was the best. She would fry sofrito for the base and simply add cooked ground beef, sazón, and jarred tomato sauce. The first time I had it, I remember thinking, "I need more. Right. Now."

My version is a bit more bougie and calls for caramelized tomato paste and white wine, but the result is the same: A sauce you will need seconds. And thirds. And fourths of.

Time: 45 minutes ● **Serves:** 4

Ingredients

1 large yellow onion, roughly chopped

1 large green bell pepper, roughly chopped

6 large garlic cloves, peeled

2 tablespoons extra-virgin olive oil

1 pound ground beef (or you can use half pork and half beef)

1 tablespoon dried oregano

½ teaspoon crushed red pepper flakes (optional)

2 teaspoons kosher salt, plus more to taste

Freshly cracked black pepper

One 4.5-ounce tube tomato paste (about ½ cup)

1½ cups dry white wine

2 cups unsalted beef, chicken, or vegetable stock

1½ teaspoons sazón with achiote

1 pound spaghetti (or another pasta of choice)

1 tablespoon unsalted butter

Grated Parmesan, for serving

¼ cup packed finely chopped cilantro leaves

Directions

1 Make the sofrito. In a blender or food processor, blend the onion, bell pepper, and garlic until smooth. Set aside.

2 Heat the oil in a large Dutch oven over high heat. Add the beef, oregano, red pepper flakes, salt, and black pepper to taste. Cook, breaking up the beef with a wooden spoon, until it starts to crisp and some parts turn a deep brown, about 10 minutes.

3 Add the tomato paste and cook until it darkens in color, about 2 minutes. Add the sofrito and stir well. Sauté until the liquid is mostly evaporated and the sofrito thickens, about 7 minutes.

●

4 Add the wine, stock, and sazón. Stir, scraping up any browned bits stuck to the bottom of the pot. Bring to a boil and then reduce the heat to medium so the sauce is at a steady simmer. It should look like bubbles in a jacuzzi. If it's barely bubbling or starts to splash violently, adjust the heat as needed. Simmer uncovered until a little more than one-third of the liquid has evaporated and the meat begins to reappear along the surface, about 20 minutes, stirring occasionally to make sure nothing is sticking. It should now have a sauce-like consistency.

5 During the last 10 minutes of the cooking, make the pasta. Add the pasta to a large pot of salted boiling water and cook according to the package instructions until al dente. Reserve ½ cup pasta water and drain.

6 Add the reserved pasta water and the butter directly to the sauce. Increase the heat to high and cook until the liquid reduces slightly and the sauce becomes glossy, about 5 minutes. Season to taste with salt and pepper. Add the pasta you are planning to eat immediately into the sauce and toss until coated. Serve with Parmesan and cilantro. When storing leftovers, store the pasta and sauce separately so the pasta doesn't absorb too much liquid. Reheat and toss together before serving.

FORGETTING SPANISH

Spanish was my first language. At least, that is, according to my initial caretaker, my grandma. She had just moved to the US from Mexico and was still in the process of learning English, so she spoke to me exclusively in Spanish. Spending whole weeks together in her small New York City apartment, we would have full conversations in her mother tongue until I was around three years old, besides the occasional *Little Mermaid* song lyrics I would belt out in English. But as I grew up, I forgot the language. My Spanish today is a one-way door: I can understand some of what is said to me, but I cannot formulate the words or grammar on my own to speak.

Whenever I meet another Latinx person, almost without fail, the first question they ask is "Do you speak Spanish?" It's not fueled by the racially motivated "What are you?" question, but it carries a weight that's heavy in another way. When they ask about my Spanish speaking abilities, it really feels like they're asking me about so much more. *Can you roll your r's without the hum of the consonant sputtering out? Can you pronounce my name the way my family wants? Can you understand the culture? Can you really be one of us?* It is a test to see if I am Latinx enough. And when I reply no, their eyes often glaze over to let me know that I've failed.

There are more than 485 million native Spanish speakers, making it the second most natively spoken language in the world, just below Mandarin. If you add people who have learned it as a second language, it is the world's fourth most-spoken language. Spanish is the official language of twenty countries, the majority of which are part of Latin America. But five hundred years ago, it was different.

It has been estimated that, before Spain's colonization, three hundred different languages were spoken in Mexico and Central America and over fourteen hundred languages in South America and the West Indies. The Spanish language was brought to Latin America by the conquistadors who annexed the land. Its spread throughout the region was not an accident but an intentional move by the European monarchy to take over—and erase Indigenous peoples and their cultures with it.

To simply call Spanish a colonizer language feels like an oversimplification, though. Over its five-hundred-plus-year history in Latin America, the Spanish language has become an integral aspect of Latinx culture to many people.

Although I am half Korean, I rarely get asked by other Asian Americans if I can speak Korean. While Latin America is far from homogeneous, Spanish is the region's predominant language. But when large numbers of people from Asia began immigrating to the US starting in the mid-1800s, a greater variety of languages was spoken, including Mandarin, Hindi, Korean, and Vietnamese; there was no single language to unite every community of Asian immigrants.

Knowing or not knowing Spanish has always felt to me like a way to gatekeep the culture. If I spoke it, the Latinx red carpet would be rolled out for me, and I could chat with someone about shared childhood memories or foods we both love. If I didn't, I wouldn't even be allowed entry on the property, usually made clear by the immediate end to the conversation. But though the language unifies a lot of Latin America, it is not the only language spoken. Brazil is the most populous country in the region, with over two hundred million people—representing about half of South America's entire population—and the national language is Portuguese. And despite colonization's devastating impact on Indigenous communities, some languages have persevered. Quechua, a fifteen-hundred-year-old language that was later adopted by the Incan empire as a lingua franca, is spoken by around eight to ten million people, mostly in Peru, Bolivia, and Ecuador. (It is also one of the most spoken Indigenous languages in the Americas.) According to a 2012 *New York Times* article, "Paraguay remains the only country in the Americas where a majority of the population speaks one Indigenous language: Guaraní." In Paraguay, Guaraní is classified as an official language, giving it the same status as Spanish. And in Guatemala, where 43.5 percent of the population identifies as Indigenous, twenty-five languages are spoken: Spanish, twenty-two different Mayan languages, and two additional Indigenous languages (Garífuna and Xinca).

Does not speaking Spanish make them any less Latin American?

I grew up around Spanish my entire life. Every guardian I've had besides my mom spoke it as their first and main language. But in the different homes I've lived in, the very common first-generation American story always played out: They would speak only in Spanish, and I would respond only in English. Like with my foster parents. They would speak to me in Spanish as if I understood it fluently, but I didn't. I could only reply back with the simplest English phrases and hope they understood my intent. Most of the time, I could get by with these kinds of exchanges. But on occasion (depending on the person's English ability), we just wouldn't understand each other and have to move on to language-neutral topics, like food. Since I was in and out of different homes so frequently, the longest exposure I had to the language lasted about one year or so before I would move and have to start over again. For the brief period I did live with my dad, he never spoke Spanish at home. I'm not sure why.

But after many years of having Telemundo playing quietly in the background and overhearing conversations in my grandparents' home, some of the Spanish I forgot came back when I was in middle school. Immersion really does work. Today when I see my very extended family at events (like second-cousin's-cousin-once-removed family), I often get teased by the older generation about my inability to converse with them. "Ella no puede hablar español. Qué triste." In my mind, I am thinking, "I can understand you!"

There are countless reasons why someone who is Latinx doesn't know Spanish; this is just my personal experience. An ironic thing I've learned from many of my friends who are Latinx *and* speak Spanish is that they're often worried they can't speak it well enough. This isn't an uncommon belief. Once even Cardi B apologized and said, "Pardón, tú sabes mi español es muy *ratata*." In the community, there's so much pressure to have such a firm grasp of Spanish that even having some language ability can still leave people questioning their identity.

Right now is the first time in my life I have fully dedicated myself to learning a new language—and it's Japanese. The Japanese language itself is far from free of its own baggage. For example, during the Japanese occupation of Korea, they stopped teaching the Korean language and forcibly imposed Japanese instead. But in my daily life, learning Japanese doesn't carry the same weight that learning Spanish has. I know when strangers ask, "Can you speak Spanish?" they are looking to connect. But through their search, rejection follows instead. Unintentionally, this pushed my desire to learn Spanish away and replaced it with a fear that I wouldn't be able to speak it well enough even if I tried for years—until now. The small progress I can see with my Japanese gives me the confidence that I can do it with Spanish, too, when I'm ready.

When it comes to learning a second language, the main thing I've accepted with Japanese is how dumb I sound. But that judgment is mostly my own doing. The outside world in Tokyo only sees someone trying to get by. Often foreigners in Japan will get hit with a "Nihongo ga jōzu!" Meaning "Your Japanese is good!" whether or not it is actually good. But the point is that I'm trying and finding that people are seeing and appreciating the effort. This experience has made me reevaluate my feelings about learning Spanish. I always felt like I wanted to learn it, but the hesitancy to do so grew for years. I no longer feel reluctant, and I think I have my many awkward, ungrammatical Japanese conversations to thank.

CARNE ASADA TATER TOTS

When I moved to California after college, I got my first taste of true freedom. I had my own job, my own car, and my own place. I was also by myself in a new city on the other side of the country for the first time as an adult. It was hard. But carne asada fries helped me make it through.

If you aren't familiar with this SoCal staple, it's a big plate of fries topped with cheese, guac, pico de gallo, sour cream, and slices of marinated carne asada. It's a dish that's meant to be shared. Over time, I met friends who introduced me to carne asada fries and we'd split them. The hangs became more frequent and the nights grew later as they filled up with laughter and pico. Carne asada fries were my freedom.

This is an ode to the classic with a slight twist: instead of fries, I use tater tots. Like the original, they're meant to be shared, preferably with good friends.

Time: 40 minutes, plus marinating • **Serves:** 4 to 6

Ingredients

FOR THE CARNE ASADA

1 pound sirloin steak

One 12-ounce can Mexican beer (such as Tecate)

2½ teaspoons kosher salt

2 teaspoons ground cumin

2 teaspoons garlic powder

3 tablespoons extra-virgin olive oil

FOR THE PICO DE GALLO

2 Roma tomatoes, diced

¼ cup diced red onion

¼ cup packed finely chopped cilantro leaves

½ lime, juiced, plus more to taste

Kosher salt

FOR THE GUACAMOLE

1 large ripe avocado

¼ cup finely chopped red onion

2 tablespoons finely chopped cilantro leaves

1 tablespoon fresh lime juice (about ¼ lime), plus more to taste

Kosher salt

FOR THE TOTS

Nonstick cooking spray

2 pounds frozen tater tots

Kosher salt

1½ cups shredded cheddar

Sour cream

Pickled jalapeño slices (optional)

Directions

1 Cut the steak in half crosswise. Place both pieces in a resealable plastic bag and add the beer. Let the steak marinate at room temperature for 15 to 30 minutes. Remove the steak from the bag and pat it dry with a paper towel. Season both sides with the salt, cumin, and garlic powder.

Recipe continues

2 While the steak is marinating, make the pico de gallo. Combine the tomatoes, onion, cilantro, and lime juice in a medium bowl. Season with salt to taste. Set aside in the refrigerator until it's time to assemble.

3 Make the guacamole. Scoop out the avocado flesh into a small bowl. Using a fork, mash it against the side of the bowl until it reaches the desired consistency. Add the onion, cilantro, lime juice, and salt to taste. Cover with plastic wrap, pressing it down over the surface to keep the guacamole from turning brown, and set aside in the refrigerator until it's time to assemble.

4 Before cooking the steak, start the tots. Preheat the oven to the temperature on the package instructions. Lightly spray a baking sheet with cooking spray. Spread the tater tots out on the prepared baking sheet and cook according to the package instructions. When done, keep in the oven to stay warm until it's time to assemble.

5 While the tots are baking, cook the steak. Heat the oil in a large skillet over medium-high heat. Once the oil is shimmering, add the steak. Discard the beer marinade. Cook until the steak is browned and medium-rare (or until it reaches your preferred temperature), about 3 minutes per side. Remove from the heat and let rest for 5 minutes. Then slice against the grain into ¼-inch-thick, bite-size pieces.

6 While the steak is resting, remove the tots from the oven. Season the tots to taste with salt and gently toss. Then sprinkle the cheddar on top. Melt the cheese with the residual oven heat or quickly broil it on low for 2 minutes. Remove from the heat.

7 It's assembly time! Layer the ingredients on top of the cheese tots in the following order: sliced carne asada, pico de gallo, scoop of guacamole, a generous dollop of sour cream, and pickled jalapeño slices on the side. Serve directly off the baking sheet and feel very, very happy.

Tajín Salad Party

Tajín is one of Mexico's most beloved seasonings. Pronounced "ta-HEEN," it is a blend of dehydrated lime, salt, and a combo of chiles de árbol, pasilla, and guajillo. I love to sprinkle it like glitter onto most things. Fruit, corn, mangonadas, paletas, candy, meat, and *even life itself* can benefit from a heavy Tajín shower.

Here are three easy recipes that celebrate the seasoning magic and pack little punches of sour, salty, and sweet. Minty pineapple and watermelon with feta is all the best parts of summer on a plate. A spicy cucumber-avocado salad with corn would be great as a light side or app. And mango strawberry fruit salad with chamoy is inspired by mangonada, one of my all-time favorite drink desserts. None of these recipes lists the exact amount of Tajín to use because you need to follow your heart (but a lot is a good place to start).

You are cordially invited to the Tajín Salad Party. ✉ ✦

MINTY PINEAPPLE AND WATERMELON WITH FETA AND TAJÍN

Time: 5 minutes • **Serves:** 4 to 6

Ingredients

1 pound watermelon, cut into 1-inch cubes

12 ounces pineapple, cut into 1-inch cubes

2 limes, juiced (about ¼ cup)

1 large orange, juiced (about ½ cup)

4 ounces feta, crumbled

½ cup packed chopped mint

Tajín, for sprinkling

Directions

1 Toss the watermelon and pineapple on a large serving plate to evenly combine.

2 Next, layer the ingredients over the top in this order: lime juice, orange juice, feta, mint, and a big shower of Tajín. Serve immediately or chilled.

SPICY CUCUMBER-AVOCADO SALAD
with CORN and TAJÍN

Time: 5 minutes • **Serves:** 6

Ingredients

1 pound Persian cucumbers, cut diagonally into ¼-inch-thick slices

1 cup raw or cooked corn kernels (from 1 to 2 ears corn)

1 ripe avocado, sliced

1 jalapeño, thinly sliced (seeds optional)

1½ limes, juiced

Extra-virgin olive oil, for drizzling

¼ cup packed finely chopped cilantro leaves

Tajín, for sprinkling

Flaky sea salt

Directions

1 Arrange the cucumbers, corn, avocado, and jalapeño on a large serving plate in an alternating pattern.

2 Pour the lime juice on top. Then drizzle with oil. Garnish with the cilantro, a big shower of Tajín, and salt to taste. Serve immediately.

MANGO STRAWBERRY FRUIT SALAD
WITH **CHAMOY** AND **TAJÍN**

Time: 10 minutes ● **Serves:** 4

Ingredients

8 ounces strawberries, thinly sliced (about 2 cups)

1½ teaspoons sugar

¼ cup packed basil leaves

2 mangoes, cut into ¼-inch slices

½ lime, juiced

Honey, for drizzling

Chamoy, for drizzling

Tajín, for sprinkling

Directions

1 Toss together the strawberries and sugar in a small bowl. Set aside to macerate for about 5 minutes.

2 Chiffonade the basil (this is a fancy French cutting term that just means we're going to make them into pretty herby ribbons!). Neatly stack a few basil leaves, working in batches. You want them to be easy to roll, so don't make the stack too thick. Then tightly roll the leaves together. While still holding the roll close, slice crosswise to create thin basil ribbons. Set aside.

3 On a large serving plate, layer the ingredients in the following order: mango, strawberries, lime juice, drizzle of honey, drizzle of chamoy, and basil. Then, make it rain Tajín. Serve immediately or chilled.

GARBANZOS GUISADOS

When it comes to guisados, or stews, the most important ingredient is time. It's the one thing that the vast range of guisados throughout Latin America have in common. This dish proves that if you're patient, you will be rewarded with the tastiest food.

This is a vegan version of a Puerto Rican guisado made with garbanzos a.k.a. chickpeas. Using canned beans will save you time, but I find the texture of dried chickpeas to be a lot better. Just another example of the reward going to those who are willing to wait. Ladle a big serving with white or yellow rice.

Time: 1 hour, plus soaking ● **Serves:** 4

Ingredients

8 ounces dried chickpeas, picked over and rinsed

1½ teaspoons kosher salt, plus more to taste

1 dried bay leaf

2 tablespoons extra-virgin olive oil

½ cup diced yellow onion

½ cup diced green bell pepper

4 garlic cloves, finely chopped

2 large Roma tomatoes (about 4 ounces)

¼ cup packed finely chopped cilantro leaves and stems

2 tablespoons tomato paste

1 teaspoon ground cumin

1 teaspoon dried oregano

12 ounces Yukon Gold potatoes, peeled and cut into ½-inch pieces

¼ cup pimiento-stuffed Manzanilla olives, drained and halved crosswise

1½ tablespoons capers, drained

2 teaspoons adobo seasoning

1½ teaspoons sazón with achiote

¼ teaspoon cayenne pepper (optional)

1 tablespoon white vinegar

Directions

1 Place the beans in a large pot or bowl with water to cover by 2 inches. Let soak for at least 4 hours or preferably overnight. Drain and rinse before using.

2 Place the soaked beans in a large pot and cover them again with water by 2 inches. Add the salt and bay leaf. Bring to a boil over high heat. Once boiling, cover and reduce the heat to medium-low. Simmer until the

beans are start to become tender, stirring occasionally, about 40 minutes.

3 During the last 10 minutes while the chickpeas are cooking, heat the oil in a large skillet over medium-high heat. Once the oil is shimmering, add the onion, bell pepper, and garlic. Cook, stirring frequently to avoid browning, until the onion is tender and translucent, about 3 minutes.

All Grown Up! Kinda ●

Recipe continues **259**

4 Add the tomato, cilantro, tomato paste, cumin, and oregano. Cook, continuing to stir frequently, until the tomato paste becomes a brick-red color, about 2 minutes. Remove from the heat and transfer the sofrito mixture directly into the chickpea pot.

5 Add the potatoes, olives, capers, adobo, sazón, and cayenne (if using). Mix to fully distribute the seasonings. Increase the heat to medium-high and bring to a boil. Cook uncovered until the potatoes are fork-tender, about 10 minutes.

6 Using a wooden spoon and fork, gently mash about ½ cup of potatoes in the pot to thicken the broth. Reduce the heat to medium and simmer for 5 minutes. Discard the bay leaf. Taste and adjust for salt. Add the vinegar right before serving.

CEVICHE POKE

Because of many, many factors totally unrelated to this book, my move to Japan got pushed back and I ended up living in Hawai'i for a year, completely unplanned. Many of the tropical details felt familiar to me because I had lived in South Florida, but so much was new. I had also eaten plenty of poke before my time in Hawai'i, but never like the kinds in O'ahu. Obviously, there's no better place for poke than its birthplace. During my time there, I fully embraced it.

Poke is a native Hawaiian dish traditionally made with a mixture of raw fish, salt, seaweed, and kukui nuts, a multifunctional nut that's rich in oil that is eaten as well as used as lighting fuel, which is how it gets its name. But postcolonial contact has introduced a huge range of ingredients and techniques. (To really do a deep dive on poke and its cultural importance to Hawai'i, I would highly recommend Martha Cheng's *The Poke Cookbook: The Freshest Way to Eat Fish*!)

This recipe is half ceviche and half poke, meaning it's not fully either dish. Instead, it's a new one that stands on its own. And it's just as delicious. Eat by itself, or pair with a side of warm white rice or freshly fried tostones.

Time: 5 minutes ● **Serves:** 4

Ingredients

1 pound sushi-grade tuna, cut into ¾-inch cubes

1 ripe mango, diced into ½-inch pieces

½ ripe large (or 1 small) avocado, diced into ½-inch pieces

⅓ cup thinly sliced red onion

½ large orange, juiced

1½ limes, juiced

3 tablespoons finely chopped cilantro leaves

1½ tablespoons soy sauce

1 teaspoon sesame oil

Kosher salt

Sesame seeds, for garnish

Directions

Combine the tuna, mango, avocado, onion, orange juice, lime juice, cilantro, soy sauce, and sesame oil in a large bowl. Mix gently until combined. Add salt to taste. Before serving, garnish with sesame seeds. Eat immediately.

CAFÉ DE OLLA

This is the type of drink that makes me feel like it's Christmas morning no matter the time of year. Traditionally brewed in ollas de barro (tall clay pots), Mexican café de olla is made with dark roast coffee, piloncillo, and tons of spices. I like the mixture of cinnamon, clove, anise, allspice, and orange, but there are many variations out there with their own spins, like cardamom, vanilla, and sometimes a little chocolate. Be sure to remove the pot from the heat and cover it while the coffee is brewing to avoid burning the grounds. Once you take off the lid, your kitchen will be filled with the smell and warmth of the holidays—even if it's July.

Time: 25 minutes ● **Makes:** 8 cups

Ingredients

5 ounces piloncillo, or ½ cup packed dark brown sugar	Two 4-inch cinnamon sticks (preferably Ceylon)	5 allspice berries	Four 3-inch orange peels (from ½ orange)
4 whole cloves	1 star anise	½ cup plus 3 tablespoons dark roast coffee	Pinch of kosher salt

Directions

1 Add 8¼ cups water, the piloncillo, cloves, cinnamon, star anise, and allspice to a medium olla de barro or large pot. Bring to a boil over medium-high heat, using a wooden spoon or ladle to gently break up the piloncillo into small chunks to help it dissolve more quickly. Reduce the heat to medium and boil until the piloncillo is fully dissolved and the water smells like Christmas, about 5 minutes.

2 Mix in the coffee, orange peels, and salt. Remove from the heat, cover, and steep for 8 minutes. Strain on through a cheesecloth–lined fine-mesh strainer. Serve immediately or refrigerate in a large pitcher. Enjoy black or with a splash of milk.

OKONOMIYAKI QUESADILLAS

Okonomiyaki is often referred to as a Japanese savory pancake, but to label it just as that is a disservice because it's so much more.

Okonomi means "whatever you like" and yaki translates to "grilled." One of my favorite things to do in Osaka is eat at okonomiyaki restaurants where the definition really comes to life. First they seat you at a table with a large built-in griddle that gets blazing hot. Next, you pick a base from a big menu and add whatever fillings you want: noodles, mochi, cheese, mentaiko . . . nothing is off limits. Then you simply mix the batter well and pour it directly on the griddle to cook yourself. Just before serving, you douse it with as many toppings as you want. An extra-thick layer of okonomi sauce? Mm-hmm. Countless strikes of Kewpie mayo? Need. Showers of aonori and beni shoga? Yes, please. It's rich and perfect.

Inspired by the classic dish from Kansai (the southern-central region of Japan that includes Osaka), this adobo-seasoned mushroom quesadilla is neither Japanese nor Latin American, but somewhere in between. I've made it the way I like, but there's nothing stopping you from adjusting it to your own taste.

Time: 30 minutes ● **Serves:** 2 to 4

Ingredients

3 tablespoons neutral oil (such as vegetable or canola oil)

8 ounces maitake mushrooms, rinsed and roughly chopped into bite-size pieces

1 cup finely shredded green cabbage

½ teaspoon adobo seasoning

1½ cups shredded cheese of choice (such as mozzarella)

Four 8-inch flour tortillas

½ cup okonomi sauce (see note)

Kewpie mayonnaise, aonori/furikake, and beni shoga (red pickled ginger), for serving

Directions

1 Heat 1 tablespoon of the oil in a large nonstick skillet over medium-high heat. Once the oil is shimmering, add the mushrooms, cabbage, and adobo. Sauté until all the moisture evaporates and the mushrooms turn a deep brown color, about 10 minutes. Transfer the mushroom mixture to a bowl and set aside.

2 Add another 1 tablespoon of the oil to the skillet and lower the heat to medium. Place one tortilla into the hot pan, sprinkle half

●

the cheese and the half the mushroom mixture evenly over the top, and then top with another tortilla. Cook until the cheese has melted and the tortilla is golden brown underneath, 2 to 3 minutes. Carefully flip the quesadilla and cook until the other side is golden, about 2 minutes. Transfer to a serving plate and cover with aluminum foil to keep warm. Repeat with the remaining quesadilla.

3 Using a spoon, evenly spread the quesadilla tops with the okonomi sauce. Then drizzle the mayo in a back-and-forth motion on top of the sauce. To get a super crisp look, use the top of a butter knife

or toothpick to gently drag the mayo in the opposite direction to create a feathered effect. Next, sprinkle on the aonori and place a spoonful of beni shoga in the center. Serve immediately.

Note: Most store-bought okonomi sauce contains oyster sauce. To make this fully vegetarian, be sure to get a vegan option like Otafuku's okonomiyaki sauce. You can also make your own by mixing equal parts ketchup and katsu sauce and adding soy sauce and sugar to taste. But I would highly recommend buying the bottled sauce if you can because it's easier and tastes gooooood.

TO BE AN AMERICAN

In Japan, corn dogs are called American dogs. And as an American, I find it hilarious. All the focus on and care we have for our regional cuisines in the US, like Texas barbecue, Louisiana po'boys, Nashville hot chicken, Florida key lime pie, Philly cheesesteaks, New York pizza . . . But the only name of a dish the US fully owns, available at every Japanese convenience store, is American dogs. Our whole gastronomic history boils down to a greasy hot dog dipped in sweet corn batter and deep-fried. This is our legacy.

While living in the US, I'd maybe eaten ten corn dogs in my entire life (discounting the mini varieties). But since I moved to Japan, I have started to eat them as often as three times a week. It took leaving the country to make me realize how much I love ~~corn~~ American dogs. My craving for the sweet fried taste makes me reflect on what else I miss. Stripping away the everyday noise of life in the US left behind only the barest, strongest desires: a missing sense of community, my friends, my family, the ability to be super loud and it not be weird, big sandwiches, and ~~American~~ corn dogs.

About two weeks after moving to Tokyo, I started school to study Japanese. Every day felt like a tiny UN meeting because the students were from all over the world: Malaysia, Indonesia, France, Hungary, Myanmar, Italy, Thailand, Brazil, Peru, Belgium, and China, to name some. Despite the range, I was the only American in class. For the first time in my life, people asked me where I was from and didn't expect a breakdown of my ethnicity. Simply replying with "I'm from the US" was enough.

It felt weird and unfamiliar to leave the answer so short. But the conversation about where we come from (as in our parents and parents' parents) and how much of what ethnicity we are does not occur the same way everywhere as it does in the US. In some places, it turns out, they just don't care. What a thought!

I still get the Japanese equivalent of "What are you?" but it doesn't come from the same place as it almost always does in the US. In the States, it feels like people need to categorize me into a racial box in their minds in order to move forward and interact with me. But in Japan, it feels like it's motivated by genuine curiosity rather than bias, unconscious or not.

The greatest realization I've had since leaving America, though, is how truly American I am. For a long time, I felt unwelcome in the US. Many first-generation writers talk about straddling two worlds: one foot in their motherland where their family speaks their native language at home and cooks only the foods from their birthplace, and another where they try to fit into the largely white-dominant US culture and hide their other self, food and all. But as someone in America who is half Latinx and half Asian, and frayed at both ends, I felt like I had nowhere . . . not Latinx enough, not Asian enough, not American enough. At least, until I left.

The famous saying "No matter where you go, there you are" is true for everyone, but it feels maybe a little extra true if you're an American. One day after Japanese class, I went to lunch with my friend from Thailand. Inside the small ramen shop, we started discussing gender equality, and I became pretty vocal both in my opinions and volume. "Kiera, you're being too loud!" She hushed me as her cheeks turned red. I knew she meant I was being too loud with my speaking volume, but also my opinions. It hit me then: My viewpoints aren't unique. They are a reflection of the US culture I grew up in. So much of my personality is a direct result of the traits that are valued and encouraged in American culture, and they are not always sought after or rewarded elsewhere. Being vocal. Not being afraid to fight for something that is just, even if I am in the minority. Celebrating individualism. Striving to be a unique, special butterfly. Some of these personality-defining beliefs used to make me think I was different, but now I realize it really means I grew up in the US.

I fully embody what it means to be an American, and it only took me moving to the other side of the world to see it.

Tres Tres Leches

Believed to have been created by Nicaraguans, this famous dessert gets its name from the three milks (whole, evaporated, and condensed) used to soak the cake. But if you go to any Latin American restaurant, you'll likely see a variation of it on the menu with different claims about where it's from. It's become a beloved dessert within the Latin American community and beyond with a huge, dedicated fandom. Tres leches has inspired things including but not limited to plushies, an indie band name, and many, many T-shirts. Personally, I like the "You, Me, Tres Leches" shirt the best because . . . romance. When I was growing up, on just about any occasion that called for cake, I ate thick slices of tres leches topped with an equally thick layer of whipped cream that was dusted with cinnamon and finished with a maraschino cherry. The light texture of the base soaks up all the milks like a sponge, making every bite airy, decadent, and rich. And the only thing better than one tres leches is tres tres leches.

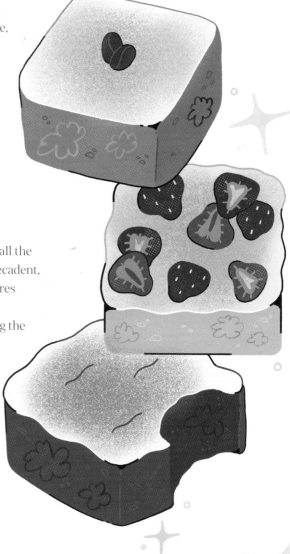

Here are three different variations utilizing the same general recipe, but each with its own colorful and unique spin. Café con ~~leche~~ tres leches with cinnamon pays homage to one of my favorite coffees and those childhood slices. When it comes to tres leches, more is more. Hojicha, or Japanese roasted green tea, is used to add a rich roasted taste. And strawberry uses dehydrated powder of the fruit to bring a concentrated berry flavor, resembling breakfast cereal in the best way.

CAFÉ CON TRES LECHES

Time: 1 hour, plus cooling and soaking ● **Serves:** 12

Ingredients

Nonstick cooking spray

1½ cups all-purpose flour

1 tablespoon cocoa powder

2 teaspoons baking powder

1¼ teaspoons ground cinnamon

½ teaspoon kosher salt

4 large eggs, separated, room temperature

1 cup granulated sugar

1½ cups whole milk

3 tablespoons instant coffee or espresso powder

1 teaspoon vanilla extract

One 14-ounce can sweetened condensed milk

One 12-ounce can evaporated milk

2 cups heavy cream

¼ cup confectioners' sugar

Directions

1 Position a rack in the middle of the oven, then preheat to 350°F. Lightly spray a 9 × 13-inch pan with cooking spray.

2 Whisk together the flour, cocoa, baking powder, ½ teaspoon of the cinnamon, and the salt in a medium bowl. In a large bowl, beat the egg yolks and ¾ cup of the granulated sugar with an electric mixer on medium-high speed until thick and pale yellow, about 1 minute. On low speed, beat in ½ cup of the milk, 2 tablespoons of the instant coffee, and the vanilla until combined.

3 Add half the flour mixture to the wet ingredients and mix on low until it starts to incorporate. Then add the remaining flour mixture and mix until just combined to avoid overworking, occasionally scraping the sides of the bowl.

4 In another large bowl, beat the egg whites with clean beaters on high speed until foamy, about 1 minute. Gradually add the remaining ¼ cup granulated sugar, about a tablespoon at a time, while continuing to beat and waiting a few seconds after each addition. Continue to mix until soft peaks form, about 2 minutes, being careful not to make stiff peaks. The texture should resemble the foamiest part of an ultrathick bubble bath, not whipped cream. With a rubber spatula, fold one-quarter of the whipped egg whites into the cake batter, then gently fold in the remaining egg whites until fully combined.

5 Pour the batter into the prepared pan. Bake until a toothpick comes out clean, about 30 minutes. Remove and let cool for at least 20 minutes at room temperature.

Recipe continues

6 While the cake is baking, make the tres leches mixture. Whisk together the condensed milk, evaporated milk, remaining 1 cup whole milk, and remaining 1 tablespoon instant coffee in a large measuring cup or medium bowl until fully combined. Set aside.

7 After the cake has cooled for at least 20 minutes, use a fork or toothpick to poke holes all over the top. Slowly pour the tres leches mixture over the top, making sure to cover the edges. Cover and refrigerate the cake for at least 1 hour or overnight to soak.

8 Just before serving, make the whipped cream. In a large bowl with an electric mixer, mix the cream on high speed until stiff peaks form, adding the confectioners' sugar after about a minute. When ready to serve, spread the whipped cream over the top of the cake and dust with the remaining ¾ teaspoon cinnamon. Use a cake server or wider spatula to help keep the slices intact when serving.

HOJICHA TRES LECHES

Time: 1 hour, plus cooling and soaking ● **Serves:** 12

Ingredients

Nonstick cooking spray

1½ cups all-purpose flour

3 tablespoons plus 1 teaspoon hojicha powder (see note)

2 teaspoons baking powder

½ teaspoon kosher salt

4 large eggs, separated, room temperature

1 cup granulated sugar

1½ cups whole milk

1 teaspoon vanilla extract

One 14-ounce can sweetened condensed milk

One 12-ounce can evaporated milk

2 cups heavy cream

¼ cup confectioners' sugar

Directions

1 Position a rack in the middle of the oven, then preheat to 350°F. Lightly spray a 9 × 13-inch pan with cooking spray.

2 Whisk together the flour, 3 tablespoons of the hojicha powder, the baking powder, and salt in a medium bowl. In a large bowl, beat the egg yolks and ¾ cup of the granulated sugar with an electric mixer on medium-high speed until thick and pale yellow, about 1 minute. On low speed, beat in ½ cup of the whole milk and the vanilla until combined.

3 Add half the flour mixture to the wet ingredients and mix until it starts to incorporate. Then add the remaining flour mixture and mix on low until just combined to avoid overworking, occasionally scraping the sides of the bowl.

4 In another large bowl, beat the egg whites with clean beaters on high speed until foamy, about 1 minute. Gradually add the remaining ¼ cup granulated sugar, about a tablespoon at a time, while continuing to beat and waiting a few seconds after each addition. Continue to mix until soft peaks form, about 2 minutes, being careful not to make stiff peaks. The texture should resemble the foamiest part of an ultrathick bubble bath, not whipped cream. With a rubber spatula, fold one-quarter of the whipped egg whites into the cake batter, then gently fold in the remaining egg whites until fully combined.

5 Pour the batter into the prepared pan. Bake until a toothpick comes out clean, about 30 minutes. Remove and let cool for at least 20 minutes at room temperature.

6 While the cake is baking, make the tres leches mixture. Whisk together the condensed milk, evaporated milk, and remaining 1 cup whole milk in a large measuring cup or medium bowl until fully combined. Set aside.

7 After the cake has cooled for at least 20 minutes, use a fork or toothpick to poke holes all over the top of the cake. Slowly pour the tres leches mixture over the top, making sure to cover the edges. Cover and refrigerate the cake for at least 1 hour or overnight to soak.

8 Just before serving, make the whipped cream. In a large bowl with an electric mixer, mix the cream on high speed until stiff peaks form, adding the confectioners' sugar after about a minute. When ready to serve, spread the whipped cream over the top of the cake and dust with the remaining 1 teaspoon hojicha. Use a cake server or wider spatula to help keep the slices intact when serving.

Note: This recipe will work with matcha powder, too! So if you prefer the taste of unroasted matcha, you can easily replace the hojicha with it. But I would strongly recommend seeking hojicha out for the deep, roasted flavor. It's available at most Japanese grocery stores and online.

STRAWBERRY TRES LECHES

Time: 1 hour, plus cooling and soaking • **Serves:** 12

Ingredients

Nonstick cooking spray

1½ cups all-purpose flour

2 teaspoons baking powder

½ teaspoon kosher salt

4 large eggs, separated, room temperature

1 cup granulated sugar

1½ cups whole milk

¼ cup plus 3 teaspoons dehydrated strawberry powder (see note)

1 teaspoon vanilla extract

One 14-ounce can sweetened condensed milk

One 12-ounce can evaporated milk

2 cups heavy cream

3 tablespoons confectioners' sugar

2 drops red food coloring

8 ounces ripe strawberries, thinly sliced, for garnish

Directions

1 Position a rack in the middle of the oven, then preheat to 350°F. Lightly spray a 9 × 13-inch pan with cooking spray.

2 Whisk together the flour, baking powder, and salt in a medium bowl. In a large bowl, beat the egg yolks and ¾ cup of the granulated sugar with an electric mixer on medium-high speed until thick and pale yellow, about 1 minute. On low speed, beat in ½ cup of the milk, ¼ cup of the strawberry powder, and the vanilla until combined.

3 Add half the flour mixture to the wet ingredients and mix until it starts to incorporate. Then add the remaining flour mixture and mix on low until just combined to avoid overworking, occasionally scraping the sides of the bowl.

4 In another large bowl, beat the egg whites with clean beaters on high speed until foamy, about 1 minute. Gradually add the remaining ¼ cup granulated sugar, about a tablespoon at a time, while continuing to beat and waiting a few seconds after each addition. Continue to mix until soft peaks form, about 2 minutes, being careful not to make stiff peaks. The texture should resemble the foamiest part of an ultrathick bubble bath, not whipped cream. With a rubber spatula, fold one-quarter of the whipped egg whites into the cake batter, then gently fold in the remaining egg whites until fully combined.

5 Pour the batter into the prepared pan. Bake until a toothpick comes out clean, about 30 minutes. Remove and let cool for at least 20 minutes at room temperature.

6 While the cake is baking, make the tres leches mixture. Whisk together the condensed milk, evaporated milk, and remaining 1 cup whole milk in a large measuring cup or medium bowl until fully combined. Set aside.

7 After the cake has cooled for at least 20 minutes, use a fork or toothpick to poke holes all over the top. Slowly pour the tres leches mixture over the top, making sure to cover the edges. Cover and refrigerate the cake for at least 1 hour or overnight to soak.

8 Just before serving, make the whipped cream. In a large bowl with an electric mixer, mix the cream, 2 teaspoons of the strawberry powder, and the red food

coloring on high speed until stiff peaks form, adding the confectioners' sugar after about a minute. When ready to serve, spread the whipped cream over the top of the cake and dust with the remaining 1 teaspoon strawberry powder. Garnish with the sliced strawberries. Use a cake server or wider spatula to help keep the slices intact when serving.

Note: Dehydrated strawberry powder is available online and in many baking stores, but you can quickly make your own from whole or sliced dehydrated strawberries. Just finely grind them in a food processor or spice grinder. For the amount called for in this recipe, you will need about ⅔ cup of whole or sliced dehydrated strawberries.

GUAVA SWIRL CHEESECAKE BARS

My foster mom always kept a huge tub of saltine crackers at the ready to spread with thick layers of cream cheese and top with chunks of sticky guava paste. Whenever she would bust out the big green aluminum tin, I knew it was cheesy guava snack time. The salt from the crackers would always hit my tongue first, then quickly mellow out with the milky taste of smooth cream cheese and a sweet tropical pop of guava to finish. These guava swirl cheesecake bars are the dessert version of my foster-care snack hour. The crust has a bit more salt, mirroring the saltines' taste, and some shredded coconut that toasts with the graham crackers while baking. The cheesecake brings that same creaminess, and the guava still offers the sweetness that lingers long after each bite.

Time: 1 hour, plus cooling   ●   **Serves:** 8

Ingredients

Nonstick cooking spray

1¼ cups graham cracker crumbs (about 10 graham crackers)

½ cup sweetened shredded coconut flakes (optional; see notes)

1 teaspoon kosher salt

7 tablespoons unsalted butter, melted

Two 8-ounce packages cream cheese, room temperature

⅓ cup granulated sugar

¼ cup sour cream, room temperature

1 large egg plus 1 egg yolk

¼ teaspoon vanilla extract

3 tablespoons all-purpose flour

⅔ cup guava jam (such as Hawaiian Sun; see notes)

Directions

1 Position a rack in the middle of the oven, then preheat to 350°F. Lightly spray an 8 × 8-inch pan with cooking spray.

2 Make the crust. Combine the graham cracker crumbs, coconut (if using), salt, and butter in a large bowl. Mix until fully combined. Transfer the graham cracker mixture to the prepared pan and use the bottom of a measuring cup to press it evenly

into the bottom. Bake until fragrant, about 7 minutes. Set aside to cool while you make the filling.

3 Reduce the oven temperature to 325°F. In a stand mixer or a large bowl using an electric mixer, combine the cream cheese, sugar, sour cream, eggs (whole and yolk), and vanilla. Mix on medium speed until well combined. Then add the flour and mix again until just combined.

4 Assemble the bars. Pour the cheesecake mixture on top of the cooled graham cracker crust. Place the pan in the freezer to chill for 5 minutes (this will help slightly firm up the base so the guava swirls don't sink into the batter). Using a teaspoon, dollop the guava jam across the top, doing your best to avoid letting the dollops touch or putting too much jam in one area. The more visible cheesecake areas there are, the more distinctive the swirl. If your jam is clumping together too much, transfer it to a heatproof bowl and microwave it in 15-second increments until it's looser. Use the tip of a small offset spatula or butter knife to lightly drag the jam across the surface in a figure-eight shape to swirl it into the cheesecake mixture. Repeat the swirling step from the opposite side to create a more striking design. Cover the top with aluminum foil.

5 Bake covered until the edges are set and the center is a little jiggly, about 45 minutes. Turn off the oven and leave the cheesecake bars to cool (still covered!) in the residual heat for 1 hour. Try not to open the oven more than you need to because a drastic change in temperature can create cracks along the surface. After 1 hour, remove the cheesecake bars from the oven, discard

the foil, and bring to room temperature, 30 minutes to 1 hour. Transfer to the refrigerator to chill for at least 4 hours. Serve chilled.

Notes: If you prefer the shredded coconut to be the same texture as the graham cracker crumbs, throw it into a food processor and pulse until it's the same size. Proceed with the rest of the steps as usual. This is a fully optional step!

Do *not* use guava jelly! It is entirely different and will not work for this recipe. There are several major guava jams available in the US. But if you're having a hard time finding it, you can make your own by combining some hot water a little at a time with guava paste in a blender or food processor until you have your desired thick-but-spreadable consistency. One 300-gram package of guava paste and ¼ cup hot water makes about 1 cup. The color won't be as vibrant as guava jam, but it's a good substitute in a pinch.

DIRTY COCONUT HORCHATA

The first time I had a dirty horchata was with my friends Michelle and Jess on a road trip from Houston to LA. We pulled up to El Tacorrido in Austin and grabbed three iced horchatas spiked with espresso for the road. Smooth horchata with sweet cinnamon washed over me while the coffee picked me up. It's truly the perfect drink.

From that moment, I knew I needed more. While living in LA, I started going to Guisados, a local taco institution. They make a mean horchata with cold brew, using whole milk to give it body. This dirty coconut horchata is inspired by both drinks but with a vegan coconutty spin.

Coconut horchata is its own long-standing, well-established aqua fresca. The combination of almonds, coconut milk, and condensed coconut milk gives it the same richness as any milk-based horchata and makes it ideal to top off with coffee. I recommend making a batch just for yourself and storing it in the fridge so you can drink well all week.

Time: 15 minutes, plus overnight soaking   ●   **Serves:** 8

Ingredients

2 cups uncooked long-grain white rice

½ cup unsweetened coconut flakes

½ cup whole raw, unsalted almonds (optional)

Three 4-inch cinnamon sticks (preferably Ceylon)

One 13.5-ounce can coconut milk

One 11.5-ounce can sweetened condensed coconut milk

1 teaspoon freshly grated nutmeg

Pinch of kosher salt

2 cups cold brew concentrate or espresso, for serving

Directions

1 Wash the rice. Using a fine-mesh strainer, rinse the rice with tap water several times, using your hand to swirl the grains around. Repeat until the water runs clear.

2 Place the rinsed rice into a large bowl. Add the coconut flakes, almonds (if using), cinnamon sticks, and 4 cups water and cover. Soak at room temperature for at least 6 hours or overnight.

3 Transfer the mixture with all the liquid to a blender and blend until all the rice and cinnamon sticks are finely ground, 1 to 2 minutes. Using a fine-mesh strainer, strain into a large pitcher or bowl. If you want the horchata to be as smooth as possible, strain the liquid at least twice. Discard the solids.

4 Add 1 cup water, the coconut milk, condensed coconut milk, nutmeg, and salt to the strained liquid. Stir until fully combined.

5 To serve, divide the horchata among ice-filled glasses and gently top each with ¼ cup cold brew concentrate or espresso, or to taste. Keep the coconut horchata refrigerated in a pitcher for up to a week. It will separate, so stir well before serving.

PANDAN COCONUT FLAN

Pandan is a tropical plant that's widely used as an ingredient throughout Southeast Asia. From wrapping chicken to making sweet green custard, its tall, palmlike leaves are used to infuse dishes with herbaceous flavor and add a gentle (or super-electric, depending on the amount of food coloring) green color. But to really bring out pandan's sweet, vanilla-like notes, it is often paired with coconut.

The two best decisions I made on my wedding day were saying "I do" and asking Chinchakriya Un to cater the reception. They run KREUNG, a Cambodian pop-up restaurant based in Brooklyn, and BONG, a forthcoming Cambodian restaurant also in Brooklyn. I fully trust them, so I wasn't too specific about what I wanted. When they asked my thoughts on a pandan coconut chocolate crunch cake, I happily obliged. This recipe is my take on the silky flan they delivered that day.

One thing I love about flan is that no one culture can take full ownership of it. It goes all the way back to the Roman Empire, and the flan fandom has since spread across the world. Spain is often credited with adding the caramel sauce to the custard, but once the Spanish began colonizing Latin America, people there created their own takes on flan. When Spain's colonization continued to the Philippines, flan de leche, a Filipino variation made using extra egg yolks to add decadence, was born. And while all of that was happening, Japan slowly began incorporating European baking techniques and eventually developed purin, another spin-off that is usually lighter and often topped with whipped cream and a cherry. Purin has become so popular to the point that there are countless purin-only stores in just Tokyo alone.

There are so many flans, puddings, purins, and crèmes out there. But this one with its tropical notes and striking green hue stands out among the eggy mix.

Time: 1 hour 15 minutes, plus cooling ● **Serves:** 6 to 8

Ingredients

¾ cup sugar

6 large eggs plus 2 egg yolks

One 13.5-ounce can coconut milk (such as Goya; see note)

One 14-ounce can sweetened condensed milk

1 teaspoon pandan extract, or ¼ teaspoon pandan flavoring

Pinch of kosher salt

Recipe continues

Directions

1 Position a rack in the middle of the oven, then preheat to 325°F. Place oven mitts or a kitchen towel and an 8-inch cake pan or heatproof flan pan of choice near the stove.

2 While the oven is preheating, make the caramel. Place the sugar in a small saucepan over medium-high heat. Cook, swirling the pan occasionally, until the sugar crystals have dissolved and the liquid becomes a rich amber color, 6 to 8 minutes. Watch it carefully because it can easily burn. (If it starts to smoke, lift it from the heat for a moment before returning it to the stove.) Remove from the heat and immediately pour the caramel into the pan. Using the oven mitts or a kitchen towel to hold the pan, quickly swirl the caramel evenly on the bottom and about ¼ inch high on the sides of the pan. If you wait too long, the caramel will harden. If this happens, you can carefully put the pan on a burner on low heat to reheat the sugar a little. Once coated, set the pan aside.

3 Make the custard. In a blender or a large bowl with a whisk, combine the eggs and egg yolks, coconut milk, condensed milk, pandan extract, and salt until smooth. If using a blender, blend on low until just combined—you don't want it foamy.

4 Place the caramel-coated pan into a 9 × 13-inch baking dish. Using a fine-mesh strainer, strain the custard mixture directly into the caramel-coated pan, then cover the pan with foil. Using a liquid measuring cup or other spouted vessel, pour hot tap water into the casserole dish until it reaches halfway up the sides of the flan dish. Carefully place on the middle rack in the oven.

5 Bake for 65 minutes, or until the flan is set but slightly jiggly in the center. Remove the flan from the water bath and let it cool uncovered for 1 hour at room temperature. Then cover and refrigerate for at least 6 hours or preferably overnight.

6 To unmold, run a thin knife along the edges. Center a big plate or serving dish larger than the flan pan on top, then carefully flip the pan and plate at the same time. The flan will release and fall to the plate. Serve chilled.

Note: Coconut milks can vary wildly. I have found through testing that Goya's coconut milk has less cream in it, resulting in less oil. If yours has a higher percentage of cream, you may get some oil separation during baking. You can tell by examining the top of the flan once it comes out of the oven and before letting it chill. If you see a thin, textured layer on top, you can gently scrape it off with a spoon. If you don't remove it, it hardens at the bottom once the flan is flipped.

A Note About My Dad

This book exists because of my dad's absence from my life. If we had spent time together in a traditional way, I would probably be writing a very different story. But we didn't. This is it, my life and reality. I've done my best to be as honest as I could with every recipe, headnote, and essay, so it felt dishonest to omit this final note: while I was writing this book, my dad passed away.

Before, I was a little anxious about what he would think about all of this, about me and how I navigated my life without him. But now I'm sad at the thought of him never being able to know.

It's incredibly difficult to grieve, especially a parent. But it feels more uncharted to grieve a parent twice, having already lost him once before.

I was never planning to write about him in the present, but his passing made me want to say: To whoever has complicated relationships, you're not alone. And it's OK to cut ties with someone if it's the healthier choice for yourself.

I have so many good and painful memories about my dad. But if he could read this, I would tell him: Thank you for inspiring my love of food and writing. Thank you for fostering creativity in me as far back as I can remember. For all the bad and good in our past, I'm the person I am today in part because of you.

Resources

Al-Anon
1-888-4AL-ANON, www.al-anon.org

Nar-Anon
1-800-477-6291, www.nar-anon.org

Narcotics Anonymous
www.na.org

Alcoholics Anonymous
www.aa.org

Acknowledgments

When I started writing this book, I felt very alone, huddled over a desk by myself in a room for hours as I quietly tapped away my story. It was as if it was just me and this book, but that couldn't have been further from the truth—it took a whole damn village to bring this to life—a massive one! From the very first moment I had this book idea to the final stages of its publication, I have never been in this alone. So many beautiful, talented, and caring people have put in so much work and made their mark on this book, and my life, too. For that, I couldn't be more grateful.

A mere written thank-you will never be enough to express my true gratitude, but let me try anyway:

To my grandpa Jorge Ruiz, grandma Veronica Ruiz, not just this book but my entire life would not have been possible without your sacrifice, love, and constant support. I love you both so much.

To Aunt TT, your cooking and stories will always inspire me. You will forever be the best cook in the family, and I am so honored you decided to share some of your recipes with me. And Mario, thank you for driving me to so many grocery stores and fueling me with your incredible cappuccinos. You're both espectacular!

Leila Campoli, my agent: From the first moment we met, you have believed that I had something worth saying, even when I wasn't sure myself. Simply put, this book (and any book before or after) would not have been possible without you.

People are lucky to have one editor, but I feel even luckier because I got two. Stephanie Fletcher, thank you for believing in this story and being the first one to officially make it a real book. Your guidance throughout the process was invaluable. Emma Effinger, thank you for your thoughtful and sharp edits. You made me sound more together and concise, which I definitely needed. I am very grateful you were the one to take this to the finish line.

To the entire Harvest team for supporting, designing, editing, marketing, MAKING (!!!) a book like this. Thank you for giving me the opportunity to tell my story. And very special thanks to Heather Rodino, Rachel Meyers, and Tai Blanche for their impeccable work making this book read and look so beautiful.

Zyan Méndez, the illustrator: Your beautiful illustrations have brought this book to life. You are soooo immensely talented, and I can't believe my words get to share the same page as your art. Thank you for your patience and for dealing with our many, many email exchanges over this process. To anyone reading this who is in need of an illustrator, hire Zyan. It will be the best decision you'll ever make. Promise.

Lauren Vied Allen, the photographer: Your stunning photos and prop styling brought the book to life as much as the illustrations. Without your creative vision, this would have been much less delicious, much less colorful, and more important, much less fun. To anyone reading this who is in need of a photographer, hire Lauren!!! Or you will regret missing your chance!

To KC Hysmith and Savannah Shoemake a.k.a. the rest of the photo squad: Thank you for your extremely hard work that crazy week in North Carolina when we all cooked our asses off. The photos would not have been able to happen without your mad cooking skills, KC. And Savannah, without your organizational skills we all would have been lost.

To my many recipe testers, thank you for taking the time to make the food in this book and welcoming it so warmly into your kitchens. Your notes made every recipe stronger and more delicious. Thank you again, Lisa Nicklin, Fatima Khawaja, Kia Damon, Asha Loupy, Jordan Johnson, Caralyn Green, Jamel Charouel, Katy Klein, Efraim Acevedo Klein, Emma Blecker, Dami Lee, Jeremie Serrano, Christian Melendez, Jacob Bukaweski, Ashley Sioson, Mel Gray, Fabiola Lara, Rudy Chaney, Alexa Tsongranis, Kevin Coutino Valade, Robin Currie, Mia McDonald, Alana Kysar, Michelle Burdin, Ashley Khawsy, Umi Syam, Tiffany Peón, Becca Jacobs, Stephanie Serna, Alexis Marie Montoya, Martha Cheng, Andy Freeland, Daniella Sawaya, Chantal Braganza, Kristine Don, Rika Hoffman, Bethany Novak, Dakota Cortez, Melissa Hirahara, Alicia Camden, Bettina Makalintal, Teresa Finney, Claire Williamson, Corrine Collins, Natalie Lennox, Rachel Trujillo, Mehreen Karim, and Jacqueline Chapman.

To the people who showed up on set to help cook/prep/wash dishes/fry a whole damn fish (*cough cough* Von Diaz), thank you for showing up so fiercely and being willing to put your all into this book even just for the day. Forever grateful to Rachel Bolaños, Ana Hoppert Flores, Forrest Mason, Jade Laurent Jackson, Christopher Jackson, Sydney Jackson, and Von.

To my friends who read my essays and/or recipe headnotes without judgment: Lucy Siguenza, Francine Tamakloe, G. Daniela Galarza, Jenny Stohlmann, Fabiola Lara, Jasmine Howard, and Michelle Burdin.

To all my other friends who provided me with much-needed emotional and creative support or just a listening ear while I worked on the hardest professional thing I have ever done. Thank you, Tetsumi (Harris) Kayama, James Park,

Caitlin Hagerty, Karla Tatiana Vasquez, Rie McClenny, Tiffany Lee, Nick Diaz, Gina Fernandez, Hannah Kirshner, Claudia Lam, Jess Lee, Chad Hicks, Gabriela González Villegas, and my other friends.

To my therapist, Melissa, boy, did I need you! Thank you for helping me get to the stage in my life where I could believe in myself to do this.

To all the Tokyo cafes and family restaurants where I sat and worked for hours, but especially to Film Coffee & Things and Beasty Coffee, my two favorite cafes in the city.

To Molly Yeh, Esteban Castillo, G. Daniela Galarza, Alicia Kennedy, and Abi Balingit, thank you for your kind words. I admire you all so much. They mean the world coming from you.

To Priya Krishna and Shauna Sever, who were some of the first people I ever told about this book idea. Thank you for sharing so much information about your book experiences and what it takes to even get started. It helped me forge my own path into this world.

To Bryan Washington and Eric Kim, thank you for sharing your book wisdom with me. Individually your knowledge could fuel the entire industry. Combined it could rule the whole damn world.

To Hetty Lui McKinnon and Tejal Rao, I am so grateful to you both for believing in me and what this book stands for. Your support helped make this book real.

To George, Benji, and Thor, thank you for being willing to let me write about our lives, especially you, Thor. I love you all so much.

To my mom, no thank you will ever cover everything you have given me. Without you, I wouldn't be here (literally, of course), and I definitely wouldn't have had the opportunity to write. Your constant sacrifice has made the person I am. I feel so lucky to have you as my mom.

And to Benjamin Korman for always being my first editor, the best eater/ dishwasher, and my partner in life. Thank you for everything.

Notes

Introduction

xiv **queer community online:** "Why Latinx/e?," Colorado State University's El Centro, July 16, 2019, https://elcentro.colostate.edu/about/why-latinx/.

xiv **Hispanic when referring to themselves:** Gene Denby, "On the Census, Who Checks 'Hispanic,' Who Checks 'White,' and Why," *Code Switch*, June 16, 2014, https://www.npr.org/sections/codeswitch/2014/06/16/321819185/on-the-census-who-checks-hispanic-who-checks-white-and-why.

Chapter 1: Growing Up (Mostly) Ecuadorian

4 **"identified as mestizo":** Britannica Online, s.v. "mestizo," https://www.britannica.com/place/Ecuador/People.

7 **three thousand years ago by fishermen:** Maricel Presilla, *Gran Cocina Latina: The Food of Latin America* (New York: W. W. Norton & Company, 2012).

38 **"Aesthetics of excess":** Jillian Hernandez, *Aesthetics of Excess: The Art and Politics of Black and Latina Embodiment* (Durham, NC: Duke University Press Books, 2020).

Chapter 2: Grandpa's Favorites

48 **most important economic center:** "Our City," Aeropuerto de Guayaquil, https://www.tagsa.aero/en_guayaquil.html.

50 **switched to the US dollar:** Eric Schnurer, "Why Ecuador and Other States Don't Use Their Own Money," *US News & World Report*, May 2, 2014, https://www.usnews.com/opinion/blogs/eric-schnurer/2014/05/02/why-ecuador-and-other-states-dont-use-their-own-money.

57 **four thousand potato varieties:** "Native Potato Varieties," The International Potato Center, September 22, 2017, https://cipotato.org/potato/native-potato-varieties/.

Chapter 4: My Cuban Foster Mother

167 **ventanita was born:** Al Diaz, "How Miami's First Ventanita Cuban Coffee Window Was Invented," *Miami Herald*, September 10, 2020, https://www.miamiherald.com/news/local/article245615500.html.

Chapter 5: Aunt TT Is a Kitchen God

203 **ninety thousand Chinese indentured laborers:** Erika Lee, *The Making of Asian America: A History* (New York: Simon & Schuster, 2016).

218 **60 percent of them were born outside the US:** "DiNapoli: Jackson Heights Economy Energized by Immigrants and Small Businesses," Office of the New York State Comptroller, October 24, 2019, https://www.osc.ny.gov/press/releases/2019/10 /dinapoli-jackson-heights-economy-energized-immigrants-and-small-businesses.

218 **160 different languages:** Sebastian Modak, "Jackson Heights: The Neighbourhood That Epitomises New York," BBC, March 22, 2023, https://www.bbc.com/travel /article/20230321-jackson-heights-the-neighbourhood-that-epitomises-new-york.

218 **identifies as Hispanic:** New York City Small Business Services, *Jackson Heights Queens Commercial District Needs Assessment,* https://www.nyc.gov/assets/sbs /downloads/pdf/neighborhoods/avenyc-cdna-jackson-heights.pdf.

219 **29 percent in New York City as a whole:** "QuickFacts New York City, New York," United States Census Bureau, https://www.census.gov/quickfacts/fact/table /newyorkcitynewyork/PST045222.

219 **the biggest population of Ecuadorians is found in New York City:** "Transcript: Mayor Eric Adams Delivers Remarks and Raises Ecuadorian Flag," Official Website of the City of New York, August 10, 2022, https://www.nyc.gov/office-of-the-mayor/news /587-22/transcript-mayor-eric-adams-delivers-remarks-raises-ecuadorian-flag.

Chapter 6: All Grown Up! Kinda

248 **485 million native Spanish speakers:** Dylan Lyons, "How Many People Speak Spanish, and Where Is It Spoken?," Babbel, April 21, 2023, https://www.babbel.com/en /magazine/how-many-people-speak-spanish-and-where-is-it-spoken.

248 **fourteen hundred languages in South America and the West Indies:** Nuno Marques, "What Languages Existed Before Colonization in America, and Which Languages Still Survive?," Babbel, July 25, 2017, https://www.babbel.com/en/magazine/what-languages -existed-before-colonization-in-america-and-which-languages-still-survive.

249 **over two hundred million people:** "Brazil," United States Census Bureau, July 1, 2023, https://www.census.gov/popclock/world/br.

249 **2012 *New York Times* article:** Simon Romero, "An Indigenous Language with Unique Staying Power," *New York Times*, March 12, 2012, https://www.nytimes.com/2012/03/12 /world/americas/in-paraguay-indigenous-language-with-unique-staying-power.html.

Universal Conversion Chart

OVEN TEMPERATURE EQUIVALENTS

250°F = 120°C

275°F = 135°C

300°F = 150°C

325°F = 160°C

350°F = 180°C

375°F = 190°C

400°F = 200°C

425°F = 220°C

450°F = 230°C

475°F = 240°C

500°F = 260°C

MEASUREMENT EQUIVALENTS

Measurements should always be level unless directed otherwise.

⅛ teaspoon = 0.5 mL

¼ teaspoon = 1 mL

½ teaspoon = 2 mL

1 teaspoon = 5 mL

1 tablespoon = 3 teaspoons = ½ fluid ounce = 15 mL

2 tablespoons = ⅛ cup = 1 fluid ounce = 30 mL

4 tablespoons = ¼ cup = 2 fluid ounces = 60 mL

5⅓ tablespoons = ⅓ cup = 3 fluid ounces = 80 mL

8 tablespoons = ½ cup = 4 fluid ounces = 120 mL

10⅔ tablespoons = ⅔ cup = 5 fluid ounces = 160 mL

12 tablespoons = ¾ cup = 6 fluid ounces = 180 mL

16 tablespoons = 1 cup = 8 fluid ounces = 240 mL

Index

Index

293

About the Photographer and Illustrator

Lauren Vied Allen is a Mexican American photographer and stylist documenting culinary traditions, food, and people as a means of understanding cultural identities and enriching her community. You can find her work in multiple cookbooks, such as *The Dinner Party Project, Islas,* and *Bodega Bakes.*

Zyan Méndez is a comic maker, doodler, and ceramic artist based in Guadalajara, Mexico. Her favorite thing to draw is frogs. Find her work at @tomboiclub.

About the Author

Kiera Wright-Ruiz is a writer, recipe developer, and the author of the picture book *I Want to Be Spaghetti!* She has written for publications like the *New York Times*, *Food52*, *Serious Eats,* and *The Kitchn*. When not writing, she is probably eating onigiri with her husband and dog somewhere in Tokyo, where she is based.

Find out more about her work at @kierawri and kierawrightruiz.com.